PUBLIC-PRIVATE PARTNERSHIP PROJECTS IN INFRASTRUCTURE

Infrastructural investment is critical to economic growth, quality of life, poverty reduction, access to education, health care, and the achievement of many of the goals of a robust economy. But infrastructure is difficult for the public sector to get right. Public–private partnerships (PPPs) can help; they can provide more efficient procurement, focus on consumer satisfaction and lifecycle maintenance, and provide new sources of investment, in particular through limited recourse debt. But PPPs present challenges of their own. This book provides a practical guide to PPPs for policy makers and strategists, showing how governments can enable and encourage PPPs; providing a step-by-step analysis of the development of PPP projects; and explaining how financing works, what contractual structures look like, and how risk allocation works in practice. It includes specific discussion of each infrastructure sector, with a focus on the strategic and policy issues essential for successful development of infrastructure through PPPs.

This second edition includes new sections on institutional frameworks, mechanisms for leveraging public financing, small scale PPP projects and more.

Dr. Jeffrey Delmon has advised governments, sponsors, and lenders on infrastructure finance and public–private partnerships since 1994 and has been with the World Bank since 2005.

Public–Private Partnership Projects in Infrastructure

An Essential Guide for Policy Makers

Second Edition

JEFFREY DELMON

The World Bank, Washington, DC

CAMBRIDGE
UNIVERSITY PRESS

CAMBRIDGE
UNIVERSITY PRESS

University Printing House, Cambridge CB2 8BS, United Kingdom

One Liberty Plaza, 20th Floor, New York, NY 10006, USA

477 Williamstown Road, Port Melbourne, VIC 3207, Australia

314-321, 3rd Floor, Plot 3, Splendor Forum, Jasola District Centre, New Delhi - 110025, India

103 Penang Road, #05-06/07, Visioncrest Commercial, Singapore 238467

Cambridge University Press is part of the University of Cambridge.

It furthers the University's mission by disseminating knowledge in the pursuit of education, learning and research at the highest international levels of excellence.

www.cambridge.org
Information on this title: www.cambridge.org/9781316645505
DOI: 10.1017/9781108163729

© Jeffrey Delmon 2017

First published 2017

A catalogue record for this publication is available from the British Library

ISBN 978-1-107-19483-0 Hardback
ISBN 978-1-316-64550-5 Paperback

Contents

About the Author

Jeffrey Delmon advises on private participation in infrastructure, transactions, finance, and policy at the World Bank. Prior to joining the World Bank, he spent eleven years in Paris and London advising on infrastructure and project finance in developed and developing countries at the law firms of Allen & Overy and Freshfields, including a secondment to the U.K. Department for International Development. He has lectured for a variety of graduate programs – including those of Oxford; Georgetown; King's College, London; the University of Dundee, Scotland; and the National University of Singapore – on public–private partnerships (PPP), private sector investment, and financing of infrastructure. His recent books include *Private Sector Investment in Infrastructure: Project Finance, PPP Projects and PPP Programs* (3rd edition, 2016); *Public Private Partnership Programs: Creating a Framework for Private Sector Investment in Infrastructure* (2014); and, with coeditor Victoria Rigby Delmon, *International Project Finance and PPPs: A Legal Guide to Key Growth Markets* (3rd edition, 2013). He holds a Ph.D. in law from King's College, London; a Diplôme d'Études Approfondies (LLM) in international law from the Université de Paris II; and a master's degree in international studies and a juris doctorate from the University of Denver.

Acknowledgments

I would like to thank Zak Rich, Robert Burch, John Scriven, Will Dachs, Scott Jazynka, and Ned White for their advice and support, and my colleagues from the World Bank in particular (in alphabetical order) Bhavna Bhatia, Tim Brennan, Amit Burman, Chalida Chararnsuk, Vickram Cuttaree, Victoria Rigby Delmon, Arnaud Dornel, Katharina Gassner, Kirsten Huttner, Tim Irwin, Alex Jett, Ellis Juan, Teuta Kacaniku, Justina Kajange, Angelina Kee, Joel Kolker, Laszlo Lovei, Cledan Mandri-Perrott, Hanna Messerli, Komal Mohindra, Mark Moseley, Yuriy Myroshnychenko, Michel Noel, Paul Noumba Um, Paul Reddel, Andres Ricover, Heinz Rudolf, Dhruva Sahai, Maria Penas Sierra, Sara Sigrist, Sophie Sirtaine, John Speakman, Fiona Stewart, Andrea Stucchi, Satheesh Sundararajan, Nozomi Tokima, Chengyu Wang, and George Wolf.

And most importantly, to Vicky, Alex, and Natasha.

1

Introduction

The links between infrastructure and poverty alleviation, equality, growth, and specific development outcomes such as job creation, market access, health, and education are well established; infrastructure's impacts are felt through multiple channels.[1] It enlarges markets (for labor, goods, and ideas), increasing output and productivity.[2] Poor infrastructure impedes a nation's economic growth and international competitiveness.[3] Insufficient infrastructure also represents a major cause of loss of quality of life as well as illness and death.[4] This raises infrastructure services from a good investment to a moral and economic imperative. In order to stimulate growth

[1] Straub, S., Infrastructure and Growth in Developing Countries: Recent Advances and Research Challenges, World Bank Policy Research Working Paper No. 4460 (2008); Calderón, C. & L. Servén, Infrastructure and economic development in sub-Saharan Africa, *Journal of African Economies* 19 AERC Supplement 1 (2010a), 13–87; Calderón, C. & L. Servén, Infrastructure in Latin America, Policy Research Working Paper 5317, World Bank (2010b); Calderón, C., E. Moral-Benito, & L. Servén, Is Infrastructure Capital Productive? A Dynamic Heterogeneous Approach, Policy Research Working Paper 5682, World Bank (2011); Agénor, P-R. & B. Moreno-Dodson, Public Infrastructure and Growth: New Channels and Policy Implications, World Bank Policy Research Working Paper 4064 (2006); Estache, A. & G. Garsous, The impact of infrastructure on growth in developing countries, *Economics Notes* 1 (2012); Schwartz, J., L. A. Andres, & G. Dragoiu, Crisis in Latin America Infrastructure Investment, Employment and the Expectations of Stimulus, World Bank Policy Research Working Paper No. 5009 (2009).
[2] Prud'homme, R., Infrastructure and Development, paper prepared for the ABCDE [Annual Bank Conference on Development Economics], Washington, D.C. (May 3–5, 2004); extracted from www-wds.worldbank.org/external/default/WDSContentServer/WDSP/IB/2004/05/13/000265513_20040513160037/Original/28975.doc.
[3] World Bank, *Infrastructure at the Crossroads: Lessons Learned from 20 Years of World Bank Experience* (2006); World Bank, *Infrastructure and the World Bank: A Progress Report* (2005).
[4] Willoughby, C., *Infrastructure and the Millennium Development Goals* (2004). For further discussion of the importance of infrastructure to economic growth, social cohesion, quality of life, education, health, social development, environmental management, mobilization of private investment, and job creation, please see www.worldbank.org.

and reduce poverty, it is essential to improve the supply, quality, and afford-ability of infrastructure services. The unmet demands are huge, and invest-ments have not matched demand.[5]

Infrastructure projects have high social rates of return; the growth gen-erated by infrastructure investment is generally pro-poor, with the income levels of the poor experiencing a proportionately greater increase than that of overall income.[6] The public sector provides financing for the vast major-ity of infrastructure services. However, many governments that would like to increase their infrastructure investment have limited fiscal space (the credit capacity/right to borrow money), with infrastructure facing stiff competition from alternative uses of public funds. The government analyzes, chooses, and implements policies intended to improve infrastructure delivery, reduce waste and corruption, and develop the information and data to manage infrastruc-ture effectively and efficiently. This cannot be done through a one-size-fits-all solution, and the government will need to choose from a range of approaches aligned with its goals and objectives.

Ultimately, the cost of infrastructure has to be borne by its users or by taxpayers, current or future (aside from limited levels of foreign aid). Investments of public infrastructure firms have traditionally been financed from the public budget (through taxing or borrowing), possibly with a con-tribution from the users of services (consumers). Funding by future tax-payers and/or consumers occurs when the government or utility borrows money, to be repaid from future revenue.

Public–private partnerships (PPP) represent an approach to procuring infrastructure services that is radically different from traditional public pro-curement. It moves beyond the client–supplier relationship when government hires private companies to supply assets or a service. PPP is a partnership between public and private to achieve a solution, to deliver an infrastructure service over the long term. It combines the strength of the public sector's man-date to deliver services and its role as regulator and coordinator of public func-tions with the private sector's focus on profitability and commercial efficiency.

PPP can provide a number of benefits:[7]

- The proportion of large-scale infrastructure projects delivered to time and budget is increased, due to alignment of incentives and access to latest construction and operation methodologies and technologies.

5   World Bank, *Sustainable Infrastructure Action Plan FY 09-11* (2008).
6   Calderón, C. & L. Servén, The Effects of Infrastructure Development on Growth and Income Distribution, Policy Research Working Paper (2004).
7   World Bank, *Public–Private Partnerships: Reference Guide Version 2.0*, documents.world-bank.org/curated/en/2014/01/20182310/public-private-partnerships-reference-guide-version-20 (2014); Andrés, L., J. Schwartz, & J. L. Guasch, *Uncovering the Drivers of Utility*

- Infrastructure shifts from a focus on inputs (construction) to a service culture, increasing innovation and competition with design better focused on minimizing the lifecycle cost and managing lifecycle risks, since the builder is also responsible for operation and maintenance.
- The service dynamic creates a positive and significant impact on coverage, quality of services, billing and collection, operational efficiency, and labor productivity.
- Project evaluation and due diligence are enhanced, using balance of interests of different stakeholders (e.g., government, investor, lender) to achieve more robust project assessment and a prioritization of value for money.
- Competition is used to improve innovation and quality.

Box 1.1. Definitions

PPP is used here in its most inclusive form to mean any contractual or legal relationship between public and private entities aimed at improving and/or expanding infrastructure services. Clearly, the more extensive the private involvement, the more supportive the investment climate needs to be. The term *government* will be used to mean the level of government responsible for the reform processes, whether it be the federal, state, or municipal government. The two counterparties to the main project contract will be referred to as the *contracting authority* on the public side and the *project company* on the private side. PPP can be implemented as a series of ad hoc projects or as a program of projects coordinated and enabled centrally – *PPP programs*.

- New opportunities are provided for local capital markets and in particular institutional investors, such as pension funds, which can match their long-term liabilities with the long-term revenue streams of PPP projects.

Performance, Lessons from Latin America and the Caribbean on the Role of the Private Sector, Regulation, and Governance in the Power, Water, and Telecommunication Sectors (2013); Gassner, K., A. Popov, & N. Pushak, *An Empirical Assessment of Private Sector Participation in Electricity and Water Distribution in Developing and Transition Countries* (2007); Gassner, K., A. Popov, & N. Pushak, Does Private Sector Participation Improve Performance in Electricity and Water Distribution? Trend and Policy Option #6 (2009); Marin, P., Public–Private Partnerships for Urban Water Utilities – a Review of Experiences in Developing Countries. Trends and Policy Option No 6, World Bank, Public–Private Infrastructure Advisory Facility (PPIAF) (2009).

- Traditional public procurement improves, as the public sector learns lessons from the PPP program.
- A focus on value for money helps governments choose the best projects to implement through PPP.
- Access to private capital is provided to increase investment.
- Demonstration effect for local businesses is achieved, with lessons learned from efficient PPP examples.
- Transition toward greater privatized services begins, in particular in the power, health, and education sectors.

In the world of PPP projects, there are numerous options, structures, solutions, and strategies. Risk allocation – balanced in line with rewards – between the public and private partners is key to the success of these partnerships.[8]

Governments need to focus more than ever on managing lenders and on creating the right framework for PPP, including the legal, regulatory, institutional, and financial interventions that a government can use to encourage:

- Selecting good, viable projects
- Carefully preparing projects to address gaps and risks, respond to market demands, and give government access to best pricing, timing, and conditions
- Attracting the best available financing solutions (e.g., government support of a type and amount that is value for money for the government)
- Locating resources for implementation and oversight, creating feedback loops to learn from projects, developing national good practice, and improving capacity for the national program

---

Box 1.2. Sample PPP Projects

A few simple examples of PPP projects might include the following:

- A power plant built, financed, and operated by the private sector delivers power to a public utility, which commits in advance by contract to purchase the power generated at a specified price over the long term. The private sector uses the purchase promise of the utility to secure lending and investment and is incentivized to build a quality facility that will meet performance requirements over the long term.

---

[8] Delmon, J. & E. Juan, *Euromoney Infrastructure Finance Book* (2008), chapter 10.

- The private sector promises to expand the airport and improve services in exchange for the right to operate the airport over a period of time. The private company promises to share a specified percentage of the revenues of the airport with the government.
- The private sector builds, finances, and operates a bus terminal and installs commercial facilities (e.g., shops, offices) around the terminal. The bus terminal must meet performance requirements; otherwise, the private sector must pay penalties or may lose the project. The private sector receives revenues from buses using the terminal, tenants of the shops, tenants of offices, and other commercial sources. If revenues seem promising, the private sector may share revenues.

One of the challenges for governments wanting to implement a conducive PPP framework is the variety of models and frameworks put forward by different countries, advisers, and commentators. This book suggests that development of a conducive framework for PPP involves a dynamic, iterative process supported by different functions and actors within the government, the private sector, and the communities in question. Instead of proposing a single model, this book discusses the different elements that together make up an effective PPP framework: the legal framework (how laws and regulatory structures can be used to encourage PPP), the institutional framework (the people involved, the decision-making power they have, and the functions they perform), the project procurement process, government involvement in each phase thereof, the use of government funding to support projects, and the mobilization of long-term local currency financing for PPP projects.

Key Messages for Policy Makers

- *Be patient.* PPP is not a quick fix; it takes time to develop and implement properly. Generally, more effort spent in advance of procurement to prepare the project properly will save much more time and frustration later. Think through contingencies in advance, and make sure you are happy with the project structure and specification before going to the market.
- *Choose well.* A good project should be financially, economically, and politically viable. Pilot projects should not be too big or too small.
- *Prepare well.* PPP requires upfront investment of staff and money to develop projects well, in particular to pay for expensive external

advisers. Project development costs the government 3 percent or more of project construction cost. The benefit of this upfront investment is obtained over time, since PPP provides for management and funding for the whole life of the assets and therefore addresses project risks early.

- *Prepare the government to play its part from project development to expiry.* Even where a comprehensive PPP is envisaged, the government will play an essential role in monitoring and regulating the project and the sector.
- *Be ready for challenges.* In any long-term relationship, change happens. PPP is, above all, a partnership, and it needs to be designed with challenges, changes, and resolution in mind. Problems need to be elevated to appropriate levels of management before they become disputes or worse.

Throughout the text, specific, candid advice is provided for policy makers. This advice is summary and generic, and should be treated accordingly.

For a more extensive discussion of the issues set out in this book, see Jeffrey Delmon, *Private Sector Investment in Infrastructure: Project Finance, PPP Projects and PPP Programmes,* 3rd edition (2016). Reference should also be made to www.worldbank.org/pppirc for further discussion of legal and contractual issues in PPP.

This book is organized into ten chapters:

Chapter 1	Introduction to the fundamentals of PPP, discussing the nature of PPP and the investment climate needed to attract PPP.
Chapter 2	PPP frameworks – including legal, institutional, and financial – needed to develop PPP on a programmatic basis.
Chapter 3	Public support and how it can be used to enable and mobilize a PPP program.
Chapter 4	Procurement of PPP, project preparation, and implementation.
Chapter 5	Financing of PPP, the source of potential funding, how project financing (also known as limited recourse financing) works, and what governments can do to improve financing flows for PPP.
Chapter 6	Key issues associated with local currency financing, in particular, how government can help to mobilize local currency financing for PPP.
Chapter 7	Risks encountered in PPP projects and how those risks are allocated among the project parties through the different project contracts.

Chapter 8	The contractual structure of a PPP and the key issues to be addressed through the contractual structure.
Chapter 9	Different elements of project implementation, from financial close through to project expiry.
Chapter 10	PPP in different sectors, from transport, power, and water to education, health, and small projects.
Appendices	Summary of the key messages provided for policy makers, a glossary of key terms, and a list of key readings and websites on PPP for further reference.

1.1 Fundamentals of PPP

Infrastructure is primarily a public sector issue, with annual global public sector investment in infrastructure vastly exceeding that of the private sector. PPP is an arrangement for the private sector to deliver infrastructure services to the public or to assist the public sector in this task. It is:

- Normally established contractually, formalizing the relationship, scope, and output-based obligations
- Focused on delivery of services and performance
- Often long term
- Focused on risk sharing to ensure commitment, buy-in, sustainability, efficiency, and balance
- Established between at least one public and one private entity[9]

Even for the most public of service providers, private involvement forms an essential part of successful service delivery, whether through construction contracts, service agreements, delivery of goods, and/or joint ventures. PPP can help mobilize this private involvement more efficiently.

Figure 1.1 sets out a number of commonly used PPP terms.[10] A few of the key acronyms are defined in the following for reference.

Corporatization – involves a utility that is in public ownership being run in a manner similar to that of a private sector entity, using incentive mechanisms for staff and management similar to those used in the private sector.

---

[9] PPPs between public entities are often known as performance contracts and raise additional challenges, in particular difficulty in enforcing obligations.

[10] For a general discussion of PPP structures, and why current nomenclature is woefully inadequate, see Delmon, J., *Understanding Options for Private Participation in Infrastructure: Seeing the Forest for the Trees: PPP, PSP, BOT, DBFO, Concession, Lease ...* (2010).

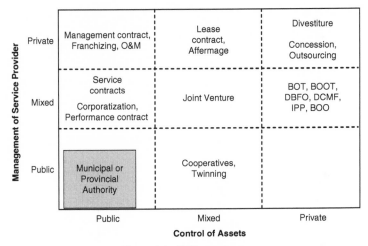

Figure 1.1. PPP structures.

For example, a corporatized utility may be structured as a limited liability company, with its share capital controlled by the public, while publishing the equivalent of an annual report containing a profit and loss statement, balance sheet, and cash flow data, giving a clear picture of the utility's finances and where any inefficiencies may be found (typical public utilities lack transparency in their accounts, making it difficult to isolate inefficiencies or properly incentivize management).

Service contracts, management contracts, operation and maintenance (O&M) contracts – are all structures whereby a private company provides services to a utility/contracting authority (for example, management services, improvement of billing and collection services, leak reduction, or marketing) with payments generally linked to performance.

Key Messages for Policy Makers

- *PPP is by nature flexible.* Look first at what you need, then design your approach based on those needs. Do not look first at what others have done, as your context may be very different. That said, a careful analysis of experiences in other jurisdictions is always useful.
- *Confirm project viability periodically to avoid losing focus.* First decide you want PPP on a rational, fundamentally sound basis, then keep reminding yourself why you chose PPP; periodically verify that the project is meeting those objectives.

- *Government must regulate and monitor PPP.* This must be an integral part of project design. PPP or not, the public sector is always the final authority and will be considered by the public to be ultimately responsible for the provision of public services. The public sector must be prepared to commit (time and budget) to the continual monitoring and evaluation of PPP projects.
- *Consider all stakeholders.* PPP will have a direct influence on some stakeholders (in particular, employees and management) and may raise political or philosophical concerns among many more. While absolute consensus will never be reached, the government needs to understand fundamental concerns and address them.

Franchizing, cooperatives, twinning – involve using an experienced operator's or utility's expertise and reputation through a local service provider's manpower and resources.[11]

Build-Operate-Transfer (BOT), Build-Own-Operate-Transfer (BOOT), Design-Build-Finance-Operate (DBFO), Design-Construct-Manage-Finance (DCMF), Independent Power Producer (IPP), Build-Own-Operate (BOO) – are similar in nature, looking to the project company to build (or refurbish if you replace the "B" with an "R") and operate a facility and deliver services to a utility (for example, to a water services company), a service delivery entity (such as a health service trust), or the consumer (be it power distribution, a road, a hospital, or otherwise). The facility may or may not be transferred to the government after a defined period of time (as sometimes indicated by the letter "T" at the end of the abbreviation).

Lease contract, affermage, concession – these generally involve the project company delivering services directly to the consumer, and differ primarily in whether the project company is responsible for new asset investment (e.g., in an affermage,[12] generally it is not) and whether the project company owns the assets (e.g., in a concession, generally it does). Performance

---

[11] See Water Operators Partnerships – Africa, *An Action Program to Enhance the Performance of African Water and Sanitation Utilities* (2008).

[12] There is a degree of confusion in the use of the term *affermage*. Certain authors have suggested that affermage agreements do not involve any obligations to make capital investments (see, for example, Guislain, P. & M. Kerf, Concessions – the Way to Privatize Infrastructure Sector Monopolies, Viewpoint, Note No. 59, World Bank (1995); Hall, D. R., *Public Partnership and Private Control – Ownership, Control and Regulations in Water Concessions in Central Europe* (May 1997), www.psiru.org). In contrast, other authors have asserted that affermage agreements can include an obligation to make capital investments,

contracts are similar but with a public sector service provider. Enforcing obligations under a performance contract can be difficult, as can governance generally, as both parties are public and appropriate formal dispute resolution mechanisms may not exist.

The preceding definitions are for reference only; they mean different things to different people and are therefore inexact and often misleading as terms of reference.[13] Further, these examples should not be viewed as an exhaustive description of the universe of PPP. PPP is ultimately flexible, limited only by the creativity of those involved and their access to funding.

1.2 Categorizing PPPs

Another way to think about the different types of PPP is to focus on the functions performed by the private party. The following provides a categorization methodology for PPP, classifying the different design options for PPPs based on their most salient elements, those characteristics fundamental to the nature of PPPs, and therefore the character of the project in question.[14] Lack of an agreed-upon categorization methodology has created confusion and limited the ability to cross-fertilize (learning lessons from different regions and sectors who use different terminology), making it difficult to know, without in-depth analysis, whether the structures being used are similar or not.

There is no universal norm as to the most appropriate approach to PPP. That analysis needs to be made on a country-by-country, sector-by-sector, and project-by-project basis. The model is therefore not meant to be normative. Instead, it is meant to give a common basis for description across projects, sectors, countries, legal systems, and cultures.

The classification model (see Table 1.1) addresses five key parameters that may or may not be relevant to any given PPP project. These parameters identify the most fundamental characteristics of a PPP project:

1. *New or existing business*: taking over existing revenues, customers, assets, or employees represents a different risk profile than a new business.
2. *The nature of project company construction obligations*: implementing a significant construction program carries with it a host of

---

so long as the cost of the investment can be recovered during the lifetime of the agreement (see, for example, Third Party Access in the Water Industry, prepared for Tasman Asia Pacific, at www.ncc.gov.au).

13   Ibid.
14   Ibid.

Table 1.1. *The Classification Model*

Business	Construction Obligations	Private Funding	Service Delivery	Source of Revenues
New	Build	Finance	Bulk	Fee
Existing	Refurbish		User	Tariff

construction- and performance-related risks that will be essential to understand the role of the project company. This obligation differs fundamentally for a new build or the refurbishment of existing assets.

3. *The need for the project company to mobilize significant private funding ab initio*: where the project company is required to mobilize private finance for any significant upfront costs (including fees, acquisition of assets, and construction costs), the risk profile for the project company and the influence of the financiers will alter fundamentally the nature of the project.

4. *The nature of the project company's service delivery obligations*: this refers to the extent to which the project company is delivering services directly to consumers ("User") or only to a single user, such as the utility ("Bulk"). Delivery of services to a large number of consumers represents a more complex context for the project company and its financiers.

5. *The source of the project revenue stream*: the source of the revenue stream influences the certainty, size, and nature of that revenue stream, for example, the collection risk associated with the revenue stream and the likelihood that the obligor will be available to pay on its obligations. "Fee" refers to a single or small number of purchasers of the offtake or service, while "Tariff" refers to collection of revenues from a large number of consumers or users.

For example, a project where the project company builds a new power plant, operates it, and sells the power to the local utilities would be a *New-Build-Finance-Bulk-Fee*. Consider the refurbishment of an existing hospital, financed by the project company, where the project company does not provide clinical services but instead makes the refurbished hospital available to the local health authority for a fee and the contracting authority delivers clinical services out of the hospital. This project would be a *New-Refurbish-Finance-Bulk-Fee*. The management of an existing water company and refurbishment of assets, financed by the contracting authority, with revenues collected from the consumers, would be an *Existing-Refurbish-User-Tariff*. The management of an existing waste management plant for the local utility with no capital expenditure, but an upfront concession fee, with revenues from anyone wanting to deposit waste at the facility, would be an *Existing-Finance-Bulk-Tariff*.

1.3 PPP Can Be Costly and Slow; Why Bother?

PPP projects, even in more efficient jurisdictions, require significant upfront project development funding for project selection, feasibility studies, and the use of expert advisers to help the contracting authority in the development and tendering process. In the United Kingdom, where a level of standardization has been achieved, these costs amount to, on average over a wide variety of projects, some 2.6 percent of capital costs over the period from prequalification to financial close, which takes an average of thirty-six months.[15] Countries with less experience in PPP will likely need to spend more and will take longer. This is a lot of resource and time commitment for the contracting authority to implement a PPP project properly, so why bother?

A variety of factors motivate the public sector to implement PPP, including the following:

- Underperformance of public sector utilities, often linked with opaque funding structures and inefficient or corrupt procurement methods.
- Inadequate technical and management resources in the public sector.
- Investment demands exceeding public resources, in particular given the large upfront capital costs associated with major infrastructure investments and the "lumpy" cost implications of periodic major maintenance; quite simply, the government may not have the resources.

PPP is generally perceived to provide the following:

- Efficiency
- Whole asset life solution
- Transparency and anticorruption
- Technology, innovation, and know-how
- New sources of financing

---

[15] National Audit Office (U.K.), *Improving the PFI Tendering Process* (March 2007).

1.3.1 Efficiency

The private sector is often considered to provide greater levels of efficiency than the public sector can.[16] This increased efficiency results from many factors, including the following:

- Commercial approaches to problem solving with focus on cost-effectiveness, in particular rationalizing the cost of labor and materials.
- Better governance to improve accountability, for example, enabling less politically oriented decision making.
- Improved transparency and competition to reduce opportunities for corrupt practices and to bring hidden costs into the open. For example, many of the high transaction costs often associated with PPP project development must also be incurred in public projects but are simply absorbed into other public budgets without being accounted for. PPP brings these hidden costs into the open.[17]

1.3.2 Whole Asset Life Solution

Public funding of infrastructure maintenance often falls short of requirements, in particular in developing countries.[18] Poor maintenance results in significant increases in future infrastructure investment requirements, representing a major disadvantage for these countries. PPP helps to manage this funding shortfall by designing sufficient funding into the project from the start and creating proper incentives to maintain assets well. The concession granted to the project company can last for twenty-five years or more, forcing the project company to adopt a more appropriate long-term commercial approach to problem solving and asset management. The project company will need to maintain assets properly to achieve performance levels, avoid performance penalties, and fulfill handover requirements at the end of the project period.

---

[16] As demonstrated by Andres, L., V. Foster, J. L. Guasch, & T. Haven, *The Impact of Private Sector Participation in Infrastructure: Lights, Shadows, and the Road Ahead* (2009); Gassner, K., N. Popov, & A. A. Pushak, *Does the Private Sector Deliver on Its Promises? Evidence from a Global Study in Water and Electricity Distribution* (December 2007), www.ppiafdev.org.

[17] Klein, M., J. So, & B. Shin, Transaction Costs in Private Infrastructure Projects – Are They Too High? World Bank, *Public Policy for the Private Sector*, No. 95 (October 1996).

[18] World Bank, *Infrastructure at the Crossroads: Lessons Learned from 20 Years of World Bank Experience* (2006).

1.3.3 Transparency and Anticorruption

Good governance endeavors to provide transparency, equal treatment, and open competition. Lack of good governance makes potential investors and lenders worry (increasing the cost of money), reduces competitive pressure on bidders (increasing costs and reducing quality and expediency of solutions proposed), and increases the likelihood of rent-seeking/bribery and other forms of corruption (adding cost and delay to project implementation and reducing quality of performance).[19] PPP provides an opportunity to implement good governance into every aspect of project implementation and thereby reduce the opportunities for corrupt practices, as in the following examples:

- The use of financial and fiduciary management, in particular ring-fencing revenue and subsidy flows to and from the project
- Improved public access to information about the project through the use of open, transparent procurement processes, for example, through a dedicated project website to attract bidders and improve competition
- Enhanced approval processes and fiscal oversight to increase competition, transparency, and consistency
- The monitoring function of the lenders

1.3.4 Technology, Innovation, and Know-How

The contracting authority may look to the private sector to provide technology, innovation, and know-how. This will include access to skills and technologies otherwise unavailable to the government or developed for the project specifically due to the alignment of incentives created by a PPP project. Private investors will have greater incentives to invest in such innovation.

1.3.5 Sources of Financing

PPP can encourage the mobilization of new or additional sources of finance for infrastructure development and provide new opportunities for the development of local financial markets, for example, by doing the following:

- Mobilizing local financial investors not accustomed to providing financing to infrastructure projects directly, but desirous of long-term, stable investment opportunities

---

[19] See generally www.transparency.org; United Nations Economic and Social Council, *Governance in Public Private Partnerships for Infrastructure Development* (2005).

- Maximizing fiscal space by using the capacity of private balance sheets and by sharing risk to increase the amount of investment globally
- Enhancing access to foreign financial markets and capital

1.4 PPP Programs and Institutions

Rather than focus solely on the development and delivery of PPP transactions one at a time, in an ad hoc manner, government may want to develop a program for PPP, coordinated and consistent to reduce transaction costs, improve the adoption of PPP, and increase the number of transactions delivered.

One of the challenges for governments wanting to implement a conducive PPP framework is the variety of models and approaches put forward by different countries, advisers, and commentators.[20] A common approach is to try to adopt the fully functioning framework used by a country that has been very successful in developing a PPP program in one fell swoop. This involves taking, for example, the PPP program in England and replicating it wholesale for any given country. But, these "best practice" PPP programs have developed over many years, through numerous challenges and innovations and for a specific legal, political, and capital context. When adopting the processes and procedures of one of these countries wholesale into a jurisdiction with little experience in PPP, the tendency is to expect the PPP program to be equally successful in a short time frame, as if a robust PPP framework will immediately result in robust PPP projects. Clearly, this is far from accurate.

The development of a conducive framework for PPP involves a dynamic, iterative process supported by different functions and actors within the government, the private sector, and the communities in question. Transparent, competitive procurement is fundamental to effective use of PPP. It ensures a level playing field for investors and provides the contracting authority with best price, terms, and conditions for the government. Instead of proposing a single model, this text discusses the different elements that together make up an effective PPP framework.

Figure 1.2 identifies what it takes to achieve a good, sustainable PPP framework:

- The political will to pursue PPP, and the legal and regulatory regime appropriate to enable and encourage PPP
- Selection of projects that are viable, feasible, and appropriate for PPP

---

[20] See generally Delmon, J., *Public–Private Partnership Programs: A Framework for Private Sector Investment in Infrastructure* (2014).

Figure 1.2. The context of a conducive PPP framework.

- Selection, design, and development of "good" projects – the most appropriate and feasible projects for PPP
- Allocation of risk to the private sector while insulating investors from those risks best borne by the contracting authority or the government
- Assurance that the financial markets are in a position (legally, financially, and practically) to provide the project with the investment it needs (debt, equity, etc.), including, to the extent necessary, by providing government support.

Generally, simpler is better. As a PPP program matures, the PPP framework may become more complex. But in the early days, it is generally better to keep the framework simple. Different constituencies will need to understand the framework – contracting authorities, line ministries, central ministries, investors, and the public at large. Simple mechanisms will help these key stakeholders more easily understand and interact with the PPP framework.

Figure 1.3 shows a more detailed depiction of the diversity of reforms and instruments that together can support a good, sustainable PPP program. The outer square shows the macro issues. The middle square identifies the key participants in achieving each of the macro drivers.

The inner square shows the tools available to those participants. One worth highlighting is "experience with PPP." It is important for the contracting authority, investors, and lenders to have access to individuals experienced with PPPs, to help them understand the risk profile, terms and conditions, market standards, and financing arrangements typical of such projects.

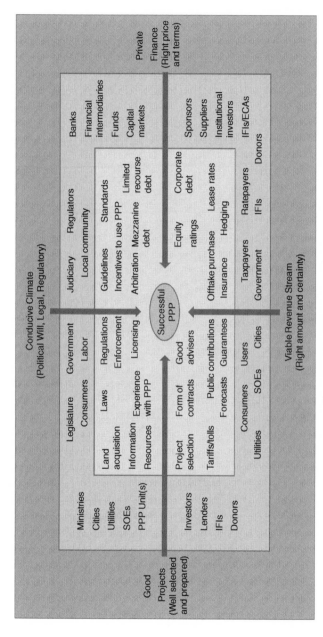

Figure 1.3. PPP investment climate.

A gap analysis identifies areas in the PPP framework that can be improved. The main activities to be addressed in this strategic plan for PPP framework reform will include the following:

- Ensure high-level government and political buy-in and understanding
- Establish/update policy
- Pass/amend necessary laws and regulations
- Create, staff, train, and coordinate institutions (e.g., units, committees, and task forces)
- Create operating guidelines and best practice guidance to establish clear, transparent, consistent, competitive processes
- Communicate PPP to government, parliament, civil servants, the private sector, and the public
- Select and develop a pipeline of good projects, including strategic demonstration projects
- Establish processes, practices, and funding for government support, including project preparation and fiscal risk management
- Implement program monitoring, knowledge capture, and sharing of lessons learned

An action plan for PPP framework reform will focus on practical actions associated with these topics. There is a tendency to approach reform of the PPP framework as a single action, generally delivered by external consultants in one massive report, with a few workshops and training sessions (in an effort to deliver the guidance in a more digestible form). But such interventions are rarely effective.

On the contrary, achieving a viable PPP framework involves a complex series of parallel, iterative initiatives and efforts. It involves updating the different elements of the PPP framework discussed in this text as each new lesson is learned from PPP transactions as they are implemented and national best practice as it develops.

Key Messages for Policy Makers

- *Keep it simple*: Complex is not necessarily comprehensive or better; the PPP framework needs to be understood by a wide variety of stakeholders.
- *Learning by doing*: An important part of identifying gaps in the investment climate is learned while "doing," while implementing PPP projects.

- *Use measured steps without being timid*: Start with easier (but not necessarily small) projects that are clearly financially viable and have political support.
- *Learn from the experiences of others without being dogmatic*: While it is important to learn from the successes and failures of others, it is generally unwise to try to simply replicate an entire framework.

1.5 PPP and Financing

The following is a general discussion of the characteristics of three of the more common sources of financing for infrastructure projects: government financing, corporate financing, and project financing (the latter two involving private borrowers). The characteristics discussed in the following may not be accurate for every project or borrower. In particular, the decision as to which form of financing to adopt will depend on government fiscal position, the market availability of financing, and the willingness of lenders to bear certain project risks or credit risks according to their view of how the market is developing and changing and according to their own internal risk management regime.

The most common sources of financing include the following:

- *Government financing* – where the government borrows money and provides it to the project through on-lending, grants, or subsidies or where it provides guarantees of indebtedness. The government can usually borrow money at a lower interest rate but is constrained by its fiscal space (in particular, its debt capacity) and will have a number of worthy initiatives competing for scarce fiscal resources. The government is also generally less able to manage commercial risk efficiently.
- *Corporate financing* – a company borrows money against its proven credit position and ongoing business and invests it in the project. The size of investment required for an infrastructure project and the returns that such companies seek from their investments may result in a relatively high cost of financing and therefore can be prohibitive for the contracting authority.
- *Project financing* – where non- or limited recourse loans are made directly to a special-purpose vehicle. The lenders rely on the cash flow of the project for repayment of the debt; security for the debt is primarily limited to the project assets and future revenue stream. By using such techniques, the investors can reduce substantially their equity investment (through debt leverage) and exposure to project

liability, thereby reducing total project cost. That said, project financing requires a complex structure of contracts, subcontracts, guarantees, insurances, and financing agreements in order to provide the lenders with the security they require and the risk allocation necessary to convince them to provide funding. This complexity requires significant upfront investment of time and resources by the contracting authority in project development. Further, project financing may increase the overall costs of debt for the project.[21]

Generally speaking, a sovereign government will be able to obtain financing at a lower cost than the sponsors or the project company.[22] The cost-effectiveness of government financing will depend on the credit profile of the government in question (as reflected in its credit rating) and any other restrictions that apply to that government in relation to assuming new debt obligations. However, government financing is often rendered less efficient by public procurement processes, failure or unwillingness to implement incentive mechanisms to achieve greater efficiency, and failure to control changes and other risks that result in higher construction and operation costs. Private sector financing may therefore prove – in certain circumstances – less expensive, less time-consuming and more flexible to arrange, or more practical than public sector financing. The private sector can provide new sources of finance (in particular, where fiscal space or other constraints limit availability of government financing), impose clear efficiency incentives on the project, and be used to invigorate local financial markets.[23]

The overall interest rate applicable to projects financed using corporate financing must take into consideration the minimum level of return on investment (ROI) demanded by sponsors to forego other investment opportunities. The corporate entity in question will borrow funds to finance the project but will compare the return earned from such financing against its other commercial activities, where it would invest these

---

[21]   Project financing is discussed in more detail in Chapter 5.
[22]   Lower interest rates obtained by a government reflect the contingent liability borne by taxpayers. Klein, M., Risk, Taxpayers and the Role of Government in Project Finance, World Bank Policy Research Working Paper 1688 (December 1996). Thus, the risk that results in higher private finance interest rates reflects actual project risk and is subsidized by taxpayers to achieve the lower public finance interest rates. Since the private sector is best placed to manage most of the commercial risk in infrastructure projects, it is argued that private finance is the most efficient method of financing infrastructure; the inherent subsidy of public finance is more appropriately used in other areas.
[23]   See Chapter 6.

funds if it did not invest them in the project (the "opportunity cost" of the project). This minimum ROI (which represents the cost of corporate financing) will normally exceed significantly the cost of project financing or government financing. Corporate financing is also less project specific than project financing, and therefore may fail to implement the project specific efficiencies and discipline generally mandated by project-specific limited recourse financing.

Project financing tends to attract a higher rate of interest than government financing, since the lenders take an element of commercial risk, but lower than in corporate financing, where the returns are needed to justify its diversion of investment funds from other opportunities. In particular, project financing offers a lower weighted cost of capital (WACC),[24] mixing cheaper limited recourse debt with more expensive private capital. It brings the following benefits:

- Highly structured risk management (including insurances)
- Fixed construction costs and time
- Fixed, or tightly controlled, operating costs
- Reduction of cost if the services are not delivered to specification

As discussed, these efficiencies are embedded in the project finance structure and form an integral part of the lenders' security package.

Financing that appears on the balance sheet of either the host government or the project sponsor will have implications for other transactions undertaken by the government or the project sponsor in that further financing will be more difficult and more expensive to obtain. By placing the debt on the balance sheet of a special-purpose vehicle in a manner that is not (or is only to a limited extent) consolidated onto the project sponsors' balance sheet or the government's liabilities, the debt becomes "off-balance sheet." For this reason, the actual cost of on-balance sheet financing may be greater than perceived. Project financing may enable the government and the project sponsor to finance the project off-balance sheet and therefore avoid these costs and risks.

The implications of project financing on a government or project sponsor will depend on the accounting treatment, and therefore the accounting standards, applied. Also, it should be noted that keeping debt off-balance sheet does not reduce actual liabilities for the government and may merely disguise government liabilities, reducing the effectiveness of government debt monitoring mechanisms. As a matter of policy, the use of off-balance

---

[24] See section 5.2.

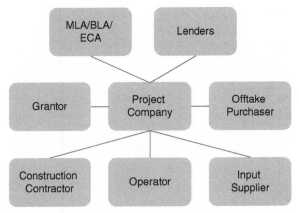

Figure 1.4. Parties to a PPP project.
Note: Multilateral agencies (MLAs), bilateral agencies (BLAs), export credit agencies (ECAs), etc.

sheet debt should be considered carefully and protective mechanisms should be implemented accordingly.[25]

1.6 Who Are the Key Actors in a PPP?

PPP is a complex process requiring input from a number of different parties, each playing an essential role in managing project risk. For the sake of simplifying our analysis, Figure 1.4 and the following discussion describe the parties typically present in a project-financed PPP project and their basic relationship with the project company. This list is not intended to be exhaustive.

1.6.1 Contracting Authority

The PPP project discussed here is based on the provision:

  i. by a national or local government, a government agency, or some regulatory authority (referred to here as the "contracting authority")
 ii. to a private party (the "project company")
iii. of the right to deliver infrastructure services.

---

[25] Irwin, T., Controlling spending commitments in PPPs, in *Public Investment and Public–Private Partnerships: Addressing Infrastructure Challenges and Managing Fiscal Risks*, eds. Schwartz, G., A. Corbacho, & K. Funke (2008).

The contracting authority will generally be responsible for the interface between the project and the government. The contracting authority will need to have the authority to grant the project to a private entity and may or may not be the public body that oversees, manages, and regulates the services provided over the long term. There will be contractual agreements between the contracting authority and the project company, such as a concession agreement, an implementation agreement, and/or a government support agreement.

1.6.2 Project Company

The sponsors will identify a project and put together a proposal or bid in an effort to be awarded the project. For a project-financed PPP project, and most forms of consortium or foreign investment, this typically means the private sector investors will form a new company (the "project company") – usually a limited liability company whose activities relate solely to the project – often known as a special-purpose vehicle (SPV) – which will contract with the contracting authority to implement the project. The use of an SPV is likely to enable the sponsors to finance the project on a limited recourse basis.[26] The contracting authority may require that the project company includes local investors in order to improve transfer of technology and provide jobs and training to local personnel.[27]

The sponsors or shareholders may include a variety of different actors, commercial, financial, and social. Companies may engage in a PPP project for social responsibility purposes rather than purely commercial ones. Nongovernmental organizations (NGOs) may also engage in a PPP project for a variety of commercial, social, and environmental reasons (see Box 1.3).

Box 1.3. Handwashing

The handwashing promotion initiative was a contractual partnership bringing together soap companies, government ministries, nongovernmental organizations, and the media in three Central American countries (Costa Rica, Guatemala, and El Salvador) to prevent diarrheal disease. This PPP, active from 1996 to 1999, focused on a handwashing campaign based on radio and television advertisements, posters, and flyers distributed by sales personnel and through mobile units to

---

[26] See section 5.2.
[27] See section 6.1.

communities, including school, municipal, and health center programs. The campaign also involved distribution of soap samples, promotional events, and print advertisements.

Source: www.globalhandwashing.org.

Most shareholders in the project company will want to be able to divest their shareholding as early as possible, in particular construction companies and equipment suppliers that are not accustomed to long-term shareholding. The contracting authority, on the other hand, will want the shareholders tied to the fortunes of the project company as long as possible to align their interests more with those of the contracting authority (e.g., a financially viable project over the long term).

Shareholders of the project company will often be both shareholder in the SPV and a contractor to the SPV. This may result in conflicts of interest and will need to be managed among the shareholders, the contracting authority, and the lenders; for example, a shareholder should not be in a position to negotiate or influence the negotiation of its contract on behalf of the SPV. These issues will typically be addressed in a shareholders' agreement between the parties when forming the SPV.[28]

1.6.3 Lenders

The profile of a lender group can range from project to project and may include a combination of private sector commercial lenders together with export credit agencies and bilateral and multilateral finance organizations. Funding is sometimes provided by project bonds, sold on the capital markets or to institutional investors. The lenders will not be in the operation, construction, or insurance business and therefore will not want to bear risks with which they are unfamiliar and that are more appropriately borne by other parties. Nevertheless, the lenders will be involved in most of the important phases of the works, including the financial structuring, the negotiation of the project documents, and certification of completion. They will generally maintain their review powers over the project with the assistance of an independent engineer (a specialist technical adviser who monitors construction and approves completion of milestones, among other things). In addition to their loan agreements with the project company, the lenders may require that direct agreements be entered into between themselves and certain other project participants.[29]

---

[28] See sections 5.2 and 8.12.

[29] For further discussion, see section 7.9; and of Scriven, J., N. Pritchard, & J. Delmon, eds., *A Contractual Guide to Major Construction Projects* (1999), chapter 29.

Multilateral Agencies (MLAs)

MLAs, for example, the World Bank, represent a grouping of nations, and are owned and funded by their members, normally sovereign nations. MLAs can participate in projects through advisory services and equity investments and by providing guarantees, insurance, or loans. An MLA can provide financing from its own funds and/or act as a conduit for funding from other sources. The World Bank Group and certain other such organizations generally refer to themselves as international finance institutions (IFIs) rather than MLAs. MLAs may provide specialized financial instruments, such as guarantees and political risk insurance (see sections 4.10 and 5.10).

It is commonly believed that governments make greater effort to ensure that loans to MLAs are repaid, even in difficult economic circumstances, a phenomenon known as the MLA "umbrella" or "halo" effect. This can work to the advantage of private lenders who cofinance alongside MLA loans. (The MLA loans from, for example, the International Finance Corporation [IFC] – a part of the World Bank – are known as "A" loans. A private lender can cofinance under "B" loans, where the IFC is the lender of record.) However, project sponsors perceive significant costs associated with MLA involvement, in particular the time needed to satisfy MLA procurement and environmental/social safeguard procedures.[30]

Bilateral Agencies (BLAs)

BLAs, sometimes described as development finance institutions, are similar to MLAs in purpose, approach, and financial instruments, but are funded by only one nation, for example, the French Agence Française de Développement (AFD) and the Dutch Development Bank (FMO). They are generally mandated to provide support to specific developing countries, in the form of debt or equity investment. They are perceived to be more politically oriented than MLAs in that they carry out the political will of their donor nation. BLA involvement may or may not be limited to projects involving investment by member country nationals; some BLAs have an "origins clause" requiring that projects funded by the BLA may not be in direct competition with opportunities being pursued by member country nationals.

Export Credit Agencies (ECAs)

ECAs are established by a given country to encourage explicitly the export of goods and services by its nationals, for example, US Eximbank or China

---

[30] Commercial banks are increasingly adopting these same requirements in order to ensure sustainable investments, e.g., the Equator Principles (see Box 7.1).

EximBank. Although traditionally governmen-trun, a certain number of these agencies have been privatized. The ECA can provide financing, insurance, or guarantees for the goods and services exported by its source country nationals. This financing is often significant, up to or exceeding 85 percent of the total price of the export. ECAs may provide direct lending or guarantee or insure repayment of commercial financing in case of political risk and/or commercial risk. The political risk borne by ECAs will generally include political violence, war, hostilities, expropriation, and currency transfer risk. In certain cases, ECAs provide extended risk cover such as change in law, changes in taxation, or a breach of a government obligation.

1.6.4 Offtake Purchaser

Where a project will deliver services to one or a limited number of purchasers/users, the offtake purchaser will promise to pay to use the project (in this context, "offtake" is an imperfect term) or to purchase any output produced in order to divert market risk away from the project company and the lenders. The purchase undertaking may be formalized by a contractual arrangement. This offtake purchase agreement will usually require the offtake purchaser to pay for a minimum amount of the project output or for all fixed costs, no matter how much output it takes, and thereby create a secure payment stream that will be an important basis for financing. An example would be a publicly owned utility agreeing to purchase power supplied by the project company, by means of a power purchase agreement (PPA).

1.6.5 Input Supplier

The input supplier assumes the supply risk for an input necessary for the operation of the project. Thus the project company is protected from the risk that the project will not reach its intended production level for lack of an essential input, such as fuel or raw materials. The input supplier ensures that a minimum quantity of input is delivered, at a minimum quality, at a defined price. The input supplier may also need to provide infrastructure to permit delivery of inputs, such as pipelines, ports, or railways. Only certain types of projects will require a form of input supply (e.g., most coal- or gas-fired power plants have fuel supply agreements [FSAs]). Other projects will rely on market availability of inputs or may not need inputs at all (e.g., toll roads). Still others will require a service rather than an input, such as the removal of sludge from a waste water treatment facility.

1.6.6 Construction Contractor

The contractor will design, build, test, and commission the project. This task is generally undertaken on a turnkey basis, placing completion and performance risk on the construction contractor, typically through some form of fixed-price, fixed-time turnkey[31] construction contract, such as a design-and-build (D&B) or engineering procurement and construction (EPC) agreement. The construction contract will, as far as possible, provide back-to-back risk allocation[32] with the project company's construction obligations, and therefore any construction risk placed on the project company will be in turn allocated to the construction contractor.

1.6.7 Operator

The project company will need to ensure operation and maintenance of the project over an extended period, from completion of construction, or the first completed section, until the end of the project period. The operator (whether one or more different companies or the project company itself) will need to manage the input supply and offtake purchase, monitor testing of the project, and ensure proper operation and maintenance. The project company will want to tie the operator's payment to the operator's performance. The operator may not want to bear the risk of operation cost or actual output, and may prefer to be reimbursed for its costs and paid a fee for its services. In any case, the payment scheme should include penalty fees and incentive bonuses to encourage efficient operation of the project. These matters will normally be dealt with in an operation and maintenance (O&M) agreement.

---

[31] The design and construction of works to completion, so that they are ready to produce cash flow – so that all the project company need do is "turn the key" and start operations.

[32] Where all risk borne by the project company is allocated to the operator, construction contractor, and other subcontractors; see Chapter 7.

PPP Frameworks

The creation of a PPP program will benefit from a well-designed institutional framework with clear and strong political support. A robust institutional framework organizes, coordinates, and focuses the resources of the government in the manner best suited to encourage and enable PPP. This chapter will review the institutional framework needed to promote PPP by describing the responsibilities to be allocated to different government entities, the project development process, the different approvals required at key decision points during the project and how the government supports PPP transaction preparation, procurement, and implementation.[1]

Key Messages for Policy Makers

- *Make sure the different roles are allocated and that the system works* ideological purity is less important.
- *Institutions are only as good as the people in them and the funding/ mandate they are given.* Real capacity building (not just the occasional training or trip abroad) is important to a sustainable program, in particular learning by doing and leveraging the experience of those who have delivered projects
- *Strong, consistent leadership is key* – providing coordination among different institutions and ensuring consistency of practices and focus of efforts generally require clear direction from the highest levels of government.
- *Seek a robust value for money assessment and transparent, competitive procurement* – these can deliver better projects cheaper and faster,

---

[1] For a more detailed discussion of PPP programs, see Delmon, J., *Public-Private Partnership Programs: A Framework for Private Sector Investment in Infrastructure* (2014).

protect the government and the project from ex-post criticism and make the project less vulnerable to change, external shocks, and the temptation of future governments to reverse decisions.

Creating a PPP program requires the mobilization of significant expertise and effort from dedicated teams, with the resources and political clout to perform their functions. Strong PPP institutions can help, as discussed previously.

A quick comparison of the PPP programs in India, South Africa, Korea, the Philippines, and the United Kingdom[2] shows a few common themes emerging:

- Multistage approvals for PPP projects with the Ministry of Finance (MoF) or equivalent agency, leading toward approvals based on economic returns, value for money, and risk allocation
- Public finance support mechanisms, such as project preparation funds and capital grants to PPPs
- Dependence on contracting authorities for project identification and acting as the procuring authority
- Publicly owned and funded PPP units

The Egyptian PPP Unit provides an interesting contrast; based in the Ministry of Finance, unlike most national PPP units, it can take on the role of procuring entity, driving the process, much like some of the subnational PPP units, such as British Colombia, Canada, or Saint Petersburg, Russia.

2.1 Setting and Implementing the PPP Legal Framework

The government will wish to create a clear and stable legal environment for PPP projects in order to reduce the perception of risk, attract more competition for projects, attract more competition for finance, and therefore reduce project costs. The legal (and regulatory) framework creates the foundation for the institutional, regulatory, commercial, and financial environment for PPP with clarity, consistency, transparency and certainty. It is particularly critical for the institutional framework, describing the interactions, relationships, and coordination that underpin that framework.[3]

---

[2] Dachs, J., *International Benchmark Comparator Report* (February 2013).

[3] For further discussion of these issues, and their application in different jurisdictions, see Delmon, J. & Delmon, R., eds., *The Law of Project Finance and PPP Projects in Frontier Jurisdictions* (2013). In relation to legal frameworks, the reader may also wish to consult the PPP in the Infrastructure Resource Center website, which describes PPP in infrastructure legal frameworks, sample laws, regulations and contracts. www.worldbank.org/PPP; United Nations Commission on International Trade Law (UNCITRAL), *Legislative*

2.1.1 Policy

Successful PPP frameworks have clear, well understood policies. The PPP policy must provide clarity to stakeholders (public and private) on how the government wants to undertake PPPs. The policy should include the following:

- Purpose of the PPP policy: vision, mission, and goals
- Definition of PPP, for example, projects will be considered PPP if
  - The private partner provides some combination of the design, construction, funding, management, maintenance, and operation of infrastructure
  - The project provides long-term, performance-based services
- Identification of responsibilities among government entities, including
  - Selection and identification of projects for PPP, project promotion, development, and marketing
  - Government support in allocation and management of fiscal risk
  - Regulation of performance and monitoring implementation
  - Gathering of know-how and lessons learned, standardization, and operating guidelines
- Government approvals that must be sought at different stages of the project
- Conditions to the allocation of government support or liabilities

---

Key Messages for Policy Makers

- *PPP policies should be clear, comprehensive, yet flexible* – periodic updates are a useful way to adopt lessons learned.
- *Keep the legal framework simple and clear* – do not confuse complexity with comprehensiveness. Simple is better, and will give more confidence to investors. Detail is best left to secondary legislation (such as regulations) and guidelines that are more easily amended to respond to change.

Guide on Privately Financed Infrastructure Projects (2000); UNCITRAL, *Model Legislative Provisions on Privately Financed Infrastructure Projects* (2003); United Nations, *UNIDO Guidelines for Infrastructure Development through Build–Operate–Transfer* (1996); European Commission, *European Commission Guidelines for Successful Public–Private Partnerships* (2003); OECD, *OECD Basic Elements of a Law on Concession Agreements* (1999-2000); European Bank for Reconstruction and Development, *Concession Assessment Project* (2004).

- Do not use the legal framework to second-guess the PPP contract by creating rights and obligations at law that should be addressed in the contract on agreed terms. If the government is keen to establish such terms, standard form documents can achieve this, where the terms can be spelled out in detail.

2.1.2 Laws and Regulations

PPP legal frameworks are often anchored in a legal instrument that implements the PPP policy.[4] These may be called PPP laws, concession laws, BOT laws, etc. Or the legal framework may be embedded in other legal instruments (laws, decrees or regulations), for example, they may be related to procurement, infrastructure sectors, government finance, or privatization.

The need for a specific law or set of regulations associated with PPP will depend on the nature of the legal system and current legal framework. In some legal systems, in particular those applying civil law, PPP laws, and the like are common, as a way to formally sanction PPP and specify the extent to which it is a permissible method of procurement for government entities; for example, Russia and Thailand have passed specific PPP laws.

In some cases, a passage of law would be too political or would simply take too long, and therefore PPP regimes are established in PPP regulations as secondary legislation. This was the approach taken in Nigeria, with PPP regulations created under the public procurement law (though a PPP law was before Parliament in Nigeria at the time of writing this text). In Indonesia, the PPP "law" was implemented through a series of presidential decrees (Perpres), which in the legal hierarchy are inferior to laws and government regulations. This has created difficulties where sector procurement processes implemented under government regulations are inconsistent with the PPP decree; the government is considering a PPP law.

In other systems, in particular common law systems, PPP laws are less common. The United Kingdom does not have a separate PPP law. The PPP function was created within the Treasury; thus the use of PPP is encouraged not by law but by the intervention of a powerful central ministry that creates incentives to ensure compliance.

Beyond its strictly legal relevance, a PPP law can also be used to demonstrate commitment across government and the legislature for the PPP agenda.

---

[4] Examples of PPP legal instruments can be found at www.worldbank.org/pppiresource.

2.1.3 Guidelines

Detailed and "plain language" operating guidelines are needed. These guidelines provide clear, simple instructions detailing each stage of the process, to ensure consistency of practice among those implementing PPP and to improve transparency. These guidelines should be drafted for the benefit of government staff and private investors alike. For example, in the Philippines, the amended Build Operate Transfer (BOT) Law is supplemented by detailed and clearly written implementing rules and regulations, the investment and coordination committee guidelines and procedures, and a series of forms and checklists that must be utilized by the contracting authorities and local government units during project selection and development. These forms and checklists are periodically reviewed and revised based on lessons learned. In Colombia, El Consejo Nacional de Política Económica y Social (CONPES) issues written policy decisions, improving the PPP legal framework as it gains experience with PPP project implementation.

Many countries with strong PPP programs use lessons learned from their experiences (and failures) to improve their subsequent efforts. South Korea revisits its PPP policy annually to adjust for lessons learned. In Colombia, CONPES has issued more than one hundred written policy decisions building on and improving the PPP legal framework as it gains experience implementing PPP projects across multiple infrastructure sectors and with evolving approaches to financing.

See section 2.13 for a brief introduction to the most critical legal issues that need to be addressed in the creation of a PPP framework.

2.2 Coordination of PPP Program

PPP involves a significant shift in mindset, processes and practices in government procurement, development, and management of infrastructure. This shift requires a strong effort from government policy makers and staff to drive PPP policy implementation and coordinate government efforts. The coordination function helps to streamline government PPP activities and ensure consistency of government support for PPP.

A separate entity or steering committee may be created to ensure coordination among the different government agencies. The coordination function is often played by a high-level group, possibly at the cabinet level, and generally supported by a technical committee. Coordinating the different government ministries and agencies that will provide critical inputs into any successful PPP program or project can be particularly challenging.

In most countries with successful PPP programs, the program and initial projects were strongly and personally backed by the president or prime minister. For example, in both Colombia and the Philippines, the president chairs the interministerial committee responsible for PPP projects. In the Netherlands, Australia, and the United Kingdom, decisions on major PPP projects, as well as the overall PPP program, are made by the cabinet, which is chaired by the prime minister. In India, the Cabinet Committee on Infrastructure (CCI) decides on national infrastructure sector projects and monitors their performance. This twelve-member committee is headed by the Indian prime minister.

In Kenya, a PPP Steering Committee has been created at the principal secretary level with representatives from key central ministries, line ministries, and the private sector as well as the attorney general.[5] The Steering Committee is a high-level body that reviews project issues periodically and solves critical problems as they arise, such as where a government agency is not providing inputs in a timely manner, where a constraint will require additional support from a government agency, or where an agency's activities are constraining the project.

Box 2.1. PPP Canada

Ontaria, Alberta, British Columbia, and New Brunswick have active PPP programs and agencies dedicated to oversee PPP procurement and implementation. These local government bodies provide advice and support, including funding and in some cases financing, to public bodies to develop infrastructure, including through PPP. At the federal level, PPP Canada (a Crown Corporation established in 2008) became operational in 2009 and is mandated to deliver public infrastructure with better value for money, timeliness and accountability through PPP. It has an independent board of directors, reports to Parliament through the minister of finance and oversees the C\$1.2 billion P3 Canada Fund, which launches annual calls for proposals for funding of up to 25 percent of a project's direct construction costs. PPP Canada can also co-fund capacity building and background studies for PPP projects.

Source: www.p3canada.ca.

---

[5] www.treasury.go.ke.

2.3 Specialized PPP Agency

Many jurisdictions use a centralized institution (often known as a *public–private partnership [PPP] unit*) to provide capacity. This institution is generally located within or attached to a key ministry that provides resources for project development or other incentives to use PPP. Typically PPP units have a number of functions, including the following:

- Improving the policy/legal/regulatory context for PPP
- Ensuring that the PPP program is integrated with overall planning, fiscal risk management, and regulatory systems
- Ensuring that projects protect government, environmental, and social interests and comply with relevant requirements
- Promoting PPP opportunities at national and regional levels among potential investors and the financial markets and developing those projects that maximize value for money, competition, and sustainability

The PPP unit can provide a single point of contact for investors and government agencies alike, coordinating PPP activities across sectors so that the PPP program is as uniform and consistent for investors as possible. A PPP unit usually works best when connected with a key ministry or department (such as the Ministry of Finance or Planning). PPP units with executive powers tend to work better than those that provide solely advisory services, as they have more influence over contracting authorities.

The most common approach is to create a single PPP unit to promote PPP, assess potential projects and help manage government liabilities. For example, South Africa created a PPP unit in the Ministry of Finance, as did the United Kingdom, with the Treasury Taskforce, which became Partnerships UK and then split into Infrastructure UK and Local Partnerships.[6]

However, there is an inherent conflict of interest where the same entity is responsible for promoting PPP and monitoring/regulating the risks borne by the government. The promotions team is incentivized to bring projects to market, which may conflict with the need to reject projects that do not represent value for money for the government.

The importance of legal, environmental and social concerns, including issues as diverse as labor unions and foreign investment criteria (often established by treaty or compacts like the Equator Principles),[7] should not

---

[6] www.localpartnerships.org.uk/.
[7] www.equator-principles.com.

Box 2.2. South Korea's PPP Unit

The Republic of Korea introduced the Promotion of Private Capital into Social Overhead Capital Investment Act (PPP Act) in August 1994. The Ministry of Strategy and Finance is responsible for developing and implementing PPP policies and chairs the high-level PPP Review Committee that must give final approval to PPP projects. The Public and Private Infrastructure Investment Management Center (PIMAC) at the Korea Development Institute (KDI) serves as a secretariat for the PPP Review Committee. PIMAC has four major functions:

1. Policy research and strategy
2. Technical support to review proposed PPPs using feasibility studies and value-for-money tests
3. Promotion of PPP to foreign investors
4. Education programs on PPP for line ministries/local governments and private partners

Approximately eighty people staff PIMAC, of whom forty-two work in the PPP Division. PIMAC is fully funded by the Ministry of Strategy and Finance, with additional resources from fees levied upon line ministries/ local governments for services provided.

Source: Dachs, *International Benchmark Comparator Report*

---

be underestimated. These issues form a key part of the public consultation, awareness and relations efforts that will be critical to the success of any PPP program. The PPP agency can help sensitize government entities to these requirements, ensure consultations are carried out and help manage backlash from different constituencies.

The PPP unit plays a political and technical function, working closely with line ministries and contracting authorities to help them use PPP, to help them select the right projects to develop, and to work through the various challenges that arise. The unit will need commercial and financial skills and, importantly, legal and political expertise.

One of the critical challenges for contracting authorities is the lack of capacity in PPP and the difficulty in allocating budget for project preparation. PPP units are therefore often given responsibility for project development funds (money provided to contracting authorities to pay for feasibility studies, transaction advisers, and other technical assistance; see sections 3.3 and 4.1), to encourage the use of PPP, help bridge the gap in capacity,

---

Box 2.3. South Africa's PPP Unit

A Strategic Framework for PPPs was endorsed by the South African Cabinet in December 1999, and in April 2000 Treasury Regulations for PPPs were first issued in terms of the Public Finance Management Act (Act 1 of 1999). By mid-2000, with technical assistance funding from the United States Agency for International Development (USAID), the German Corporation for International Cooperation (GTZ), and the U.K.'s Department for International Development (DFID), the PPP unit was established as a unit within the Budget Office in the National Treasury.

The PPP unit also administers a project development facility (PDF) as a "trading entity" – a government financing facility that funds project development as well as recovers funds from successfully closed PPP projects. The PDF cannot appoint the transaction advisers itself; these will either be appointed by the contracting authority or by an intermediary such as the Development Bank of Southern Africa (DBSA) on behalf of the contracting authority.

Source: Dachs, *International Benchmark Comparator Report*

---

and ensure the use of best practices and high-quality advisers. Contracting authorities may be loath to use the PPP unit, concerned about sharing information and adding complication to the project process. However, access to such funding will encourage contracting authorities to use the PPP unit and increase the quality of projects accordingly.

In addition, PPP desks or nodes are often created in different sector ministries, state-owned enterprises (SOEs) and local governments to capture skills and funding at the project implementation level, with close links to central PPP institutions to ensure cross-fertilization, development of best practice and greater economies of scale for advisers, capacity-building programs, and other knowledge functions.

2.4 Project Team

A technical team will be formed to support, prepare, and implement each project. The contracting authority's project team will be responsible for overseeing the preparation of the PPP project and implementing of the PPP procurement process through the final negotiation; signing of the PPP agreement; and design, construction and operation of the project.

> ### Box 2.4. The Importance of Capacity
>
> *The lack of commercial skills to match those of the private sector can put the public sector at a disadvantage in the negotiation and management of contracts. Since our 2009 report on commercial skills for complex projects, the government has taken steps to improve commercial skills across the public sector. Despite this, the public sector's skills are generally not as well developed as their private sector counterparts, which puts value for money at risk.*
>
> Source: U.K. National Audit Office, 2011

The project team is responsible for providing the key management, oversight and decision-making functions for the PPP on behalf of the contracting authority. It will need to address key issues in PPP, such as those with the following aspects: technical, legal, financial, commercial, environmental, social, stakeholder management, regulatory, etc.

The team will change in role, mandate, capacity, staffing and funding requirements as the project develops and moves from phase to phase of the PPP cycle

When establishing a project team, contracting authorities should provide it with clear authority and resources to make timely decisions on behalf of the public authority.

2.5 Fiscal Support

To encourage line ministries and state-owned enterprises to procure infrastructure services through PPP, support may be provided to fund project development costs such as the hiring of suitable expert transaction advisers or the provision of extrabudgetary support like capital grants to defray contracting authority costs. Such financial support reflects the value (implicitly or explicitly) of the benefits to be obtained by the government and society generally from the project. Chapter 3 provides more detailed discussion of government support for PPP.

The government needs to decide whether government support would represent value for money, should it be provided, and if so, how much, when, by whom, and on what conditions. In the Netherlands and South Africa, the amount of direct fiscal support to a project can be as much as 100 per cent of the cost of the project – for example, in the form of an availability payment made over the life of the facility. Such high levels of direct fiscal support are common for education and health facilities and government accommodation PPPs. In India, the government provides direct fiscal support of up to 40 percent of cost or the amount needed to make them commercially viable (whichever is less), provided the project is justified on a cost-benefit basis. In contrast, many government officials believe that PPPs should be largely self-funded, with infrequent and strictly limited use of direct government support. The unintended consequence of this approach is that opportunities to stretch public funds and increase their impact are lost, and time is wasted in preparing projects that never proceed because direct fiscal support is not approved in needed amounts.

Box 2.5. Cost of Public versus Private Capital

It is often assumed that public capital is cheaper than private capital, but the two are difficult to compare; the cost of public debt is often (though not always) cheaper than private debt, but the actual cost of public capital should include the hidden risk premium of the implicit guarantee of taxpayers for public debt (the taxpayers' support making the debt cheaper). The equivalent risk premium is included in the cost of private debt. The actual cost of public capital should also include the opportunity cost for the country of using its capital for different purposes. Chile, for example, applies a "social discount rate" when it uses its capital for infrastructure as compared to other sectors that would be less likely to attract private financing.

Source: Klein, M., The risk premium for evaluating public projects, *Oxford Review of Economic Policy*, 13, no. 4 at 29 (1997); McKinsey Global institute, *Infrastructure Productivity: How to Save $1 Trillion a Year (January 2013)* at 25.

2.6 Communication Strategy

Communications is an essential aspect of project development and implementation. The communications strategy for the PPP program and for each project should be developed early, to ensure timely engagement of stakeholders. Principles of communications strategy include the following:

- *Proactivity* – communicate issues early and often; do not wait to respond to issues, be the one to raise them from the beginning before they become concerns.
- *Transparency* – key decisions and processes need to be shared openly to ensure buy-in, manage stress/concerns and elicit feedback.

- *Listening* – communication must be two-way; stakeholders will have valuable contributions to project design and implementation.
- *Inclusiveness* – ensure public consultation, in particular with those groups most directly implicated, such as staff to be transferred, consumers or adjacent residents, and responsible officials. Information provided must be balanced and fair, providing pros and cons to help stakeholders understand decisions taken and issues analyzed.
- *Coordination* – establish communications protocol to manage communication, in particular written communications, by the government to ensure management and consistency of messaging.

2.7 Project Selection

Not all projects are appropriate for PPP. Government should consider total investment needed, total funding available, and what part of its investment needs to develop through PPP. Government will have many investment projects, but only a limited number of them will have potential for implementation as PPPs. The process of selecting which projects to implement as PPP (as compared to public financing or purely private) is complex, requiring a preliminary analysis of each project based on sufficient data.

It is tempting to try to identify the most "strategic" projects to focus efforts on PPP. However, in many countries, the projects identified as "strategic" are often large, complex, politically driven, and generally very difficult to achieve through PPP. To be implemented as a PPP, a project needs to be technically, financially, and commercially viable. As discussed later in this chapter, in parallel with such large strategic projects, it may be preferable to develop some smaller, less complex, and more financially viable projects to help demonstrate that PPP can deliver as promised.

Government needs to focus on investment projects that have greatest potential to be viable PPP projects. Given limited time and resources, selecting the wrong projects for PPP can undermine the entire PPP program and also waste government resources and render the investment program ineffective.

The planning function needs to help allocate projects among public and private solutions most effectively. Equally, those responsible for investment decisions, prioritizing some projects for public investments and selecting those appropriate for PPP, must have the knowledge and data needed to make those decisions.

Projects identified for development through PPP must also:

- Comply with national, local, and sector plans and performance targets
- Be affordable within the contracting authority's budget projections or to end-users
- Be attractive to the private sector, including clear scope, robust revenues, and manageable risk
- Not rely on new, untested, or experimental technologies

Government should avoid the temptation to require perfect results. This early selection process involves a limited amount of information and is therefore likely to be imprecise, but is a critical part of the decision process.

When selecting projects and formulating a pipeline strategy, government should note that the PPP program may need to be phased, in particular where a number of large projects are contemplated. The contracting authority may have difficulty implementing multiple projects in parallel, given the staffing, skills, and financial requirements. Also, the debt markets have limited capacity and appetite. Phasing will allow the market to absorb demand without increasing costs.

The committees that make PPP decisions in countries with successful PPP programs have a value-for-money ethos, viewing PPPs primarily as a way to increase the total value of services to the public and not simply as a substitute for public finance. For example, in the Philippines, the National Economic Development Agency (NEDA) presents all relevant information to a powerful committee of ministers (including the Department of Finance and the Sector Ministry) who decide simultaneously whether a project should go ahead, whether it should be a PPP, and what fiscal support it should be allocated.

2.8 Project Preparation

A properly prepared project can only be achieved by the investment of time and resources in project development. The government will need to form a project team, with appropriate skills, focused on the transaction. Many of these skills can be bought in through short-term contracts and transaction advisers, though the project team will need the capacity to manage those advisers and the underlying issues to be resolved.

Box 2.6. The Indian PPP Institutional Framework

In 2005, the Cabinet Committee on Economic Affairs (CCEA) of India established the procedure for approval of PPP projects and the establishment of a Public Private Partnership Approval Committee (PPPAC). The PPPAC is constituted with the secretaries of MoF's Department of Economic Affairs (DEA), the Planning Commission, MoF's Department of Expenditure, the Department of Legal Affairs, and the secretary of the department proposing the project. The DEA secretary chairs the PPPAC. A PPP cell was established in the DEA and undertakes the appraisal on behalf of the PPPAC, screens identified proposals for funding under the India Infrastructure Project Development Fund (IIPDF) and provides an advisory function to support state cells and municipalities.

Source: Dachs, *International Benchmark Comparator Report*

The contracting authority will need experienced and professional financial, legal, technical, insurance, and other advisers when identifying, designing and procuring a project. Each of these advisers will be subject to different agendas and incentives that will influence the nature of their advice and the ease with which the government will be able to manage their involvement. The project team (possibly through the PPP institutions) should have access to expertise in managing such advisers. To provide capacity to the project teams, the United Kingdom arranged for secondment of staff from commercial banks and law firms with expertise in project finance into the PPP unit. South Africa and Egypt initially hired long-term expert consultants who had experience in successful PPP programs to work in their PPP unit to improve access to global best practices.

Box 2.7. The U.K.'s Erstwhile PPP Unit

Partnership UK (PUK) was formed by the U.K. government in June 2000 following the recommendation in the second Sir Malcolm Bates review of 1999, and absorbed back into HM Treasury in 2012. It was a PPP, majority owned (51 percent) by private sector shareholders and the remainder retained by government (HM Treasury 44.6 percent and Scottish Executive 4.4 percent). PUK supported the following:

- Individual projects before, during, and after procurement – by using its commercial experience and expertise

- Government in developing policy and monitoring compliance – by using its market knowledge to ensure that outputs are effective and practical

PUK financed itself by charging fees to the public sector for its services, benchmarked against private advisory companies.

Source: www.treasury.gov.uk/public-private-partnerships.

2.9 Demonstration Projects

There is no substitute for experience. Most countries with successful PPP programs adopt a "learn-by-doing" approach, using the experience with early projects to improve the PPP framework. Equally, most of these countries experienced problems with their early projects, but they learned from these and revised their rules, policies, and guidelines to avoid repeating those same mistakes. For example, in South Africa, the initial project scope specified for the first maximum security prison procured on a PPP basis proved to be fiscally unaffordable. As a result, the project required two years of design and scope changes after the preferred bidder stage was reached to correct this. Learning from this experience, the PPP guidelines now require the strict testing of fiscal affordability at the earliest stage of project preparation.

Governments are well advised to select viable, strategic projects to test their PPP framework. In implementing such projects, they will identify legal and institutional gaps and other opportunities to improve the framework. These early projects also send a clear message to the market that the government is serious about PPP and is adopting a reasonable model for risk allocation.

Box 2.8. The Challenges of Large Demonstration Projects

In Russia, the government of the City of Saint Petersburg decided to launch the Western High Speed Diameter toll road as a large, single project with project costs exceeding Euro 12 billion in 2007. The subsequent tender process resulted in a single bidder, due primarily to the size of the project. After efforts at negotiation, the city chose to cancel the bidding process, restructure the project, and retender based on smaller phases of the project with more creative use of available financing, which led to the successful implementation of the project.

There is a tendency to select early PPP projects that are large, complex, and politically popular rather than financially viable (ironically often known as "transformational" projects). This is generally a mistake. PPP is a difficult structure to adopt, and large complex projects can add to that difficulty. Early projects create precedent that will apply to later projects and create expectations among investors. These early projects should therefore have the following characteristics:

- Of sufficient size to attract experienced PPP investors, but not so large that they are overly complex; in fact, smaller projects may be better
- Well developed, that is, feasibility study done and agreed upon, with sufficient funding and staffing for preparation
- Politically strategic, but not so high profile that political interference is likely

This is, of course, the ideal. It is rare that a PPP program has the luxury of selecting only feasible, viable projects. Most governments have a long list of large, politically driven, high-profile projects that do not meet the criteria or public financing and are often the first projects proposed for PPP. It may not be politically feasible to reject all such projects. However, it may be possible to focus on the most viable for such projects. In parallel, it may be possible to develop some demonstration projects, smaller, less political and more likely to succeed. Where large, complex projects are implemented, the government needs to have the patience and courage to restructure or change direction where necessary (see Box 2.8).

2.10 Preparation of Good Practice Contracts and Bid Documents

The standardization of risk allocation and contract terms helps reduce the cost of financing and project development. Standardization should be implemented gradually, using an iterative process for market feedback. Reference should be made to the suites of standard documents developed by different PPP programs, many of which can be found at www .worldbank.org/pppirc.

The standardization achieved in the United Kingdom[8] and South Africa[9] demonstrates the benefits available, including the reduction of time and cost of procurement. They also demonstrate the need for these provisions

---

[8] www.hm-treasury.gov.uk/documents/public-private-partnerships/ppp_index.cfm.
[9] www.ppp.gov.za.

to evolve over time, as investors and lenders become more comfortable with the PPP framework and program.

Box 2.9. Lessons from London Underground – Allocating Too Much Risk to the Private Sector

Contracts that were supposed to deliver 35 station upgrades over the first three years in fact delivered 14–40% of the requirement; stations that were supposed to cost Metronet SSL £2 million in fact cost £7.5 million – 375% of the anticipated price; by November 2006, only 65% of scheduled track renewal had been achieved. They have ended in collapse and chaos. It was a spectacular failure.

The Government should remember ... that the private sector will never wittingly expose itself to substantial risk without ensuring that it is proportionally, if not generously rewarded. Ultimately, the taxpayer pays the price.

Source: House of Common, Transport Committee, "The London Underground and the Public–Private Partnership Agreements," Second Report of Session 2007–08, HC 45 (January 2008)

The Philippine national planning agency continues to revise its model PPP agreements on the basis of lessons learned from prior deals and international best practices and in conformance with the applicable rules and regulations for PPPs. The Netherlands has standard contracts for roads, schools and government buildings. South Africa issued in 2004 a set of "Standardized PPP Provisions." India has developed model concession agreements for its national and state highway, port, airport, passenger, and freight rail projects.[10]

Colombia does not utilize standard or model PPP contracts, but it has established broad policy guidelines with respect to risk allocation for PPP projects involving transport, energy, communications, and water and wastewater.

2.11 Value for Money

Value for money (VfM) is a measure of the net value that a government receives from a PPP project. The assessment of VfM helps the government decide whether a project should be implemented as a PPP and how much support the government should provide to that project. Assessing VfM is as much an art as a science, given the various and changing concepts of "value" that the government will want to access and apply to PPP.

---

[10] Available at infrastructure.gov.in/mca.htm.

Box 2.10. Quantitative versus Qualitative VfM

The U.K. National Audit Office emphasizes that financial appraisal and cost modelling is just one part of the overall assessment of projects and has sought to discourage appraisers striving for disproportionate levels of accuracy. Qualitative considerations – viability, desirability, achievability – should frame the approach to quantitative assessment. The quantitative assessment should form part of the overall value for money judgement rather than be seen as a stand-alone pass/fail test. Neither the quantitative or qualitative assessment should be considered in isolation.

Source: Infrastructure UK, *A New Approach to Public Private Partnerships* (December 2012)

Various approaches and models endeavor to quantify VfM, in particular through public sector comparators (see Box 2.11), cost-benefit analysis and shadow models (where a financial model is developed from the bidder's perspective to test likely bidder concerns). Best practice uses such quantitative analysis as important data but looks to a qualitative analysis to respond to all relevant parameters rather than seek measurable accuracy in assessment (see Box 2.10).

Box 2.11. Public Sector Comparator (PSC)

A comparison between the cost of public delivery of the project and that through PPP can provide a useful mechanism in assessing value for money. But a PSC is difficult to assemble with any accuracy. In order to assess PSC properly, full information is needed on how the project would be implemented by the public sector, including actual cost of construction, cost of operation, cost of financing, and risk borne by the public sector (which is difficult to calculate with any accuracy).

For further discussion of PSCs, see www.treasury.gov.uk.

In some cases, VfM is used as an ex-post rationalization of a political decision to implement a project. This can jeopardize the sustainability of the project and PPP program. A robust VfM exercise at the time of project selection and procurement can protect a project from ex-post challenges. See Section 4.2 on feasibility studies and value for money.

2.12 Approval Process

Approvals help raise key questions and issues during preparation of the project. They are important for quality control but also for buy-in from different agencies, achieving greater ownership and certainty for investors. But these layers of different agencies with approval rights can complicate the process. To the extent possible, these approval requirements should be streamlined, to facilitate efficient application, reduce the cost of approvals and fast-track the investment process.

The following describes a few of the key parties that often have approval rights and the points in the project process at which such approvals are usually required:

- *Sector line ministry* will be responsible for sector strategy, prioritization and risk management, in particular during project selection and feasibility verification (based on the feasibility study), before issue of bid documents and during award/financial close and renegotiation.
- *Ministry of Finance/Budget/Planning* will be responsible for allocation of government support and fiscal risk management, in particular during feasibility verification (based on the feasibility study); before issue of bid documents; and during award/financial close, and renegotiation.
- *Sector regulator* may be responsible for some combination of economic impact (e.g., tariff levels, cross-subsidization among consumers, and cost allowances), environmental impact, and consumer protection.
- *Procurement agency* is often responsible for monitoring the use of transparent, competitive procurement.
- *Environmental agency, land agency, central bank, attorney general, etc.;* there may be a variety of agencies with regulatory authority over specific issues.

2.13 Key Legal Constraints

This section provides a brief introduction to the most critical legal issues that need to be addressed in the creation of a PPP framework.[11] It describes issues and sets out the kind of questions that an investor will ask when doing due diligence on a country's legal system.

---

[11] A more complete discussion of the legal issues that are important to PPP projects can be found in Delmon, J., & R. Delmon, eds., *International Project Finance and PPPs: A Legal Guide to Key Growth Markets* (2013).

Box 2.12. Delusion and Deception in Risk Assessment

As human beings, our risk assessment tends to be influenced by personal beliefs or biases, for example:

- Underestimating the time and cost required to complete a task
- Believing we understand risk better than we really do
- Underestimating risks associated with familiar tasks, for example, traffic accidents while driving to work and slipping in the bathtub
- Validating prior decisions

There may be collaboration in these influences. This collaboration may have pure motives, for example, exaggerating the benefits and underestimating costs and time to help decision makers justify a project they believe is important. And yet, this deception ends up costing the taxpayer, since risks that are ignored are not managed.

Source: Flyvbjerg, B., M. Garbuio, and D. Lovallo, Delusion and deception in large infrastructure projects: two models for explaining and preventing executive disaster, *California Management Review, vol.* 51, *no* 2, *Winter* 2009; Delmon, J., *Project Finance, BOT Projects and Risk* (2005); Delmon, J., *Increasing the efficiency of risk allocation in project financed public private partnership (PPP) transactions by reducing the impact of Risk Noise, Part I and II (International Construction Law Review).*

2.13.1 Vires

The PPP legal framework will need to describe which government authorities and entities have the power to perform different functions associated with a PPP project. An *ultra vires* act is one performed outside of a party's legal rights, for example, where a party enters into an obligation or agreement that it is not empowered to undertake. An *ultra vires* obligation or agreement may be void by law. This doctrine can affect the acts of private companies and government bodies. See further discussion in section 7.1.

2.13.2 Government Obligations and Support

PPP projects are often not viable without some form of government support, such as the provision of land, assets, subsidies, guarantees, or other value, in particular when the central government is not a party to the key project agreements, or the infrastructure service does not in and of itself generate sufficient revenues.[12]

---

[12] See Chapter 5 for further discussion of government support.

Investors will need to know the forms that government support can take, the processes and criteria for approval of government support, and whether government support is binding on the government or is it voidable, such as where budget allocations are insufficient.

2.13.3 Creation of Limited Liability Project Company

Project financing relies on the limited liability nature of project vehicles to achieve limited recourse financing (where the liability of shareholders is limited to the equity invested in the project; see section 5.2) and is subject to the ability of courts to look through the limited liability nature of the entity, for example, by piercing the corporate veil (where the level of control of the company by the shareholder exceeds permissible levels).[13]

2.13.4 Procurement

Procurement requirements are generally aimed at maximizing the efficiency of the process, reducing opportunities for corruption, and encouraging open competition.[14] The selection process should be specified, creating a fair and transparent set of tender rules, with limited exceptions allowing direct negotiations, mechanisms for implementing unsolicited proposals (or rejecting them entirely), and the applicable regime for challenging project awards. See section 4.5.

2.13.5 Land Rights and Acquisition

PPP projects, particularly in the transport sector, can be land intensive. Therefore, the ability of the government to use compulsory acquisition (expropriation) of land without undue delay is essential. This acquisition generally involves judicial and administrative proceedings to set the land aside (to avoid squatters inhabiting the land once the project becomes known or speculators depriving land owners of their entitlements), allow the government to seize the land, and establish the amount of compensation to be paid to the owner of the land and any other affected party. Ideally, this regime will allow the government to acquire the land quickly while providing clear rights to compensation and resettlement, to provide certainty to all stakeholders.

---

[13] See Delmon, *Private Sector Investment in Infrastructure*, 2nd ed., for further discussion of limited recourse structures.

[14] For further discussion of public procurement requirements, see chapters 4 and 5 of Scriven et al., eds., *A Contractual Guide to Major Construction Projects*.

2.13.6 Setting and Collecting Tariffs

To the extent the project company must rely on tariffs from consumers as the basis for its revenue stream, the legal framework will need to define the following:

- How those tariffs are set, whether they can be set by contract, and on what basis they are adjusted over time
- Any limitations to the basis on which tariffs can be set; for example, can they be set based on profit margin/rate of return, foreign exchange rates, or cost of debt?
- Whether the project company is entitled to collect tariffs from consumers. Can the project company enforce its right to collect tariffs through penalties or disconnection/denial of access?

2.13.7 Penalties, Sanctions, and Bonuses

The project, in order to align incentives, will include a regime of sanctions or penalties for situations in which project parties fail to comply with their contractual obligations; for example, sanctions for the project company for substandard service delivery and for the construction contractor for late completion.

Jurisdictions treat penalties or liquidated damages differently. Some jurisdictions allow them so long as they are reasonable, others require them to be a genuine pre-estimates of the damage likely to be suffered, as in England, for example. Still others allow the court to modify such penalties in order to achieve reasonableness, in particular where one of the counter-parties is a public entity, for example, as in France. There may be limitations on charging interest on interest or on imposing a rate of interest on judgments that is different from that prescribed by the court.

2.13.8 Security Rights over Assets

The lender will seek remedies or opportunities to control the management of borrower assets in the event of its bankruptcy or insolvency.[15] Each jurisdiction will place different rules on the taking of security over different project rights or assets (existing or future), for example, real or movable assets, contractual rights (including future rights as they crystallize), endorsement of insurance policies to the benefit of third parties, rights over bank accounts (ideally fixed and floating charges), and the pledge of shares.

---

[15] See Chapter 5 for further discussion of security rights.

2.13.9 Dispute Resolution

Parties to a PPP project generally prefer to submit any disputes that may arise to arbitration, because of its flexibility and greater ease of award execution,[16] rather than to state courts. International arbitration benefits from sophisticated arbitrators, speed of process, and international conventions on enforcement of international arbitration awards, such as the New York Convention[17] (which require enforcement of international arbitration awards as if they were domestic awards and do not allow the enforcing court to open up the award and make a qualitative assessment of its merits, except for a few specified reasons). See sections 8.13 and 9.11 for further discussion.

2.13.10 Sovereign Immunity

States generally benefit from two forms of immunity: jurisdiction and execution. State entities are immune from the jurisdiction of the courts of another state. This immunity results from the belief that it would be inappropriate for one state's courts to call another state under its jurisdiction, since this would erode the principle of independent national sovereignty. However, this immunity can generally be waived by the state entity. The state will also have immunity from execution, since it would be improper for the courts of one state to seize the property of another state. Just as courts do not have jurisdiction over foreign sovereign states under international law, they are also prevented from seizing the property of such sovereign states.[18] Immunity from execution generally may also be waived.[19]

2.13.11 Employment

Some of the most important reasons for granting the project company the right to operate a public sector service are to improve efficiency, to streamline the relevant corporate and management structures, and to transfer commercial know-how from the private sector. However, this improved efficiency may be inconsistent with the interests of existing public sector

---

[16] Execution of arbitral awards is supported by a number of international treaties and conventions, in particular the United Nations Convention on the Enforcement of Arbitral Awards (1958) (the "New York Convention").

[17] United Nations Convention on the Recognition and Enforcement of Foreign Arbitral Awards (1958).

[18] O'Connell, M. E., *International Law*, 2nd ed. (1970), at 864.

[19] Maryan, Negotiating with the monarch; special problems when the sovereign is your partner, *Project Financing in Emerging Markets* (1996).

employees. Applicable law may create restrictions governing the project company's relationship with its employees, such as the following:

- Whether it is possible to transfer or second public employees to another entity/contracting party
- Whether public sector employees who have been transferred to the project company retain their rights and benefits, and whether new employees enjoy the same rights and benefits as the transferred employees
- Whether employers can remove dishonest or ineffective workers; whether it is possible to impose disciplinary procedures; and whether the project company can release employees or make them redundant, and if so, what sort of compensation is required by law, if any applicable law exists

2.13.12 Tax

PPP projects raise a number of issues associated with taxation of assets, revenues, interest payments, and profits. Limited recourse financing creates particular challenges for tax liabilities, such as transfer pricing, depreciation, value-added tax (VAT) offsetting, and taxation of subsidies. In jurisdictions where limited recourse financing is not common, the application of those tax liabilities to limited recourse financing for PPP may not be fully understood.

2.13.13 Regulatory Frameworks

The government may be assisted in its monitoring/management function by third parties. For example, an independent specialist may be appointed under the contract to act as the monitor of compliance with contract obligations by the parties.[20] Equally, the sector regulator (e.g., the water sector regulator) will be monitoring the project company's performance and may agree to monitor generally the parties' compliance with their obligations under law, which may well coincide with their obligations under the relevant contracts. The difficulty with this approach is the need for the regulator to operate in accordance with its mandate, with the usual discretion given to regulators. Often, this discretion cannot be limited (or "fettered"), and therefore the regulator must comply with its legal mandate first and its contractual role as a secondary function.

---

[20] Tremolet, S., P. Shukla, & C. Venton, *Contracting Out Utility Regulatory Functions* (2004).

Where the site country has a history of regulation, the regulatory structure may be predictable and may provide comfort to the project company and especially to the lenders. However, in many cases the regulator's role may be new, possibly the product of a hasty response to the involvement of the private sector, or it may not yet exist, creating uncertainty for investors.

Box 2.13. U.K. Reforms to Improve Transparency

In order to improve transparency, in 2012 the U.K. government implemented plans to do the following:

- Monitor and disclose all commitments arising from off-balance sheet PPP contracts
- Require the private sector to provide equity return information for publication
- Publish an annual report detailing project and financial information on all projects where government holds a public sector equity stake
- Introduce a business case approval tracker on the Treasury website
- Improve the information provisions within the standard contractual guidance

Source: Infrastructure UK, *A New Approach to Public Private Partnerships*

2.13.14　Trusts, Agency, and Other Legal Relationships

Project-financed transactions are highly structured, often with multiple lenders and investors needing to share in the protections provided by such structuring. For these reasons, trust and agency arrangements are often used, where available, to help manage common rights and flow of funds.

2.13.15　Currency

The recurring balance of payment difficulties of many host countries and their need to conserve foreign exchange to pay for essential goods and services greatly reduce their ability and willingness to grant investors the unrestricted right to make monetary transfers, hence many countries have exchange-control laws to regulate the conversion and transfer of currency abroad. The host country may limit the extent to which local currency can be converted into foreign currency, the rate that can be obtained in such a transaction, and how much of such currency can be transferred offshore, which will be essential to pay foreign lenders and to repatriate profits offshore.

3

Public Support

PPP requires both public and private financial contributions. Public resources should be provided only to the extent they represent value for money. The PPP framework should include processes and criteria to ensure the efficient allocation of public resources. Figure 3.1 maps out key opportunities to use public money to mobilize PPP, including through the project development cycle, by supporting project preparation, through the bidding process, through investment mechanisms that can support project financing, and finally through contingent support to reinforce and target the incentives fundamental to the project revenue stream and possibly refinancing.

Moving chronologically through the project process, the following are some of the key areas the government can support to help implement PPP:

- Project preparation – funding and technical support for feasibility studies, hiring and managing transaction advisors, and providing technical assistance to the contracting authority and sector ministries
- Capital grants and in-kind support – for example, offsetting construction costs, acquiring land and rights of way, etc.
- Debt or equity into the project – to supplement available private capital
- Contingent support – to address key project risks, for example, guarantees of demand risk, foreign exchange risk, or payment risk
- Revenue support during implementation – for example, as key milestones are achieved, possibly as a feed-in/shadow tariff or availability payment

3.1 The Fundamentals of Public Support

The government will need to consider carefully which projects to support, how much support to provide, the terms of such support (in particular,

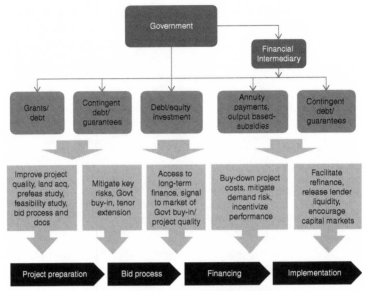

Figure 3.1. Mechanisms to encourage PPP.

which incentives to create and how to maximize leverage of private invest-ment) and how to ensure that support is properly managed. Public funds should be targeted toward the most strategic, economically viable, and fea-sible projects.

There is a temptation to approach a project assuming that no government support will be needed and to contemplate such support only when nego-tiations with investors and lenders fail without it. However, this results in an ad hoc support package, developed when the government's negotiating strength is low; achieving maximum leverage and minimum exposure will be even more difficult. Allocation of government support must be decided and announced before the bid date to maximize benefits for the contracting authority and avoid perceptions of discrimination by those who would have bid had they known that such support was available.

Box 3.1. The U.K.'s Erstwhile Private Finance Initiative (PFI) Credits

Until relatively recently, the U.K. Treasury allocated PFI credits for both local government and central-level government departments – a speci-fied amount of funding for a specific project over a period of time beyond that of the immediate budget allocation framework. It allowed the local authority (or department in the case of central government) certainty as to a revenue stream from the central budget for meeting its obligations under a PPP agreement and provided a strong incentive for departments and local authorities to implement projects as PPPs. The use of PFI credits was heavily criticized for creating significant long-term liabilities for the government. The program has been abandoned officially.

Source: www.treasury.gov.uk/public-private-partnerships

It is advisable for government to consider government support as a package – funded and contingent – to ensure that maximum leverage and optimal exposure (fiscal risk) is achieved.

The government needs to be very careful about de-risking debt. To the extent debt is de-risked, incentives on lenders to ensure project success are diminished.

It is tempting to use available public support to simply improve those projects that do not achieve the levels of viability or feasibility required by private investors. To ensure the public support is not wasted on simply compensating private investors for failures in the government's PPP framework, appropriate investments should be made in identifying weaknesses in, and improving the framework for, PPP in parallel with maximizing the effectiveness of government support.

Key Messages for Policy Makers

- *Government support* can improve financial viability and make a project more attractive for investors, but it *will not turn a bad project into a good one.*
- *Use government support efficiently,* in a targeted manner, to ensure government goals are achieved.
- Ensure funding mechanisms are properly resourced and incentivized to *avoid political capture or inertia.*
- *Avoid perverse incentives* created by government support – ensure private and public sectors are motivated to make the project a success.

3.2 Purposes for Public Support

Public resources can be used to do the following:

- Improve access to, and quality of, services provided, creating financial incentives to achieve government strategic priorities (see Box 3.2).

Box 3.2. Targeted Support

Output- or performance-based subsidies or aid makes a clear link between the intended results and payment.[1] While requiring evidence of the ultimate output (e.g., healthier children or improved industrial output) is impractical for a number of reasons, governments can require the project company to perform a task or provide a service that achieves a stated objective before aid or subsidies are paid out, for example, a specified number of additional poor households connected to the electricity grid and using the service. These outputs need to be targeted to ensure they achieve the desired impact (e.g., connections alone will not create an output unless the service delivery is sustainable).[2]

- Improve the quality of project preparation, which in turn improves competition, drives down prices, and increases the likelihood of success of the PPP program. Funding mechanisms for project development are important to a successful PPP program, enabling and encouraging government agencies to spend the amounts needed for high-quality advice.
- Increase use of PPP. The benefits of PPP (efficient procurement, life-cycle improvements, well-planned maintenance, and service improvements) may not be captured by the relevant contracting authority. Government support can provide the incentives required to motivate even reluctant users to implement PPP effectively.
- Redue the amount of private finance needed. Public financing may be easier to access, at a lower rate of interest. Reducing the amount of project finance needed may reduce the cost of the project and increase the amount of risk the private sector will bear.
- Improve opportunities for specific parties, for example, local lenders, local equity investors, smaller investors, and new/poor consumers. Public support can be conditional on such opportunities or may alter the requirements of the project such that opportunities are created.

---

[1] Brook, P. J. & M. Petrie, *Output-Based Aid: Precedents, Promises and Challenges*, www.gpoba.org/docs/05intro.pdf.
[2] See generally www.gpoba.org.

Box 3.3. Project Development Funds (PDFs)

South Africa: The PDF began operations on October 21, 2003. It is a single-function trading entity (public account), created within the National Treasury. Disbursed funds may be recovered from the successful private party bidder when the PPP reaches financial close, as a "success fee." The PDF is exposed to the full risk of the project not reaching financial closure. The PDF is capitalized by the South African government as well as donors.

India: The India Infrastructure Project Development Fund is a revolving fund that is replenished by the reimbursement of investments through success fees earned from successful projects. The project development fund will cover up to a maximum of 75 percent of the project development expenditures incurred by the contracting authorities. The fund is capitalized by contributions from the government of India and multilateral institutions.

The nature of the government support instruments chosen will depend on the intended impact of that support, the volume and currency of liquidity (or other funding) available to the government, the fiscal position of the government, and the financial gaps identified in the relevant PPP projects or program.

3.3 Funded Instruments

The most common form of government support involves instruments that provide cash, assets, or some other form of funding, often known as "funded" instruments, such as loans, grants, land, assets, or equity. This is different from contingent support, where the government support must be paid out or crystallizes only in certain circumstances, for example, standby capital (debt, equity, or grants), guarantees, or indemnities.

3.3.1 Grants/Capital Contributions

The government may choose to provide funded support that does not give the government an ownership interest, for which the government does not charge interest and that may not require reimbursement, often known as a contribution, subsidy, or grant. The process for selecting which project will receive government contributions should focus on the relative benefit of the project to the country given the amount of contribution required.

Box 3.4. (Mis)use of the Term "Viability Gap Funding"

The Indian government has created a mechanism to pool capital contributions for PPP transactions (open to many sectors, but used primarily to date to support the roads sector); see Box 3.5. The popularity of this mechanism has resulted in the term "viability gap funding" entering the common parlance in certain circles as a generic term for all government support or capital contribution programs. There is a strong risk of confusion with the Indian program (which involves only one form of, and approach to, government support), and therefore this generic version of the term will not be used in this text.

Similarly, it may be difficult to assess the amount of contribution for a given project that represents value for money. Many jurisdictions use competition to set the amount to be allocated, such as in India (see Box 3.5), the procurement process uses the lowest government contribution as the key criteria to select the winning concessionaire. Brazil, Colombia, and Mexico use similar competitive pressure to identify the appropriate level of government contribution to be provided. But this approach leads to some concern that politically motivated but not economically viable projects are being enabled through such contributions.[3] Russia's Investment Fund allows the contracting authority to use a value for money analysis to set the level of contribution (using the competitive process to achieve additional advantages).

Some countries run their contribution commitments through state-owned enterprises (which can roll budgeting and commitments over from one year to the next, as compared to many government budgets that only cover one year); for example, the public power utility is often used to pay such contributions for power PPPs. In Mexico, Fondo Nacional de Infrastructura (Fonadin – see Box 6.12) is funded through capital set aside by the government and revenues from existing public toll roads. It granted over $1 billion worth of government contributions to PPP projects during 2008–9 alone.[4]

---

[3] Private sector interest in a project is an inexact indicator of viability or value for money. The private sector suffers from the same optimism bias as the public sector and also from ill-founded negative perceptions. Projects with high economic returns may not attract competition, in particular where they suffer from other constraints. Where competition or access to financing is weak, relative levels of public contribution will increase despite constant value for money.

[4] World Bank, *Best Practices in Public Private Partnership Financing in Latin America: The Role of Subsidy Mechanisms* (2012).

Box 3.5. India's Viability Gap Fund

In 2004, the government of India launched the Scheme for Financial Support of PPPs in Infrastructure, now more commonly known as the Viability Gap Funding (VGF) scheme. VGF provides upfront capital grants at the construction stage. These grants may not exceed 20 percent of the project cost and are disbursed only after the private company has made its required equity contribution. Sponsoring ministries or state governments may provide additional grants, but these may not exceed an additional 20 percent of the project cost. No economic cost-benefit assessment is performed, as the scheme relies instead on sector regulation and competitive procurement to identify the need for government contribution.

Source: www.pppindiadatabase.com.

Russia (see Box 3.6) has created a nominal fund in order to establish rules and regulations applicable to government contributions, but the funding comes directly from annual budget allocations rather than a stand-alone fund. Colombia has a special mechanism for future budget allocations, while Brazil treats government contributions as "interest payments" to mitigate the risk that annual legislative budget approvals might be delayed or rejected.[5]

Box 3.6. Russia's Investment Fund

The Russian government allocates a line item in its national budget to support PPP and other regional projects with grants, managed by the Ministry of Regional Development, and referred to as the Investment Fund. These funds can cover up to 50 percent of the project capital cost and are subject to a variety of rules and procedures on the condition of their allocation and use. The Western High-Speed Diameter toll road (which reached financial close in mid-2012) is one of the most high-profile and largest recipients of Investment Fund contributions.

3.3.2 Payments for Services Rendered

The government may choose to pay the project company directly for services rendered (or some part thereof). For example, where a road is being developed through PPP, rather than ask the investor to rely wholly on tolls collected, the government may pay directly to the investor an availability

---

[5] Ibid.

payment (also called an annuity payment in India). The payment is made to the extent the project company provides services to a specific performance standard. There is generally a minimum level of service below which no payment is made.

Availability payments provide more certainty of revenues to investors, with the government as obligor (which may help the project access cheaper debt). While the downside risk is largely absorbed by the government through this payment stream, the upside potential of high profits from tolls or tariffs will also belong to the government, potentially reducing the incentives on the private investor to ensure success of the project.

The government can also prepurchase, or promise to purchase, a certain amount of output. For example, a fiber-optic network may have a clear advance commitment by the government to purchase a portion of the network's capacity. Such payments generally reduce demand risk and provide a guaranteed revenue stream, which in certain cases can be used as collateral for debt.

Box 3.7. Availability Payment Mechanism for Roads

Availability payment mechanisms place downside risk clearly on the government, but also ensure the government benefits from the upside benefits. (If the road is not used, the government still pays, but if it is very successful, the benefits accrue primarily to the government.) Under a toll-based concession, government reforms can reduce concessionaire revenues, giving the concessionaire the right to claim lost revenues from the government. The availability payment allows the government to make changes without concerns of liabilities to concessionaires.

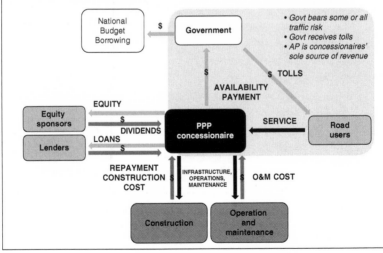

3.3.3 Loans

The government may choose to provide access to debt, in particular in local currency and of an appropriate tenor, grace period, and terms. However, government provision of debt should be approached with caution. Any of the following may apply:

- It may be subject to legal restrictions, in particular where the government lends money to a private entity.
- It may be subject to approval, control, governance, auditing, and other oversight mechanisms that may complicate the project structure.
- It may require project assessment skills and capacity when first deciding to make the loan that are not typical of the skills found among government personnel.
- It may reduce opportunities for private lenders and therefore create political backlash.
- It may require the government to play the due diligence, monitoring, and oversight role of a lead commercial bank that the government may be ill equipped to play.

3.3.4 Equity

Government support in the form of equity is sometimes used to offset equity requirements from private investors, maintain control by the government over certain project decisions, or obtain access to information about the project company that would normally be difficult to achieve. However, government equity contributions raise particular challenges for governments and investors:

- Conflict of interest – where the government is on both sides of the concession agreement, private investors will be concerned that when difficult decisions must be made, government will be incentivized in a manner different from the commercial priorities of the project.
- Decision processes – government procedures are often a poor fit with good corporate governance, such as procedures for voting, appointing board members, and selecting management.
- Management and monitoring of government shareholding – often government staff are not familiar with private corporate governance and are unlikely to be able to protect the government's interests among corporate shareholders.

3.4 Contingent Support

Contingent support (as compared to funded support; see Section 3.3) only becomes payable (or "crystallizes") in certain specified situations. Contingent support can include the following:

- Guarantees, including against breach of contract, nonpayment of debt service, adverse movements in exchange rates, lack of convertibility of the local currency or availability of foreign exchange, credit risk of an offtake purchaser, tariff collection risk, the level of tariffs permitted, the level of demand for services, payment of termination compensation, etc.
- Indemnities, such as against failure to pay by state entities or damages associated with undue government intervention
- Standby funding (debt, equity, or grants) that the project company can draw on, such as in the event demand is insufficient or for cost overruns

Key Messages for Policy Makers

- Contingent support can be a powerful instrument.
- However, the risk borne by the government must be assessed honestly and managed carefully.
- Taking too much risk away from private lenders or enabling reduced equity investment, or overprotecting investors, limits the private investors' "skin in the game," so when crisis befalls the project, the investor and lender may be less motivated to help.

Contingent support instruments can be used to address challenges that may arise, such as the following:

- Construction cost increases, for example, to address underestimates in construction costs due to information provided by the government or where there are delays in the provision of land by the government.
- Revenue shortfalls, such as where revenues do not meet forecasts, for example, during ramp-up or where traffic does not meet expectations.
- Exchange rate and other financial cost shifts, requiring revenue support, such as to meet debt service obligations.
- Operating cost increases, such as where circumstances change during operation, such as increases in the cost of labor and materials,

government agencies delay permits or require changes in operating methodologies.

Box 3.8. Using Government Payment Obligations to Secure Debt

Availability payments provide more certainty of revenues to investors, with the certainty of the government as obligor (which may help the project access cheaper debts). While the downside risk is largely absorbed by the government through this payment stream, the upside potential of high profits from tolls or tariffs will also belong to the government, potentially reducing the incentives on the private investor to ensure success of the project.

The credit strength of this government payment obligation can be used to secure funding. French law allows these government guaranteed payments to be assigned to creditors (a Dailly assignment), allowing part of the project debt to be considered quasigovernment debt with pricing and tenor implications.[6] The Peruvian Certificados de Reconocimiento de Pago Anual de Obras (CRPAO) provides another interesting example, breaking the government payment obligation into certificates to be paid out on completion of milestones. These certificates (equivalent to government payment obligations) can be pledged to secure debt.[7]

3.4.1 Government Guarantees

The government can use its credit position to guarantee certain risks, in order to increase private sector appetite for the project and reduce the cost of investment. Government guarantees tend to be "partial," as blanket guarantees are generally less than effective, because they create perverse incentives for the beneficiary not to manage the risk well, and should be avoided in most cases.

Chile has had great success in developing its PPP portfolio. Since 1994, the government has established a solid institutional framework; well-developed procedures to identify, evaluate, and tender projects; and financial markets well placed to provide financing for PPP projects. But even such a successful program involved extensive government guarantees and protections for investors in the early days, including guarantees from

---

[6] Crothers, J. D., M. Bonnet, & J. Brusau Cuello, Assignment of receivables under the French "Dailly" law: legal and practical applications in PPP projects, International Business Law Journal, RDAI/IBLJ (2011).

[7] World Bank, *Best Practices in Public Private Partnership Financing in Latin America: The Role of Guarantees* (2012).

multilaterals and credit wraps from monoline insurers. The extent of such guarantees was reduced as the program matured, until such guarantees became the exception.[8] A similar dynamic can be seen in most developed PPP programs.

3.4.2 Contingent Debt/Equity

Debt and/or equity structures can be created to draw down only after certain circumstances have arisen, in a specified time frame and/or when requested by specified persons. These structures are known as standby, contingent, or callable capital.

Box 3.9. Lessons from the London Underground: the Importance of Private Liability

The London Underground project involved three parallel concessions to run different metro lines. Two of these "infracos" could claim additional funds if total cost increases exceeded 50 million pounds sterling ($80 million), the third if it exceeded 200 million pounds sterling ($320 million), giving it a powerful incentive to make savings in order to offset any cost increases, rather than seeking additional payments from London Underground. This has encouraged a considerable level of innovation by the third "infraco," but much less so among the first two.

Source: House of Common, Transport Committee, "The London Underground and the Public–Private Partnership Agreements," Second Report of Session 2007–8, HC 45 (January 2008)

3.4.3 Contingent Contributions

Government grants may also be provided on a contingent basis, once certain construction milestones, financial ratios, investment commitments, or other performance criteria have been met. Examples include funding of capital investment paid out only on delivery of outputs or performance, such as connections for poor households and delivering of services to the vulnerable.

3.4.4 Bilateral/Multilateral Guarantees

Contingent support mechanisms are also available from development finance institutions (DFIs) and donors, for example, the contingent support

---

[8] International Monetary Fund (IMF), *Public Private Partnerships* (2004).

mechanisms available from the World Bank[9], the Multilateral Investment Guarantee Agency (MIGA),[10] and the International Finance Corporation (IFC).[11] For a full comparison of these facilities, see www.ppp.worldbank .org. Some private sector providers of capital view bilateral or multilateral involvement as improving the likelihood of priority being given to their interests in the event of restructuring by the host government. This is known in the market as the DFI "umbrella" or "halo."

Box 3.10. GuarantCo

GuarantCo is an independent, regionally focused provider of partial credit guarantees. It is a private company owned by the members of Private Infrastructure Development Group (PIDG)[12] and run and managed on a commercial basis. It provides a variety of contingent products, including partial credit and partial risk guarantees.

Source: www.guarantco.com.

3.5 Managing Government Liabilities

PPP involves important government liabilities that must be managed carefully to avoid exposing the public accounts to undue risks. While PPP debt is generally off-balance sheet for the government, it creates important fiscal risks that the government must assess, monitor, report, and manage.

3.5.1 Assessing Liabilities

The ability to value and assess risk associated with PPP is often created within the debt management function of the Ministry of Finance, but it might also be tasked to a PPP unit in some other part of government, for example, planning or economic coordination. The assessment of government liabilities should be assessed at different stages of the project to

---

[9] For further discussion, see www.worldbank.org/guarantees; Delmon, *Private Sector Investment in Infrastructure*.

[10] www.miga.org.

[11] www.ifc.org.

[12] The PIDG is a multidonor, member-managed organization. Current PIDG members include the U.K. Department for International Development (DFID), the Swiss State Secretariat for Economic Affairs (SECO), the Netherlands Ministry of Foreign Affairs (DGIS), the Swedish International Development Cooperation Agency (SIDA), the World Bank, and the Austrian Development Agency (ADA).

confirm what level of liabilities represents value for money for the government for a given project.

The government's objective is to expose liabilities associated with PPP projects to an appropriate level of scrutiny:[13]

- Creating risk awareness – for example, collecting information on PPP contracts and using it to discuss fiscal implications of PPP projects
- Disclosure of PPP risks – promoting transparency of PPP contracts and the fiscal risks associated with those contracts
- Risk management – coordinating or even centralizing fiscal risk monitoring and authorization and providing for auditing mechanisms of the government's risk analysis and risk management functions

---

Box 3.11. Integrated Health PPP – Lesotho PPP

In 2006, the government of Lesotho adopted a PPP to replace Queen Elizabeth II (QE II), the one-hundred-year-old national referral hospital in the capital of Maseru, and to upgrade the network of urban clinics. The PPP included construction of a new 425-bed national referral hospital (QMMH), a gateway clinic adjacent to the hospital, and the refurbishment and re-equipment of three urban "filter" or feeder clinics.

Through a competitive tender process, the government of Lesotho selected a consortium to build, operate, manage, and deliver clinical and nonclinical services through this integrated network over the next eighteen years. The project had an overall capital value of over $100 million USD with capital expenditures jointly financed through public (38 percent) and private funds (62 percent). The unitary payment is calculated based on the estimated cost to serve up to 310,000 outpatients and 20,000 inpatients per year. At volumes above this ceiling, the consortium is entitled to incremental payment per patient from the government.

The PPP hospital network delivered more and higher-quality services and achieved significant gains in clinical outcomes compared to the government-managed hospital system at baseline.

However, the project was a victim of its own success. Based on Ministry of Health records, the PPP has absorbed an average of 34.8 percent of the total government recurrent budget for the health sector for 2012–2015. This has attracted intense criticism from NGOs as being unaffordable, despite the performance improvements. Government needs a careful

---

[13] Adapted from Public–Private Partnerships in the New EU Member States: Managing Fiscal Risks, World Bank Working Paper No. 114 (2007).

assessment of project affordability, under various scenarios, and in view of different project risks.

Source: World Bank: Lesotho Health Network PPP (February 2016); *Guardian Newspaper UK*, Half of Lesotho health budget goes to private consortium for one hospital (April 14, 2014).

3.5.2 Monitoring/Accounting for Liabilities

The government will either apply a cash accounting (where liabilities are accounted for once they crystallize) or accrual accounting (where liabilities are accounted once they accrue). Cash accounting will not show the contingent liability unless a contingency fund is created, as discussed later in this chapter. Even if accrual accounting is not used, governments can still use the reporting of such liabilities (for better transparency) to create the necessary accountability of policy makers and help to manage the relevant contingent liabilities. This has been successfully implemented in a number of countries, for example, the Czech Republic and South Africa.[14]

3.5.3 Paying for Liabilities Once They Crystallize

The government will need to decide how to fund liabilities associated with PPP as they arise. It may simply be able to find space in its budget from time to time for the relevant amount or may have other sources of funding. Another useful mechanism is an undertaking by a bank or development financial institution that will provide credit to the government in the event the contingent liability crystallizes.

Several countries have established schemes that reduce government payment risk, creating a fund able to support guarantee payment obligations as they come due, from accumulated budgetary transfers, fees, or taxes collected. Canada, Sweden, and the Netherlands have such funds (though not specific to PPP). The expected payouts under these contingent liabilities are deducted from the annual budgetary allocation for the relevant line ministries and are set aside for use in the event the contingent liability crystallizes.[15]

3.6 Coping with Crises

Economic and financial crisis of 2008–2009 had a significant impact on PPP globally. From the first half of 2008, investment in PPP declined by

[14] Irwin, T., *Government Guarantees: Allocation and Valuing Risk in Privately Financed Infrastructure Projects* (2007).

[15] Ibid.

48 percent in the second half of 2008. The first half of 2009 saw a recovery to first half 2008 levels, driven by large, high-priority projects in a handful of countries. Following the crisis, there was a clear "flight to quality," with projects more likely to reach closure characterized by strong economic and financial fundamentals, the backing of financially solid sponsors, and government support.[16] Other crises have had similar impact, for example, the Mexican crisis of 1994–1995, the Asian crisis of 1996–1997, and the Argentinean crisis of 2001. In particular, such crises have been marked by the following challenges:

- Difficulty to access, and increased cost of, debt and equity
- Reduced demand for infrastructure services (in particular from industrial users)
- Reduced ability to pay and therefore less political appetite to increase tariffs
- Reallocation of government budget funding away from project preparation
- Reduced appetite of international sponsors to take developing market risks

These challenges tend to result in the following:

- Delay or cancellation of PPP projects still in the preparation stage
- Difficulty obtaining financing or even failure of those PPP projects that have been awarded but not yet reached financial close
- Inability of existing PPP projects to access refinancing or to restructure to the extent that challenges arise
- Increased financial vulnerability of offtakers due to the inability to set tariffs at a cost recovery level while financing costs increase
- Failure of governments to develop new projects, resulting in a significant lag in the PPP project pipeline – with parts of Latin America and East Asia experiencing a "lost decade" of slow growth due to such lags in their infrastructure project pipelines

This section discusses key lessons learned from financial and economic crises (section 3.6.1) and what governments can do when faced with financial or economic crisis to protect existing PPP projects and maintain the pipeline for the continued development of PPP (section 3.6.2).

---

[16] World Bank, *Assessment of the Impact of the Crisis on New PPI Projects – Update 4 (09/28/09)*, PPI database of the World Bank, ppi.worldbank.org/.

Key Messages for Policy Makers

- *Crisis does not change the fundamentals of PPP,* and PPP is sufficiently flexible to be adjusted to market conditions. Be willing to reconsider each aspect of the PPP to find the best solution. For example, phase or scale down investment to fit accessible finance and reduced demand, and consider replacing some of the desired private financing with public funding (to the extent public funding is available) until such time as market conditions make private financing a better value.
- *Continue developing the PPP pipeline* during the period when private financing may not be available, to avoid a significant lag in the pipeline later. Similarly, sector reform to encourage PPP should continue, to the extent possible. Don't lose momentum.

3.6.1 The Impact of Crises

Each crisis is different, but the following general observations can be made.

Demand Profile

Any major crisis will have a negative impact on consumer confidence and therefore on corporate investment programs and on budget allocations (both household and organizational) for infrastructure services, and therefore demand suffers. Reduction in demand and increase in financing costs may result in increased tariffs. In a vicious circle, increased tariffs may simply result in further reduced demand, depending on its elasticity. It may also pose affordability problems, in particular among the poorest consumers. Where tariffs are not increased, the utility will be placed under greater financial pressure, which may hurt the utility's credit position, which may in turn further increase the cost of the utility's debt. Also, when revenues fall, maintenance is usually one of the first expenses to be cut. However, shortfalls in maintenance will have an exponential impact on future capital expenditure requirements (for asset replacement). The money saved on asset maintenance now will cost much more over time.

Availability and Cost of Capital (Debt and Equity)

For those projects that have not yet reached financial close, accessing new debt or equity undertakings (in local and/or foreign currencies) may be extremely difficult or merely more expensive. The complete inability to access investment is generally short-lived; however, large increases in the cost of money (debt or equity) can threaten the financial viability of the project and its value for money for the government. This increased cost of money arises from (i) reduced liquidity, and therefore higher cost of money reflected in a reduction in the supply of money; and (ii) increased perception of risk and therefore increased credit risk, resulting in lenders and equity investors demanding larger margins to cover that credit risk.

The increased cost of debt (due to reduced liquidity and increased credit risk) will be exacerbated by the increased time and cost to reach financial close. The syndications markets is likely to be disrupted, and therefore lending for a project will need to rely on a single bank or a club of banks, leaving the project exposed to the demands of even the smallest club member and the time and complexity needed to manage a club of banks. This will be more of a problem for large projects, where the size of the club increases. Debt tenors may also shrink in times of crisis, making it difficult for projects to be financially viable unless tariffs are increased accordingly or government grants take up the slack.

Equally, sponsors who are relied upon to provide much of the energy to drive project development and coordination of lenders may experience a weakening of their balance sheets and in the level of funding they can make available for project development. Therefore, governments will see a reduction in the number of active bidders for projects, and, where bids are received, their pricing will reflect the increased cost of debt and equity due to perceptions of higher financial risk. Bids are also less likely to have fully committed funding before financial close, creating moral hazard that lenders will use this reduced competitive pressure to argue for better terms or pricing for their financing. This may result in further flight to quality, as private investors are interested in pursuing only the most attractive projects, and competition among private investors is limited. Government will need to assess whether the savings to be made in a bid made after the markets are rebalanced are worth the cost of delay.

Availability of Hedging and Other Financial Mechanisms
To help manage various financial risks, in particular in relation to foreign exchange and interest rates, project companies will look to enter into a number of different hedging and other financial mechanisms (see sections 8.7–8.10 for further discussion of these mechanisms). In times of crisis, project companies have more difficulty accessing these mechanisms, and those that are available have shorter tenor and higher prices.

Availability of Government Funds
For many PPP projects, government support, be it funded or contingent, is key to the viability of the project. In times of financial or economic crisis,

the government may find its tax receipts reduced and its budget reallocated to other priority expenses, reducing the amount of support it can provide to PPP projects. Equally important are the government resources used to fund project development and ensure the pipeline of PPP projects is maintained. Reduction in the amount of public funding for project development can result in weaker, more vulnerable projects and an increased likelihood of expensive failures.

Availability of Donor Funds

Where a financial crisis is global in nature, reductions in fiscal receipts across the globe will also have a direct impact on the availability of donor funding for poor countries. Where governments are scrambling to rescue their own economies, focus on the problems of others is likely to diminish. Support provided by wealthy countries may take on a clearly nationalistic bent.

3.6.2 What Can Be Done?

The first piece of advice is: don't panic. Markets eventually normalize and financial and economic crises do not change the fundamentals of PPP. They merely alter the way PPP should be structured to address the government's needs and the realities of financial markets. The following is a discussion of what can be done to support PPP in difficult times. It will discuss mechanisms that may be used for existing projects and/or new projects that have not completed the bid process. This menu will clearly need to be adjusted to the context of the country, the project, and the appetite of the government in question.

Revenue Support and Cost Reductions

To respond to the risk of demand reductions and increases in the cost of financing, the government may want to support portions of the project revenue streams, in particular where tariff increases are no longer feasible from a political or affordability perspective. For example, subsidies can be used to reduce the consumer tariff burden on certain parts of society or allow a more gradual increase of tariffs to improve affordability (see section 3.3). The government may want to increase tariffs to support cost recovery and therefore the long-term sustainability of the utility. Government funding can be used to mitigate the impact of higher tariffs on those unable to afford them, such as through subsidies to the utility to offset lower tariffs for low-income consumers or subsidies directly to consumers to offset cost increases. Tariff support needs to be specifically targeted, with proper incentives to improve efficiency and achieve performance requirements. Badly targeted tariff support can merely encourage inefficiency and divert incentives away from service delivery. Extensions of the project period can also add value and reduce tariffs.

In parallel, efforts can be made to reduce costs, in particular by reducing the size of the facility or refurbishment being undertaken or phasing project investments (in particular, to respond to reducing demand).[17] Cost reductions should not be permitted to create maintenance shortfalls or otherwise degrade key performance specifications or increase long-term capital deficits. Additional contingent support such as government or International Financial Institution (IFI) guarantees can also reduce financing costs or provide comfort as to offtaker payment risk.

Replace Private Debt/Equity with Public Resources
Where access to private investment is difficult or too costly, and the government has access to debt or other funding, the government may consider replacing private investment with public funding (subsidies, debt, equity, or otherwise). Such a publicly funded project can later be refinanced using private money once the financial markets improve, and the PPP project should be structured accordingly from the outset. For example, following the 2008–9 crisis, the U.K. created the Infrastructure Finance Unit in the Treasury to act as a direct lender to projects. France, on the other hand, chose to provide guarantees to encourage private lenders.

However, it should be noted that in privately financed PPP projects the contracting authority will rely on the presence of the lenders to monitor financial flows and the shareholders' equity investment to ensure their medium-to-long-term commitment to the project. To the extent the government provides debt or guarantees, the lender's incentive to perform careful project assessment may be diminished. The contracting authority will therefore need to take on an even more proactive role in project development where the lenders are not involved at the outset to establish mechanisms to protect financial flows. The U.K. Treasury has assembled a specialist team, the Infrastructure Finance Unit, to provide some of this project assessment function. To ensure that project company incentives are aligned with delivering services, the PPP project will need to be structured accordingly, for example, paying out profit over time or obtaining

---

[17] However, consideration should be given to the cost of expanding the infrastructure later, once demand grows; if the facility is too small, it may be significantly more expensive to expand it later.

shareholder guarantees for long-term service delivery. The structure of a PPP can be maintained by using performance- or output-based contracting and by requiring the shareholders to invest a level of equity sufficient to ensure that the project company incentives are properly focused.

When providing such support, the government will need to set clear policies, particularly on the following:

- How much support to provide, for example, what proportion of the total project cost
- What intracreditor or other rights the government will require
- The terms on which the government will sell down its position at a later date
- How to avoid political capture of the support mechanism, including the projects to which the government provides support, the amount of support provided, and the terms on which this support is provided
- Where the support is to be provided by a public entity, and how to establish an efficient capitalization, selection, and credit function in an otherwise public entity.

Locally Sourced Debt/Equity

In some cases, a financial crisis will impact international financial markets, but some local financial markets may not be as severely impacted. Liquidity in these markets can be used to support PPP projects, with the added benefit of increasing long-term opportunities in those local markets. Where local financial markets have the depth and liquidity needed to help finance PPP projects, but merely lack the asset/liability mix needed for long tenor debt or the expertise in PPP project financing debt, another effective mechanism available to the government is the use of a financial intermediary. This intermediary would assemble the expertise and attract the right asset/liability mix needed to issue project finance debt in local currency and mobilize additional local currency funding from local banks or capital markets by taking risk out of the project to the extent needed to permit these local entities to participate (see section 3.3).

Alternative Sources of Debt/Equity

Where private sources of financing are no longer sufficient to meet the requirements of PPP projects, multilateral lending agencies (MLAs) and bilateral lending agencies (BLAs) may be able to provide additional support or help mobilize other sources of financing (for example, for funding from local financial markets where the local financiers do not have experience in PPP, MLAs and BLAs can effectively mobilize the available liquidity). As noted previously, there is a likelihood that concessional financing from donors will be reduced during the period of crisis; however, a certain number of the MLAs may be able to mobilize additional capacity in the face of the crisis. Sovereign wealth funds may also provide an additional source of financing for PPP, in particular on a cofinancing basis to leverage the PPP experience of other lenders such as the MLAs.

Tenor Extension

Where private lenders are not able to provide long tenor debt as is commonly preferred for PPP projects, some combination of government and sponsor support can be used to remove the refinancing risk that the lenders are not willing to bear. For example, the lender may be willing to provide a "soft miniperm" facility with a short tenor (five-to-seven-year debt), after which the margin increases significantly, creating a strong incentive for the project company to refinance. A similar structure can be used, where the refinancing is compulsory, a "hard miniperm." In either case, it will be important to allocate risk of the increased cost of debt clearly, including any mechanisms to manage that risk (e.g., standby equity). The parties will also want a clear allocation of refinancing gain-sharing.

Increased Contingent Support

In times of crisis, when perceptions of risk are at their highest, the government may wish to provide additional contingent support to reduce the credit risk of the project or other isolated project risks. This was adopted by the French and Portuguese governments, for example. The government can isolate specific concerns of potential investors and lenders and adjust the nature of it support as the impact of the crisis changes over time. However, contingent support is complex, and the potential for significant government liabilities arising out of such support, often unknowingly, is high. Government debt management departments may not be properly staffed to assess, monitor, and manage these liabilities.

Project Development Funding

Contracting authority access to project development funding can have a dramatic impact on projects in the process of procurement and on the pipeline of PPP projects in the short to medium term. The government will want to ensure that this funding is maintained (particularly in the face of reducing donor support), either directly through budget allocations or possibly through project development facilities. This support for broader preparation, and government capacity, will be even more important given the likelihood of a flight to quality by private investors once the markets start to recover.

Dispute Resolution

Finally, for projects that have reached financial close, the government will need to increase its monitoring of projects and thereby increase its vigilance to identify problems with revenue streams, the need to access additional debt, and other warning signs of trouble. By identifying PPP project stress early, many problems can be avoided or mitigated and the relevant impact of the crisis reduced. The government will need to allocate sufficient funding and experienced staff to monitor projects and ensure timely responses. As discussed in section 9.9, renegotiation can be an opportunity to improve the project, and times of economic and financial crisis may provide many such opportunities.

4

Preparing, Procuring, and Implementing
Transactions

This chapter describes project preparation and implementation. Competitive procurement of PPPs involves careful preparation, reviewing risks and their allocation, identifying market requirements, and creating a competitive process for selection of the right private partner. In its most basic form, the tender (or bid) process involves a party offering a project to the market and asking for bids from parties interested in performing the project or some part of the project. Tendering procedures are meant to achieve efficiency, manage costs, maintain quality, encourage expediency, and maximize value for money. PPP transactions take time to prepare and need the attention of experts to ensure that risks and financing are managed properly and efficiently and that they are taken to market in a form and manner designed to attract as many high-quality bidders as possible and thereby keep costs down and improve delivery.

4.1 Inception/Prefeasibility/Preliminary Viability
Study/Outline Business Case

A prefeasibility study (also known as an outline business case or preliminary viability study) tests the fundamentals of the project, based on a preliminary technical survey identifying key constraints and assessing the basic technical and financial project fundamentals such as site selection, concept design, and possible forms of implementation, revenue, and financing. A first-level financial model will be developed at this stage, to test the viability of the project and the potential appetite of investors. This is an important stage of project development, to avoid wasting preparation costs on projects that do not satisfy these basic criteria. As part of the prefeasibility study, the contracting authority makes a preliminary assessment of value for money,[1] which tests the value provided by PPP.

Key Messages for Policy Makers

- *Do not cut corners in procurement.* It may seem easier to enter into direct negotiations instead of using competitive procurement, but it isn't. It takes longer and costs more money. Maximize competition (where possible) through good, transparent, competitive procurement.
- *Invest in preparation.* PPP preparation takes time and money, if done well.
- *Be clear to bidders about what you want.* Indicate clearly what results, milestones, and indicators you want the investor to achieve, in particular in the bid evaluation criteria and their weighting. Help bidders to give you what you want; don't make them guess.
- *Be cautious when selecting the winning bid.* If a bid seems too good to be true (financially, technically, or otherwise), then it probably is.

Once a preliminary decision to undertake the project through private investment has been made, a feasibility study is undertaken to identify key project issues and constraints.

4.2 Viability/Feasibility Study/Full Business Case

The decision on implementation of a project through PPP will follow a "viability" or "feasibility" study (also known as a "full business case"), which is a more detailed version of the prefeasibility study. The contracting authority performs a feasibility study to commence project structuring and key risk allocation decision making. It is at this stage that the fundamental design of the PPP solution is defined.

The feasibility study will build on the prefeasibility study, providing a more detailed analysis. It will include the following:

4.2.1 Demand Drivers

- Contracting authority and sector strategic objectives – whether the project is in national or local plans; meets critical public needs; and

---

[1] For further discussion of value for money, see section 2.11.

has political support, including from key stakeholders, for example, user groups, consumer groups, local government, and so on
- Capability of contracting authority and the project team to effectively manage the project, for example, to determine whether there is sufficient budget allocation for the project

4.2.2 Economic Valuation

- Fiscal affordability and consumer/end-user affordability
- Public/government/contracting authority benefits, for example, taxes, customs, duties and excise levies, employment generation, regional development, improvements in quality of life, attracting private investment (in particular, foreign direct investment), economic growth, and revenue share
- Government costs, such as likely environmental impact, impact on the site and the community, and available mitigation measures

4.2.3 Financial Analysis

- Revenue estimates, source of revenues (e.g., tariff collection), demand forecasts, tariff profile, credit risk of offtaker, willingness to pay, and elasticity of revenues with demand/tariffs charged
- Cost estimates for construction, operation, and financing, including inflation risk, interest rate risk, foreign exchange risk, and refinancing risk (e.g., where debt/tenor is insufficient)
- Public money support approved and sufficient (amount and terms)
- Base financial model (showing return on equity, return on investment, net present value, financial internal rate of return, and debt service cover ratio, with assumptions on debt: equity, debt currencies, debt tenor inflation rate, discount rate, depreciation, interest rate, foreign exchange rate and tax risk, and summary of results), including sensitivity analyses for cost increases and revenue reductions.[2]

4.2.4 Technical Analysis

- Full demand assessment, with elasticity of demand against toll levels and sensitivities for possible changes in circumstances

---

[2] Sensitivity analysis determines the resilience of the financial model to changes in assumptions and risk components over the PPP term; assesses the impact of these risks; assesses the likelihood of these risks arising; calculates the value of risk (and ranges of possible outcomes); allocates risks to the party best able to manage risk; and identifies strategies for mitigating risk.

- Selection of process and technology, process description, engineering, layout and basic if not more detailed design, technical options, construction methods, project construction schedule, costs, time, likelihood of failure, and interface with other technologies
- Performance/output specifications and whether the project meets the needs and requirements of the government
- Schedule of approvals, processes, regulatory matters, licensing, and permitting regime – risk of renewal, withdrawal, change in standards – in particular, environmental (including Equator Principles[3]) and social requirements, potential blockages, and critical path issues
- Access to land and process for acquisition/compensation/resettlement, with assessment of subsurface risk, archaeological remains, man-made obstacles, zoning and planning, utility supplies, nature of existing facilities, and interconnection with other facilities

4.2.5 Legal Assessment

- Key legal compliance challenges, including approvals, procurement, regulations, environmental laws, and the creation of security rights
- Legal authority to apply PPP approach and enter into project agreements (vires assessment)[4]
- Key terms for all contracts and documents, including tender documents, project contracts, and project information brief
- Access to justice, including enforceability of arbitral awards, and ability of private parties to challenge government actions in court

4.2.6 Comprehensive Risk Matrix

- For all project risks, identify the party that would be negatively affected in the event of the risk materializing, how much they would be affected, the likelihood of the risk, how those risks could be managed or mitigated, the cost of mitigation, who is incentivized to mitigate, and how the risks should be allocated.

The feasibility study is intended to demonstrate value for money (VfM), a measure of the net value that a government receives from a PPP project. The assessment of VfM helps the government decide whether a project should be implemented as a PPP and how much support the government

---

[3] www.equatorprinciples.org.
[4] See section 2.13.

should provide to that project. Assessing VfM is as much an art as a science, given the various and changing concepts of "value" that the government will want to access through PPP. VfM's very definition can be adjusted to respond to changes in government priorities and requirements over time.

The process of assessing value for money is iterative. From the earliest project selection processes, government should use value for money as its standard. This assessment will gain in detail and sophistication throughout

---

Box 4.1. Optimism Bias or Bad Incentives – How Planning Goes Wrong

Planning and forecasting need to reflect benefit to the government (as a proxy for the broader society) through cost-benefit or value-for-money assessments. But such assessments tend to involve incentives for those performing them to emphasize benefits and deemphasize costs, whether consciously or not.[5] There is a similar bias toward building something new rather than refurbishing what exists and maintaining it properly. Maintaining a road properly is three to seven times less expensive than maintaining it poorly and rebuilding later. But the sociopolitical incentive is to build something big and new that can carry the name or be identified with a politician or political party. Khan and Levinson (2011) highlight the failure in the U.S. national highway system to maintain roads properly due in part to the tendency for federal monies to be allocated to new building projects rather than maintenance or refurbishment.[6]

Proper planning and monitoring can help. The Private Infrastructure Investment Management Center in South Korea routinely rejects 46 percent of proposed projects (compared with 3 percent before its creation) at a savings of 35 percent to the government on poorly planned or selected projects. Similarly, Chile's national Public Investment System rejects 25 to 35 percent of projects proposed.[7]

Source: McKinsey Global institute, *Infrastructure Productivity*

---

[5]   See Flyvbjerg, B., Survival of the unfittest: why the worst infrastructure gets built – and what we can do about it, *Oxford Review of Economic Policy*, 25, no. 3, 2009; McKinsey Global institute, *Infrastructure Productivity: How to Save $1 Trillion a Year* (January 2013).

[6]   Kahn, M. & D. Levinson, Fix it first, expand it second, reward it third: a strategy for America's highways, Hamilton Project discussion paper 2011–2013 (February 2011); McKinsey Global institute, *Infrastructure Productivity*.

[7]   Ibid.

the project cycle, as more information is gathered from prefeasibility studies, feasibility studies, procurement, and implementation.

Various approaches and models endeavor to quantify VfM, in particular through public sector comparators, cost-benefit analysis, and shadow models (where a financial model is developed from the bidder's perspective to test likely bidder concerns). Best practice uses such quantitative analysis as important data but will give specific consideration to a qualitative analysis to respond to all relevant parameters rather than seek measurable accuracy in assessment.

As in most such exercises, a balance needs to be found between the time and expense of the "perfect" feasibility study and a feasibility study that addresses enough to meet market, contracting authority, and government approval requirements.

Failure to implement properly the different stages of project preparation, with sufficient time, funding, and expert advice, has doomed many PPP projects and programs; this preparation process should not be curtailed. As in most such exercises, a balance needs to be found between the time and expense of the "perfect" feasibility study and a feasibility study that addresses enough to meet market, contracting authority, and government approval requirements.

Key Messages for Policy Makers

- *Select good projects.*
- *Select robust, viable projects for PPP*; these are more likely to be financed on a competitive basis and are therefore more likely to provide value for money. Projects suffering from bad design, dubious demand, or weak fundamentals (even if politically popular) are more likely to fail and may weaken the entire PPP program in the process.
- If a project needs government support, *get approvals early* to avoid wasting time and money on projects that do not meet viability and value-for-money criteria. It can be awkward to reject support for a project later after preparation.
- A good, transparent selection process (for commercial rather than political reasons) can reassure investors and increase competition. Projects selected for political reasons or priorities will create a perception of increased political risk among investors.

Interested parties – such as potential investors, funders, or contractors – may offer to develop, or may produce of their own accord, "feasibility studies." Governments need to be cautious. Even with the best of intentions, such studies will be biased toward the interests and context of the proponent. Governments will need their own independent study to ensure that feasibility is properly tested, key choices are well founded, and the government has critical information needed to negotiate with eventual investors and funders.

Having the project approved as a PPP following from a completed and approved feasibility study ensures political buy-in of the process before the government and potential bidders start investing further in project development. Following the feasibility study and associated approvals, the contracting authority is ready to commence the tender process.

4.3 Direct Negotiations and Unsolicited Proposals

Governments often receive proposals directly from private investors. These proposals can be a good source of innovative ideas for the government and can help governments identify new project concepts. However, unsolicited proposals are difficult to manage and can be a source of significant mischief. Serious technical capacity is needed to manage them well.

Direct negotiations generally take longer, are more expensive, and are more likely to fail than projects procured through competitive processes.[8] Directly negotiated arrangements are also more vulnerable to challenges by new governments or opposition groups; without the validation of a transparent, competitive process, direct negotiations are more vulnerable to claims of bias, corruption, incompetence, and inappropriate use of government resources.

- *Where permitted, the circumstances allowing the award of the project without competitive procurement should be limited,* for example, by applying the following criteria:
  - ○ Where the project is of short duration and a small value, such that the added efficiency of a competitive process is outweighed by the cost of the process
  - ○ Where the project is critical to national defense or national security, and the competitive process would require disclosure of sensitive security information that cannot be managed safely

---

[8]   See, inter alia, Inadomi, H., *Independent Power Projects in Developing Countries: Legal Investment Protection and Consequences for Development* (2010); U.K. National Audit Office, *Getting Value for Money from Procurement* (2001).

Key Messages for Policy Makers

- *Prepare the government to play its part from project development to expiry.* Even where the investor proposes the project, produces the feasibility study and is to provide a comprehensive service solution, the government will play an (even more) essential role in reviewing, approving, monitoring, and regulating the project and the sector.
- *Be ready for challenges.* In any long-term relationship, change happens. PPP is, above all, a partnership, and it needs to be designed with challenges, changes, and resolution in mind. Problems need to be elevated to appropriate levels of management before they become disputes or worse.
- *Consider all stakeholders.* PPP will have a direct influence on some stakeholders (in particular, employees, management, and the local populace) and may raise political or philosophical concerns among many more. While absolute consensus will never be reached, the government needs to consult widely, understand fundamental concerns, and address them.

- Where there is only one possible source of the services (due to the skill set of the provider or exclusive intellectual property rights)
- Where there have been repeated efforts to implement a competitive process, but with no success, yet there is one party willing to undertake the project on the same terms that failed to attract competition

Whenever a project is proposed to be awarded without competitive procurement, the mechanism to apply for such a waiver should be managed by an appropriately high-level authority. The decision process should be made public and transparent, to allow other stakeholders to comment if they have issues, and there should be a mechanism for those disgruntled stakeholders to appeal against the decision. These mechanisms help protect the decision and the project from vulnerability to legal and political challenge.

Where competition is not possible or practicable, legislation often provides for market testing (see Box 4.2) to ensure that the pricing and terms agreed upon for a directly negotiated project meet market standards (consistent with what the government would have achieved through competition). A robust, independent feasibility study is invaluable in such circumstances.

Box 4.2. Benchmarking

Where a project is not subject to competitive pressures, or that competition is insufficiently robust, the government should submit that project to benchmarking to verify that the price represents best value as compared to similar projects, in the sector and in similar countries. This can be a challenging process where equivalent projects are not readily available or where relevant information is not available.

Some countries reject unsolicited proposals outright, providing no benefit or compensation to those offering such proposals. In particular, in countries without the resources and sophistication to manage unsolicited proposals, this offers a robust method to avoid the complications and dangers of unsolicited proposals; but it also deprives the government of the advantages.

Unsolicited proposals are often attractive to contracting authorities as the proponent offers to prepare a feasibility study for the project at no or low cost in exchange for the award of the project. However, the contracting authority cannot rely on the feasibility study. Even if the study is provided in the detail and with the rigor that the contracting authority would apply to its own study, the proponent is naturally biased to show the project is viable and should use the technology and methodology familiar to the proponent. The study will need to be reviewed and verified by independent advisers before the contracting authority can rely on it.

Mechanisms have been developed to encourage unsolicited proposals, while also ensuring that competitive tendering is used, where possible, when selecting the best investor.[9] These mechanisms involve a careful review of such unsolicited proposals to ensure that they are complete, viable, strategic, and desirable. The project is then put out to competitive tender, with the proponent of the unsolicited proposal receiving some benefit, for example:

- Automatic prequalification of the proponent
- A bonus on the proponent's scoring in the formal bid evaluation (i.e., additional points allocated to the proponent's total score when its bid proposal is evaluated)
- A first right of refusal, enabling the proponent to match the best bid received (also known as the "Swiss challenge"), in some cases only

---

[9] Hodges, J. T., & G. Dellacha, *Unsolicited Infrastructure Proposals: How Some Countries Introduce Competition and Transparency* (2007).

where the proponent's bid score is within a defined margin of the
best bid

- The right to automatically participate in the final round of bidding,
  where there are multiple rounds of bidding (the "best and final offer"
  system)
- Compensation paid to the proponent by the government, the winning
  bidder, or both.

Box 4.3. Unsolicited Bids in Colombia

The Ministry of Transport, the National Department of Planning (DNP),
and the MoF enacted detailed regulations regarding the acceptance of
unsolicited proposals from the private sector.[10] If accepted as a viable
project, an unsolicited proposal must then go through a competitive,
open procurement.[11] The proponent participates in this selection process like any other bidder. If the proponent's bid is not selected, however,
then the winning bidder must reimburse the proponent for certain of its
expenses, as approved by the responsible government agency prior to the
start of the tender process. In such cases, the proponent is responsible to
the winning bidder for the quality of the relevant studies.

The unsolicited proponent is often viewed as having an unfair advantage,
so any preference given (such as a right of first refusal or bonus during bid
evaluation) may stifle competition.[12] A more robust approach is to use competitive tendering, but without any advantage to the unsolicited proponent.
Instead, a fee is paid to the proponent if he does not win the bid, as compensation for the value added by his efforts to develop the project (see the
example of Colombia in Box 4.3). The fee should be sized to reflect actual
benefit of the proposal to the government.

4.4 Prequalification

The bidding process is generally lengthy and costly, for the bidders and for
the contracting authority. In order to manage the cost and time outlay, the
contracting authority may wish to prequalify those parties most likely to
provide an attractive bid and avoid the time and cost of managing bidders

---

[10] MOT Decree No. 4533 of 2008.
[11] See requirements of Laws 80 of 1993 and 1150 of 2007.
[12] This is not the case in countries such as Chile, with a very sophisticated regime that gives
confidence to other bidders that the proponent will not have an unfair advantage in the
process.

who do not have the fundamental qualifications or financial substance that would enable them to undertake the project. Prequalification also encourages good bidders, who will prefer a smaller field of equally qualified competitors. Low-quality bidders are more likely to lowball a bid, and their presence among short-listed bidders may scare off high-quality bidders.

Box 4.4. Prequalification Criteria for an Airport Concession

Each sector and project has its own specificities. For example, prequalification criteria may include the following:
- Level of owned total assets in excess of a set amount
- Recent experience managing the construction and operation of a project of similar size and complexity in a similar market
- Recent experience raising similar amounts of debt and equity
- Exclusion of air carriers, companies owned by air carriers, or operators of airports located close to the site (e.g., within 800 kilometers), to avoid any conflict of interest

The criteria will reflect sector and market context.

4.5 Bid

The contracting authority provides the prequalified bidders with tender documents (including project documents and technical specifications) and access to relevant data. Bids received will be evaluated against specified criteria. The criteria need to be described thoroughly in the bidding documents to help bidders understand the contracting authority's needs and improve the quality of bids received.

Box 4.5. Sample Bid Evaluation Criteria

Bid evaluation criteria may include the following:
- A technical solution compliant with the government master plan and with specifications provided
- A legal solution compliant with bid documents
- A financial proposal indicating the extent of government funding, investment, or guarantee needed or the share of project revenues
- A financing plan showing how and from whom the bidder intends to mobilize debt, equity, and other financial instruments to fund the project, how much due diligence has been completed, and the extent of commitments provided by lenders in the bid package

---

4.6 Single Bids

Even in the most sophisticated markets, creating investor appetite can be a challenge. Even before the financial crisis, some 30 percent of PPP projects in the U.K. only received two bids.[13] The procurement process should put the contracting authority into a strong negotiating position if there is only one bidder, limiting the opportunity of that bidder to hold the contracting authority hostage. The contracting authority needs to be prepared to start the bidding process over if it is not happy with the bidder's proposal. Where a single bid scenario is encountered, benchmarking of the bid may be a useful mechanism to help the government understand if it is getting good value and to help reassure other stakeholders that the lack of competition is not a fatal flaw in the process.

4.7 Preferred Bidder

Once bids are received, the contracting authority will evaluate compliant bids and select the preferred bidder. The contracting authority will negotiate with the preferred bidder any open issues (to the extent permitted by the bid documents or by law), finalize the commercial and financial arrangements, award the project, sign the concession agreement and other key contracts (subject to the conditions precedent discussed later in this section), and reach financial close. More than one preferred bidder may be selected for additional rounds of competition, for example, through best and final offer (BAFO – see Box 4.6) or competitive dialogue (see Box 4.7). Additional rounds need to be carefully managed, to maintain transparency, avoid any perception of favoritism or corruption, and limit the added cost and delay such a process implies.

Box 4.6. BAFO

The contracting authority may choose to include additional stages of competition, for example, reducing the competition to two bidders who will then be asked to further refine their bids and submit a best and final offer (BAFO), after which the contracting authority chooses the preferred bidder. This process allows the contracting authority to use the available competitive pressure to further motivate bidders and possibly obtain firm financing commitments.

---

[13] National Audit Office (U.K.), *Improving the PFI Tendering Process.*

Lenders will not be finally committed to the project until financial close is achieved. Before financial close, lenders will want to confirm that the risk allocation for the project is "bankable," a general term referring to the level of comfort that a lender will require from a project given the context of the project (see section 5.2).[14] The lenders will then agree with the project company and the government a list of conditions precedent (CPs) that must be satisfied before the lending arrangements become final and before first drawdown can be made.

Box 4.7. Competitive Dialogue

The European Union uses a "competitive dialogue procedure" that allows governments to enter into a dialogue with prequalified bidders before finalizing the tender documentation. It allows structured discussions with each of the prequalified bidders and helps identify key issues and amendments needed for the project.[15]

---

[14] See Delmon, *Private Sector Investment in infrastructure*, 2nd ed.
[15] European PPP Expertise Centre, *The Guide to Guidance: How to Prepare, Procure and Deliver PPP Projects* (2012).www.eib.org/epec/resources/guide-to-guidance-en.pdf.

Financing PPP and the Fundamentals of Project Finance

Ultimately, the cost of infrastructure has to be borne by its users or by taxpayers, current or future (aside from the limited concessionary component of foreign aid). The investments of public infrastructure firms have traditionally been financed from the public budget (through taxing or borrowing), possibly with a contribution from the enterprises' retained earnings (consumers). Funding by future taxpayers and/or consumers occurs when the infrastructure company borrows money, to be repaid from future revenue. Public infrastructure companies may do this by issuing bonds or shares or borrowing directly from commercial banks or the government. These options are only available to well-managed infrastructure firms in favorable investment climates.

Key Messages for Policy Makers

- *Be flexible when considering sources of financing.* Be ready to mix public and private money to improve value for money, especially in the early days of PPP or when private markets are weak. Public money also helps worthwhile projects that are not necessarily financially viable become more robust projects, increasing the opportunities for private investment.
- *Efficiency of financing is key.* There is no free ride; someone will have to pay (consumers and/or taxpayers), so make sure you get the best value for money.
- *Beware of creating significant risks when using highly structured financing.* Overly complex, highly leveraged financing, while cheaper, may create a project vulnerable to risk and change. A robust project is often worth the higher cost in times of trouble – and trouble happens.

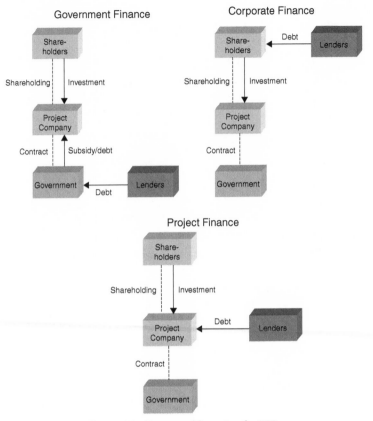

Figure 5.1. Sources of financing for PPP.

PPP offers alternatives to attract new sources of private financing and management while maintaining a public presence in ownership and strategic policy setting. These partnerships can leverage public funds and offer advantages of contracting with well-qualified private enterprises to manage and deliver infrastructure services. Three of the more common sources of financing for infrastructure projects, as shown in Figure 5.1, are the following:

- *Government financing* – where the government borrows money and provides it to the project through on-lending, grants, subsidies, or guarantees of indebtedness. The government can usually borrow money at a lower interest rate, but is constrained by its fiscal space (the amount it is able to borrow) and will have a number of worthy initiatives competing for scarce fiscal resources; the government is also generally less able to manage commercial risk efficiently.

- *Corporate financing* – a company borrows money against its proven credit profile and ongoing business (whether or not that debt is secured against specific assets or revenues – whether the debt is "secured" or "unsecured") and invests it in the project. Utilities and state-owned enterprises often do not have the needed debt capacity and may have a number of competing investment requirements. External investors may have sufficient debt capacity, but the size of investment required and the returns that such companies seek from their investments may result in a relatively high cost of financing and therefore can be prohibitive for the contracting authority.
- *Project financing* – where non-recourse or limited-recourse loans (these terms can be used interchangeably) are made directly to a special-purpose vehicle. The lenders rely on the cash flow of the project for repayment of the debt; security for the debt is primarily limited to the project assets and revenue stream. The debt can therefore be off-balance sheet for the shareholders and possibly also for the contracting authority (see section 5.2).

The proportion used of each source of financing and the decision as to which form of financing to adopt will depend on market availability of financing and the willingness of lenders to bear certain project risks or credit risks according to their view of how the market is developing and changing and of their own internal risk management regime.

This chapter will provide further discussion of types of financing contributions needed for PPP (section 5.1), project financing (section 5.2), and what the government can do to improve the ability to mobilize private financing for PPP (section 5.3).

5.1 Sources of Financing

A PPP project will involve financing from various sources, in some combination of equity and debt.

5.1.1 Equity Contributions

Equity contributions are funds invested in the project company that comprise its share capital and other shareholder funds. Equity holds the lowest priority of the contributions. For example, debt contributors will have the right to project assets and revenues to meet debt service obligations before the equity contributors can obtain any return or, on termination or insolvency, any repayment; and equity shareholders cannot normally receive distributions unless the company is in profit. Equity contributions bear the highest risk and therefore potentially receive the highest returns.

5.1.2 Debt Contributions

Debt can be obtained from many sources, including commercial lenders, export credit agencies, bilateral or multilateral organizations, bondholders (such as institutional investors), shareholders, and sometimes the host country government. Unlike equity contributions, debt contributions have the highest priority among the invested funds (e.g., senior debt must be serviced before most other debts are repaid). Repayment of debt is generally tied to a fixed or floating rate of interest and a program of periodic payments.

The source of debt will have an important influence on the nature of the debt provided.[1] PPP generally involves the construction of high-value, long-life assets with stable revenues and therefore seeks long-term, fixed-interest debt. This debt profile fits perfectly with the asset profile of pension funds and other institutional investors.

Bond financing allows the borrower to access debt directly from individuals and institutions rather than using commercial lenders as intermediaries.[2] The issuer (the borrower) sells the bonds to the investors. The lead manager helps the issuer to market the bonds. A trustee holds rights and acts on behalf of the investors, stopping any one investor from independently declaring a default. Bond financing generally provides lower borrowing costs and longer tenors (duration) if the credit position of the bond is sufficiently strong. Rating agencies may be consulted when structuring the project to maximize the credit rating for the project. Rating agencies will assess the riskiness of the project and assign a credit rating to the bonds, which will signal to bond purchasers the attractiveness of the investment and the price they should pay.

Different types of credit enhancement can be used to increase availability and reduce the cost of debt. For example, a monoline insurer (or a multilateral lending agency [MLA] such as the World Bank) may provide credit enhancement to bond investors, also known as an "insurance wrap."[3] The monoline insurer has a superior credit rating and provides

---

[1]   For further discussion of different lenders, see section 3.3.1.

[2]   For further discussion of documenting a bond issue, see Vinter, G. & G. Price, *Project Finance: A Legal Guide*, 3rd ed. (2006).

[3]   Although the collateralized debt obligations (CDO) and the subprime mortgage crash of 2008 have seriously reduced the availability of such instruments.

some undertaking to investors using that superior credit rating to reduce risk for investors, thereby improving the rating for the bond and reducing the yield required, justifying the cost of the insurance wrap.

5.1.3 Mezzanine/Subordinated Contributions

Located somewhere between equity and debt, mezzanine contributions are accorded lower priority than senior debt but higher priority than equity. Examples of mezzanine contributions are subordinated loans and preference shares. Subordinated loans involve a lender agreeing not to be paid until more "senior" lenders to the same borrower have been paid, whether in relation to specific project revenues or in the event of insolvency. Preference shares are equity shares, but with priority over other "common" shares when it comes to distributions. Mezzanine contributors will be compensated for the added risk they take either by receiving higher interest rates on loans than the senior debt contributors and/or by participating in the project profits or the capital gains achieved by project equity. Use of mezzanine contributions (which can also be characterized as quasi-equity) will allow the project company to maintain greater levels of debt-to-equity ratio in the project, although at a higher cost than senior debt. Shareholders may prefer to provide subordinated debt instead of equity to achieve the following:

- Benefit from tax deductible interest payments
- Avoid withholding tax
- Avoid restrictions on some institutions not permitted to invest in equity
- Allow the project company to service its subordinated debt when it would not be permitted to make distributions
- Permit shareholders to obtain some security, for example, to rank senior against trade creditors.

But, unlike equity holders, subordinated lenders face the following:

- Do not share in profits
- Do not normally have voting and control rights
- May be subject to usury laws on the amount of interest they are allowed to charge, where equity distributions would not

5.2 Project Finance

One of the most common, and often most efficient, financing arrangements for PPP projects is project financing, also known as limited recourse or nonrecourse financing. Project financing normally takes the form of limited recourse lending to a specially created project vehicle that has the right to carry out the construction and operation of the project. One of the primary advantages of project financing is that it can provide off-balance sheet financing, which will not affect the credit of the shareholders or the contracting authority and shifts some of the project risk to the lenders, in exchange for which the lenders obtain a higher margin than for normal corporate lending. Project financing achieves a better/lower weighted average cost of capital than pure equity financing. It also promotes a transparent risk-sharing regime and creates incentives across different project parties to encourage good performance and efficient risk management.

Key Messages for Policy Makers

- *Project finance is complex.* Get the right advice and be ready to pay for it. If properly managed, it can save you time and money.
- *While protecting the contracting authority's interests, listen to lender concerns.* Focus on the lender's key needs and perceived risks, but don't let the lender drive the agenda. Take the time and effort to make life a little easier for the lenders. It is likely to make your life easier in the long run.

5.2.1 Off-Balance Sheet and Limited Recourse Financing

Project finance debt is held by the project company, which is a sufficiently minority subsidiary so as not to be consolidated onto the balance sheet of the respective shareholders. This reduces the impact of the project on the cost of the shareholder's existing debt and on the shareholder's debt capacity, releasing such debt capacity for additional investments. To a certain extent, the contracting authority can also use project finance to keep project debt and liabilities off-balance sheet, taking up less fiscal space.[4] Fiscal space indicates the debt capacity of a sovereign entity and is a function of requirements placed on the host country by its own laws or by the rules applied by supra- or international bodies (such as the International Monetary Fund) or by market actors (such as credit rating agencies).

---

[4]   It should be noted that keeping debt off-balance sheet does not necessarily reduce actual liabilities for the government and may merely disguise government liabilities, reducing the effectiveness of government debt-monitoring mechanisms. As a policy issue, the use of off-balance sheet debt should be considered carefully, and protective mechanisms should be implemented accordingly.

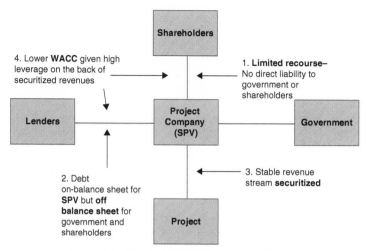

Figure 5.2. Key characteristics of project finance.

Another advantage to the shareholders of project financing is the absence, or limitation, of recourse by the lenders to the shareholders. The project company is generally a limited-liability, special-purpose project vehicle; therefore, the lenders' recourse will be limited primarily or entirely to the project assets. The extent to which some recourse is provided to shareholder assets is commonly called "sponsor support," which may include contingent equity or subordinated debt commitments to cover construction or other price overruns. These key characteristics of project financing for PPP are set out in Figure 5.2.

5.2.2 Bankability

The lenders' recourse for repayment of debt will be limited primarily to the revenue flow from the project. Due to the limited recourse and highly leveraged nature of project financing, any interruption of the project revenue stream or additional costs not contemplated in the project financial plan will directly threaten the ability to make debt service payments. This makes lenders extremely risk averse. The lenders will want to ensure that the risks borne by the project company are limited and properly managed and that the project involves a solid financial, economic, and technical plan. Therefore, before committing themselves to a project, the lenders will perform an in-depth review of the viability of the project (their "due diligence"). This is known commonly as verifying the project's "bankability."

Bankability requirements will vary based on the identity of the lenders, who will have different interests, concerns, and perceptions of risk. The lenders' vigilance is a key benefit of project finance, helping the contracting authority and shareholders alike to assess project viability. Clearly, an overly anxious lender can delay, complicate, or even undermine a project. Equally, a lender that is not sensitive to risk – for example, where the government provides a comprehensive guarantee of the debt – will not be as concerned about due diligence, and therefore the benefits of the lender's incentive to assess and monitor the project are lost. A lender's due diligence will include the following.

Economics and Politics

The lenders will wish to review the effect that the local economy and the project will have on each other. Although it is the contracting authority and not the lenders who should be verifying that the project will have an overall beneficial impact on the site country and the local economy, the lenders will need to assess the net political and socioeconomic benefit the project can have on the site country generally.[5] A commonly used measurement is the economic internal rate of return (EIRR[6]), which is the project's rate of return after taking into account economic costs and benefits, including monetary costs and benefits. EIRR captures the externalities (such as social and environmental benefits) not included in financial internal rate of return (IRR[7]) calculations.

The lenders will also use this macro-level assessment to ask certain fundamental questions about the project, such as the following:[8]

- What are the historical and likely future trends in prices, costs, production, availability quality, competition, demand, and the nature of the demand?
- Who are the input supplier and other service providers, and where are they located?
- What is the flexibility, sophistication, skill, and depth of the labor market?

---

[5] For further discussion of this issue, see Haley, G., *A-Z of BOOT* (1996), at 34.

[6] EIRR is the project's internal rate of return after taking into account externalities (such as economic, social, and environmental costs and benefits) not included in normal financial internal rate of return (IRR) calculations.

[7] FIRR is the discount rate that equates the present value of a future stream of payments to the initial investment. See also economic IRR.

[8] As modified from United Nations Industrial Development Organisation, Guidelines for Infrastructure Development through Build-Operate-Transfer (1996) at 130.

- What are the historical and likely future trends in inflation rates, interest rates, foreign exchange cost, and availability of labor, materials, and services (such as water, power, and telecommunications)?
- What is the condition of local infrastructure?
- What administrative burden will be placed on imports, in particular specialized labor and equipment?

Legal/Regulatory

The lenders will want to consider the legal system (including regulation and taxation) applicable to the project in view of the following:

- A long-term commercial arrangement based on undertakings by the public sector, property rights, taking of security asset management, likely tax exposure and corporate structures, and the likelihood of changes in law and taxation during the project
- Whether and to what extent the legal system is accessible to the project company and the lenders, including the time and resources required to access judicial review and whether such decisions can be enforced (courts or arbitration)
- Availability of security rights and priority given to creditors

Financial

In asset financing, it is the value and rate of depreciation of the underlying assets that defines the lenders' security and willingness to finance a project. In project financing, it is the viability of the project structure, the business plan, and the forecast revenue stream that will convince the lenders to provide financing. The revenue stream is only as secure as the credit position of the offtaker (e.g., the power utility that plans to buy the electricity generated), so lenders will assess carefully the credit risk of different project counterparties, including of course the project shareholders. Financial due diligence will include issues associated with financing risk, such as historical information on exchange rate movements, inflation, interest rates, availability of hedging and swaps, availability of insurance and reinsurance, and remedies available against different counterparties for losses or damages.

The lenders will develop their financial model from the information available. This model will identify the various financial inputs and outflows of the project. By calculating project risk into the financial model, the lenders will be able to test project sensitivities, that is, how far the project can absorb the occurrence of a given risk, for example, a 10 percent increase in construction costs or a 10 percent reduction in revenues. When assessing financial viability, the lenders will use the financial model to test a number of financial ratios, in particular debt-to-equity, debt service cover, loan life cover, and rates of return. (Some of these concepts are defined in Box 5.1 and in the glossary.)

Box 5.1. Financial Terms

A number of financial ratios are used to test financial viability, including the following:
- *Debt to equity ratio* compares the amount of debt in the project against the amount of equity invested.
- *Debt service cover ratio (DSCR)* measures the income of the project that is available to meet debt service (after deducting operating expenses) against the amount of debt service due in the same period. This ratio can be either backward or forward looking.
- *The loan life cover ratio (LLCR)* is the net present value of future project income available to meet debt service over the maturity of the loan against the amount of debt.

Technical

The review of the project carried out by the lenders will also focus on the technical merits of the design or intended design and the technology to be used in the project. The lenders will prefer not to finance projects using cutting-edge or untested technology. They will want to have relatively accurate performance forecasts, including operation, maintenance, and lifecycle costs; the capacity of the technology to be used and its appropriateness for the site; and the type of performance required from the project. Lenders will therefore prefer tried and tested technology used in similar projects with well-documented performance. Technical due diligence will also consider administrative issues, such as the likelihood of obtaining permits and approvals using the technology in question and the reasonableness of the construction schedule and price.

5.2.3 Refinancing

After completion of construction, and after construction risk in the project has been significantly reduced, the project company will look to refinance project debt at a lower cost and on better terms, given the lower risk premium. In developed economies, the capital markets are often used as a refinancing tool after completion of the project, since the bondholders prefer not to bear project completion risk, but are often able to provide fixed rates at a longer tenor and lower margin than commercial banks. Refinancing can be very challenging, in particular for lesser developed financial markets, but can significantly increase equity return, with the excess debt margin released and the resultant leverage effect, where the project performs well and where credit markets are sufficiently buoyant. While wanting to incentivize the project company to pursue improved financial engineering, in particular through refinancing, the contracting authority will want to share in the project company's refinancing gains, often in the form of a 50–50 split. The contracting authority may also want the right to require refinancing in certain circumstances.

5.3 What the Government Can Do to Improve the Financial Climate

Governments can and should provide a number of financial mechanisms to support and enable PPPs.[9] Few PPP projects are viable without some form of government technical or financial support. Efficient financing of PPP projects can involve the use of government support to ensure that the government bears risks that it can manage better than private investors and to supplement projects that are economically but not financially viable; that is, where infrastructure projects have large public externalities, some level of direct financial support from the government may be appropriate. Also, local financial markets may not be able to provide the financial products (in particular, long-term, fixed-interest debt) needed for PPP, even though such products would benefit the entire financial market. The government can do much to resolve these issues, by providing funded or contingent products or creating entities that provide some form of financial support necessary for PPP to flourish (see Figure 5.3).

Each project is likely to require tailor-made support, but the individual instruments to be used should be carefully designed to provide the perceived predictability that the private investor needs and the flexibility the government needs.

---

[9] Delmon, *Private Sector Investment in Infrastructure*, 2nd ed.

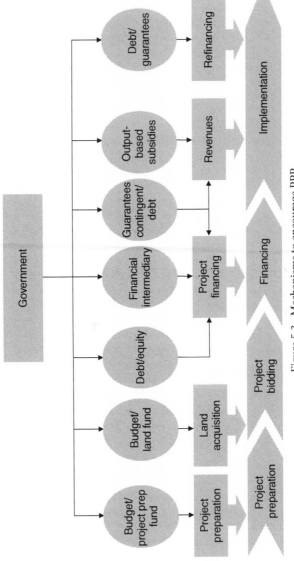

Figure 5.3. Mechanisms to encourage PPP.

When considering government support, the government will need to consider carefully the following:

- Which projects to support
- How much support to provide
- The terms of such support
- How to ensure that support is properly managed, for example, through transparency and proper governance

In particular, government support can create conflicts of interest or misaligned incentives, as the government will be playing different roles on different sides of the transaction; for example, it may be contracting authority and shareholder at the same time. Government support therefore needs to be designed, implemented, and regulated carefully.

Key Messages for Policy Makers

- *Government money can be used effectively to improve PPP projects. Government is a key partner in PPP and government support is a key element in successful PPP.*
- *Government support can improve financial viability and make a project more attractive for investors, but it will not turn a bad project into a good one.*
- *Use government support efficiently, in a targeted manner, to ensure government goals are achieved.*
- *Ensure funding mechanisms are properly resourced and incentivized to avoid political capture or inertia.*

These mechanisms are particularly useful where the project does not on its own merit achieve bankability or financial viability or is otherwise subject to specific risks that the private investors or lenders are not well placed to manage. In developing countries, where private finance is most needed, these constraints may necessitate more government support than would be required in more developed countries.

The decision on providing government support should be finalized and announced well before the project bid date, to improve the private investor's appetite, increase the number of bids, and reduce project costs for the contracting authority. The commercial and pricing benefits from government support packages are achieved best only if the support is announced in advance of the competition and if it is well designed. Allocation of government support after the bid date will deprive the contracting authority of most of these benefits.

5.3.1 Funded Products

Funded support involves the government committing direct financial support to a project, such as the following:

- Providing grant contributions – in cash or in kind (e.g., to defray construction costs, procure land, provide assets, compensate for bid costs, or support major maintenance)
- Waiving fees, costs, and other payments that would otherwise have to be paid by the project company to a public sector entity (e.g., authorizing tax holidays or a waiver of tax liability)
- Providing financing for the project in the form of loans (including mezzanine debt) or equity investment
- Funding shadow tariffs and topping up tariffs to be paid by some or all consumers (for example, to subsidize those least able to pay) to reduce the demand risk borne by the project company

These mechanisms can be used in combination, and can be more or less targeted (see Box 5.2).

Box 5.2. Targeted Support

Output- or performance-based subsidies or aid makes a clear link between the intended results and payment.[10] While requiring evidence of the ultimate output (e.g., healthier children or improved industrial output) is impractical for a number of reasons, governments can require the project company to perform a task or provide a service that achieves a stated objective before aid or subsidies are paid out, for example, a specified number of additional poor households connected to the electricity grid and using the service. These outputs need to be targeted to ensure they achieve the desired impact (e.g., connections alone will not create an output unless the service delivery is sustainable).[11]

5.3.2 Contingent Products

The government may choose to provide contingent mechanisms; that is, where the government is not providing funding, it might instead take on certain contingent liabilities. For example, the government may provide the following:

---

[10] Brook & Petrie, *Output-Based Aid.*
[11] See generally www.gpoba.org.

- Guarantees, including guarantees of debt, exchange rates, convertibility of local currency, offtake purchaser obligations, tariff collection, the level of tariffs permitted, the level of demand for services, termination compensation, and so on.
- Indemnities, such as against nonpayment by public entities and for revenue shortfall or cost overruns
- Insurance
- Hedging of project risk, such as adverse weather, currency exchange rates, interest rates, or commodity pricing
- Contingent debt, such as take-out financing (where the project can only obtain short tenor debt, the government promises to make debt available at a given interest rate at a certain date in the future) or revenue support (where the government promises to lend money to the project company to make up for revenue shortfalls, enough to satisfy debt-service obligations)

For example, on the Zagreb–Macelj toll road, the Croatian government provided in-kind support in the form of land and contingent subordinated debt drawn down whenever revenues were insufficient to cover debt service. Thus, lenders were protected, but the risk remained with the equity holders.

The government will want to manage the provision of government support, and in particular any contingent liabilities created through such support mechanisms. Governments seek a balance between (i) supporting private infrastructure investment and (ii) fiscal prudence.[12] Striking this balance will help the government make careful decisions about when to provide public-money support and manage the government liabilities that arise from such public-money support while still being aggressive in encouraging infrastructure investment. Government assessment of projects receiving such support is doubly important given the tendency of lenders to be less vigilant in their due diligence when government support is available, since this reduces lender risk and exposure.

Governments actively managing fiscal risk exposure face challenges associated with gathering information, creating opportunities for dialogue, analyzing the available information, setting government policy, and creating and enforcing appropriate incentives for those involved.[13] Given the

---

[12] For further discussion of this issue, see Irwin, T. C., *Government Guarantees: Allocating and Valuing Risk in Privately Financed Infrastructure Projects* (2007).
[13] Brixi, H., Irwin, T., & Budina, N., *Managing Fiscal Risk in Public–Private Partnerships* (2006).

complexity of these tasks, it is becoming more popular for governments, and in particular ministries of finance, to create specialist teams to manage fiscal risk arising from contingent liabilities, in particular those associated with PPP. This is often achieved through debt management departments, which are already responsible for risk analysis and management.[14] The government may also consider creating a separate fund to provide guarantees, allowing the government to regulate this function better and ring-fence the associated government liabilities.

5.3.3 Financial Intermediation

The government may wish to use its support to mobilize private financing (in particular, from local financial markets) where that financing would not otherwise be available for infrastructure projects. The government may want to mobilize local financial capacity for infrastructure investment to mitigate foreign exchange risk (where debt is denominated in a currency different from revenues), replace retreating or expensive foreign investment (for example, in the event of a financial crisis), and/or provide new opportunities in local financial markets. But local financial markets may not have the experience or risk management functions needed to lend to some sub-sovereign entities or to private companies on a limited recourse basis.

To overcome these constraints, the government may want to consider the intermediation of debt from commercial financial markets, creating an intermediary sufficiently skilled and resourced to mitigate the risks that the financial markets associate with lending to infrastructure projects. To achieve this, the government may want to use a separate mechanism (the "intermediary") to support such activities without creating undue risk for the local financial market, for example, by doing any of the following:

- Using the intermediary's good credit rating to borrow from the private debt market (e.g., providing a vehicle for institutional investors who could not invest directly in projects), then lend these funds to individual entities or projects as local currency private financing of the right tenor, terms, and price for the development of creditworthy, strategic infrastructure projects
- Providing financial products and services to enhance the credit of the project and thereby mobilize additional private financing, for example, by providing the riskiest tranche of debt, specialist expertise needed

---

[14] Different structures may be needed to track and manage risks created by central and local governments.

to act as lead financier on complex or structured lending, syndication credit enhancement, and specialist advisory functions, and/or

- Providing support to finance or reduce the cost or improve the terms of private finance for key utilities. These entities may need first to learn gradually the ways of the private financial markets, and the financial markets may need to get comfortable with lending to infrastructure operators. This mechanism can help slowly graduate such subnational entities or state-owned enterprises from reliance on public finance to interaction with the private financial markets.

Box 5.3. Infrastructure Development Finance Company (IDFC) of India

IDFC was set up in 1997 by the government of India along with various Indian banks and financial institutions and IFIs. IDFC's task was to connect projects and financial institutions to financial markets and by so doing develop and nurture the creation of a long-term debt market. It offered loans, equity/quasi-equity, advisory, asset management, and syndication services and earned fee-based income from advisory services, loan syndication, and asset management to capitalize on its established knowledge base and credibility in the market. IDFC also developed a project development arm, taking early positions in some project vehicles.

In its early years, the IDFC invested significant efforts in policy and regulatory frameworks advice to government.

IDFC began operations with a strong capital base of approximately U.S.$400 million. Growth was initially slower than expected. After six years of operations, IDFC had a loan portfolio of around U.S.$550 million, and growth accelerated. After eight years, an initial public offering (IPO) in July 2005 introduced new equity and allowed early investors to realize their gains. An additional U.S.$525 million equity was raised through an institutional placement in 2007, by which time the Indian government's stake had fallen to 22 percent.

Source: www.idfc.com

Current best practice indicates that such intermediaries should be private financial institutions with commercially oriented private sector governance. Intermediaries meant to create space in an existing financial market must have commercial incentives aligned to this goal, with appropriately skilled and experienced staff, and a credit position sufficiently strong to mobilize financing from the market. Existing private financial institutions with appropriate skills and capacity can help to perform this function. However, private entities often suffer from conflicts of interest (e.g., holding positions in the market such that their interests are not aligned with the role of intermediary) or would be constrained from taking positions in the market due to their role as intermediary (crowding out vital market capacity). The government may therefore want to create a new private entity to play this role, despite the cost and time required.

5.3.4 Project Development Funds

In the U.K., arguably one of the more efficient PPP markets, advisory costs during project development average 2.6 percent of project capital costs.[15] Advisory costs in less developed PPP markets run even higher. The large amount of upfront costs for procuring PPP projects, in particular the cost of specialist transaction advisers, often meets with strong resistance from government budgeting and expenditure control. But quality advisory services are key to successful PPP development and can save millions in the long run.[16] Therefore, funding, budgeting, and expenditure mechanisms for project development are important to a successful PPP program, enabling and encouraging government agencies to spend the amounts needed for high-quality project development.

The government may wish to develop a more or less independent project development fund (PDF), designed to provide funding to contracting authorities for the cost of advisers and other project development requirements (see Box 5.4). The PDF may be involved in the standardization of methodology or documentation, its dissemination, and monitoring of the implementation of good practices. It should provide support for the early phases of project selection, feasibility studies, and design of the financial and commercial structure for the project, through to financial close and possibly thereafter, to ensure a properly implemented project. The PDF may provide grant funding, require reimbursement (for example, through a fee charged to the successful bidder at financial close) with or without interest, or obtain some other form of compensation (for example, an equity interest in the project), or some combination thereof, to create a revolving fund. The compensation mechanisms can be used to incentivize the PDF to support certain types of projects.

---

[15] National Audit Office (U.K.), *Value for Money Drivers in the Private Finance Initiative* (2007).
[16] Department of the Treasury (U.K.), *Strengthening Long-Term Partnerships* (March 2006).

Box 5.4. South Africa's PDF

South Africa's Project Development Facility (PDF) is a single-function trading entity, created within the National Treasury in accordance with the Public Finance Management Act. Its primary function is to support governmental entities with the transaction costs of PPP procurement. The PDF does the following:

- Collaborates with the Department of Provincial and Local Government's Municipal Service Partnerships Unit
- Provides funding for the preparation of feasibility studies and procurement of service providers
- May consider funding the costs of procuring the project officer

---

Support from the PDF can be acquired only if the project receives support from the National Treasury's PPP unit.

The PDF recovers its disbursed funds either in part or in full as a success fee payable by the successful bidder at the financial close of the project. The risk of the project not reaching financial close is taken by the PDF in all cases other than an institutional default.

6

Local Currency Finance

Financing for PPP ideally involves long tenor debt at fixed rates. This allows the high cost of infrastructure to be spread out over its long lifecycle (as much as thirty to fifty years) and therefore makes the infrastructure more affordable; the fixed rates help avoid sudden changes in financing costs and therefore user tariffs. Long-term financing (twelve to eighteen years tenor), either with fixed interest rates or with variable interest rates that are supported by interest rate swaps to become fixed, are generally available in the global currencies, such as U.S. dollar, the euro, the yen, and the pound sterling (with notable exceptions, e.g., during the credit crunches in 2008–2009 and 2011–2012) but is more difficult to access in developing financial markets.

Long-term infrastructure investments can provide opportunities to debt capital markets, help to increase the depth and breadth of the markets, establish robust yield curves, and provide long-term placement opportunities in local markets that are often starved of such opportunities. Long-term capital for infrastructure, and its associated long-term returns, can provide a platform for reforms and market dynamism.

Accessing long-term financing for infrastructure in local currency is not so simple. Commercial banks in many countries do not have access to long-term liquidity. They fund themselves primarily through short-term deposits. The debt capital markets may offer only short to medium term positions (e.g., three to five years), depriving banks of the opportunity to lay off long-term loans against long-term bond issuances. These banks will face a "liability mismatch" to the extent they lend long term (long-term loans funded with [the volatility of] short-term deposits).

Governments can do much to help mobilize long-term local currency debt. Governments regulate financial markets, setting rules for banking and capital markets, to protect different market actors and encourage activity in those markets. They also enable and provide market information, clearing functions, rating of credit risk, exchanges for different instruments, and so on. One of the key sources of long-term local currency financing is institutional investors, such as pension and insurance funds. Government reform programs can do much to protect institutional investors and thereby enable them to invest in good projects.

While not a focus of this chapter, it should be highlighted that, in PPP, one of the most important efforts a government can make to mobilize local currency financing is to prepare projects well, ensuring financially viable projects with bankable risk allocation. Government reforms of financial markets can help address these challenges and release the capacity of financial markets to support PPP development.

This section discusses government efforts to mobilize long-term local currency finance for PPP, in particular through the use of "intermediaries," such as state-owned enterprises (SOEs). Section 6.1 summarizes the sources of long-term private capital. Section 6.2 discusses different types of government intervention to help mobilize long-term capital. Section 6.3 analyzes the use of intermediaries (e.g., state-owned enterprises) to mobilize long-term private capital, and section 6.4 concludes.

6.1 Sources of Long-Term, Local Currency Funding

This section discusses sources of long-term local capital and how to attract such resources to infrastructure.

Local commercial banks – Local banks (public and private) may provide a very convenient source of long-term financing. While often less sophisticated than their global counterparts, local banks have more access to local currency. Local banks also tend to be less risk averse when assessing projects in their own country, having better "on-the-ground" knowledge of factors affecting the project, taking a more pragmatic view of government and political risk, and having the confidence that local bureaucratic and technocratic challenges can be resolved in a satisfactory manner.

Global commercial banks – Global commercial banks are often more sophisticated, with experience in construction risk, operation of infrastructure, and structured finance that will give them a clear competitive edge (though this capacity may be located in other offices and not in the local office). Global banks may also have superior access to the global financial markets, with their deep pools of liquidity and long tenors, well suited to infrastructure finance. Global banks may have local activities, giving them access to local currency liquidity but generally in limited volumes. There are exceptions where the global bank has a strong local subsidiary or branch, but the local offices of global banks may have competing interests and are unlikely to have serious capacity on infrastructure finance located in the local offices, as they will be staffed for local operations. For these reasons, global banks tend to focus on foreign currency finance for infrastructure and are less competitive in local currency finance for infrastructure.

Box 6.1. Hard Miniperm Financing

The Al Dur IWPP in Bahrain was financed in 2009 using an eight-year hard miniperm structure. The sponsors and lenders took the refinancing risk. According to the sponsors, Al Dur had to refinance by year five or the sponsors would have been liable for a margin increase of 50 basis points and a 100 percent cash sweep for the remaining term. Before application of the cash sweep (see Box 6.2), the deal amortizes in line with a twenty-year amortizing loan. Under the base case model, an 80 percent balloon payment is left for repayment at the end of the eight-year term. Of the remaining 20 percent of the loan, 10 percent is repaid in accordance with the repayment schedule, and the other 10 percent is repaid by base case cash sweeps. There is an automatic event of default if the project is not refinanced before the end of the eight-year term.

Source: Al Dur: Enter the mini-perm, *Project Finance* (2012)

Development financial institutions – External development financial institutions (DFIs), including multilateral institutions such as the World Bank and the IFC and bilateral institutions such as Agence Française de Développement (AFD) of France, are ideally placed to support infrastructure finance and are increasingly critical to PPP in developing countries. They tend to have relatively low interest rates, long tenors, and grace periods. In addition to debt, they can also provide guarantees and insurance that may address specific financing risks faced by the project. However, DFI financing tends to be in foreign currencies and can involve additional costs related to the conditions imposed (such as procurement, safeguards, and financial management), complying with DFI practices and the time it takes to access finance.

Institutional and retail investors – Long-term liquidity may be available in local currency, in particular from institutional investors such as pension and insurance funds. Pension and insurance funds may hold large volumes of long-term capital; in most countries, such funds have difficulty finding long-term placements outside of government bonds and real estate. Long-term liquidity may also be available from retail investors, such as wealthy individuals otherwise tempted to move capital offshore, retirees looking for long-term security, and so on, in particular where other long-term investment opportunities are not available in local currency. Access to these investors is often facilitated through capital markets.

Box 6.2. Soft Miniperm

A soft miniperm sets out the contractual remedies available to funders. The incentives for the sponsors to refinance the loan by an earlier date include the following:

- A margin ratchet: incremental step-ups of, for example, 25 to 50 basis points at certain dates, which make the cost of borrowing more expensive in the event the loan isn't refinanced.
- A cash sweep: this triggers at a certain date, after which some or all free cash flow is used to prepay the debt outstanding rather than being directed to shareholder distributions. Sometimes the cash sweep is structured so that, for example, 50 percent of free cash flow is "swept" for prepayment in year five and increases to 100 percent in years eight or ten. But the effect is the same – the loan is fully repaid several years short of its legal maturity, and the shareholders suffer a long period of zero distributions.

In the event that a refinancing does not occur, the public sector pays for the margin ratchets (which are priced into the base case model), and the sponsors take the impact of deferred distributions and lower IRRs resulting from the cash sweep.

Source: KPMG, *The Use of Mini Perms in UK PFI (2009)*.

Debt capital markets – Capital markets often hold depth of liquidity in addition to, and often in excess of, that available from commercial banks. Debt capital markets (through the issuance of debt securities often called "bonds") may provide access to credit at lower interest rates and longer tenors than commercial banks by providing access to retail investors and to institutional investors. However, the financing available through capital markets is often less flexible than the financial instruments available from commercial banks. For example, they are not designed to provide grace periods (where the lenders agree to defer payment of debt service during an initial period and instead to capitalize these payments) nor to provide debt in tranches (where the borrower must pay a commitment fee from financial close but pays interest only once it has drawn down the amount needed). Instead, under a bond issuance, the project company must borrow the full amount of debt needed at financial close and pay interest on that full amount until repayment (the extra interest charged for funds not yet needed is called "carry cost"). Also, the most active purchasers of debt securities (i.e., pension funds, insurance funds, and other institutional investors) do not generally have the expert staff and processes of commercial banks, designed to assess and manage risk and respond to changes and requirements of dynamic investments such as infrastructure, and must hire advisers or investment banks and other intermediaries to provide such expertise.

Box 6.3. Prudential Rules for Pension Funds

In general, Anglo-Saxon countries adopt the prudent person rule (PPR) in pension fund investment. This rule requires only that funds be invested "prudently" rather than limited according to category. Furthermore, there are few restrictions on investment in specific assets. Such a system in fact requires an efficient court system with well-trained and informed judges, capable of establishing clear jurisprudence on prudent investor behavior and of guaranteeing its swift enforcement for market participants. In many other countries, different quantitative restrictions have traditionally been applied, normally stipulating upper limits on investment in specific asset classes, including equity.

Source: OECD, *Pension Fund Investment in Infrastructure: A Survey* (September 2011)

Global capital markets – The global capital markets have access to deep and long-term capital from sophisticated investors likely to be more interested in infrastructure investments. However, these investors are likely to have limited appetite for local currency placements. Even in foreign currency, these investors will be subject to certain limitations on the credit rating of the securities they purchase; in particular, the prominence of pension, insurance, and other prudential funds in the global markets may limit appetite for anything less than investment grade or even higher international credit ratings. Global capital markets are unlikely to be a significant source of local currency debt. There have been local currency bonds issued in the global markets (e.g., diaspora bonds) with some success, but usually not in large volumes. These efforts often focus on currencies from countries with large emigrant communities with close contact with their home country and desiring investments in local currency.

Box 6.4. Index Linked Debt and Pension Funds

The Regulated Asset Base (RAB) model takes changes in generic costs of financing into account during periodic reviews of utility tariffs. This effectively transfers the refinancing risk onto consumers or onto government, where an availability payment is used. However, this puts little if any incentive on the private sector to manage the risk, unless the RAB review only accounts for lowest cost financing, second-guessing the decisions of the private sector.

The N33 highway project was the first transport project in the Netherlands where pension funds were involved in the financial structure. Rijkswaterstaat (RWS) awarded a PPP project to the sponsor, a 50–50 joint venture between BAM PPP and PGGM, on October 1, 2012. The sponsors provided equity of €13 million. The project was financed at a gearing ratio of 90:10. Three banks, BTMU, KfW-IPEX, and Rabobank, provided the construction loan and a long-term project loan of €47.1 million (38 percent of the debt financing). The remaining 62 percent of the debt financing was secured from Dutch pension fund ABP (managed by its APG subsidiary, which administers the ABP pension scheme) in the form of an index-linked loan to be issued after construction was over, refinancing the banks' capital expenditure (capex) facility.

The payment mechanism from RWS was inflation-linked to help attract long-term debt from institutional investors. Following a six-month evaluation of the progress of the N33 PPP project, the Dutch government announced in June 2013 that it would not publish new tenders for infrastructure projects with inflation-linked payments. While the pricing of the inflation-linked loan was very attractive at financial close, the government regrets having taken this risk and believes that it is better allocated to the private sector.

Source: *Partnerships Bulletin*, Taking the risk, at 20.

Domestic capital markets – Local capital markets have more appetite for local currency positions and will be less sensitive to political and other country-specific risk. However, for the purposes of financing PPP, local debt capital markets often elicit a number of challenges:

- Lack of liquidity, in particular long term
- Short tenors and lack of a long-term yield curve; in sum, there are no comparable long-term financial instruments freely traded in the local market, so no objective basis to set a price
- Local investors unfamiliar with the risk profile of infrastructure

Equity investment – Investors in equity in PPP projects (often known as shareholders or sponsors) can provide a variety of types of financing. This section will focus on two major types: equity contributions and shareholder loans.

Equity contributions earn returns from distributions by the project company. When the company earns a profit, the lending agreements allow distributions and the board of the company approves. Distributions will be paid in the currency of revenues; therefore, shareholders take foreign exchange risk to the extent their investment was made in foreign currency.

Shareholder loans are generally subordinated debt treated as quasi-equity. There are various benefits to providing debt rather than equity, including tax and priority of repayment (see Chapter 5).

Shareholders tend to be one of three project actors. Project participants are often shareholders, such as construction companies, operators, and suppliers. They take on a shareholding position often as much to obtain the contract for the project as to earn returns on their equity investment. They often seek to sell-down their equity position as soon as possible, since equity investment is not their core business. Contractors may form a separate company to act as investor. Financial investors may also be shareholders. These are equity funds, banks, or other financial entities that invest solely to obtain equity returns. The government may also be a shareholder. The government may insist on equity shares as part of the project, but may not provide additional capital in the process. Government equity is discussed further in section 3.3.

Box 6.5. Securitization of Infrastructure Revenues

Dubai hired local and international banks to raise $800 million by securitizing road toll receipts to fund infrastructure projects in the Gulf emirate. Securitization requires a reliable revenue stream, careful structuring from experienced and well-respected advisers, and possibly credit enhancement to ensure the placement is sufficiently credit worthy to attract debt at the cost and tenor desired.

6.2 Possible Government Interventions

A variety of instruments are available for government to help mobilize long-term local currency financing for infrastructure, including the following:

- *Advisory services* bring the assistance of experienced transaction advisers to the aid of contracting authorities or private investors, depending on the need. Mobilizing debt for infrastructure projects requires particular skills, for example, packaging debt efficiently and managing lender groups and their due diligence requirements. One of the key advisory roles is the "arranger" of debt. An arranger needs to know, and be known by, the market to facilitate arranging and negotiation with other lenders.
- *Equity and "equitylike" instruments* for infrastructure projects can be large in value and risky, with long periods before equity distributions are realized. Sponsors are often the construction companies, infrastructure operators, or other service providers whose principal focus is the provision of services to the project. The government can provide equity investment and mandate an intermediary to act as an equity investor. Equity investment in infrastructure is a difficult function to fulfill well; it requires a level of sophistication different from most equity investment. It is not just a question of funding but rather the governance, the ability to make critical decisions in times of need and to provide technical and commercial support, given the complexity of an infrastructure transaction.

Box 6.6. Bonds Using Subordinated Debt to Credit Enhance

Subordinated debt can be used to credit-enhance a project, to facilitate bond financing. One structure might involve tranched debt, a senior tranche as A Notes and a subordinated tranche as B Notes. The A Notes are issued to the capital markets, and the B Notes are placed with a fund that provides a "first loss" tranche of debt. For example, A Notes might represent 70 percent, with B Notes representing 15 percent and equity 15 percent. The aim would be to take the total project debt with a rating of BBB–/BBB and use the fund to enhance the risk profile of the A Notes to at least BBB+. The structure could use the principle of some real estate funds where the B Notes are the controlling creditor of the project unless the project performance falls below predefined thresholds, in which case the A Notes take control. This alleviates the need for bondholders to manage the project on a day-to-day basis unless the project is in distress.

- *Long-term liquidity for equity investors* – Equity investors also need access to large amounts of capital. Project sponsors will normally have less robust balance sheets than banks and will not be able to leverage like lenders. In many countries, the shortage of equity investment is a major challenge for infrastructure programs, reducing competition and making projects expensive. This is equally important for the secondary market, where equity investors will seek to on-sell shares once the project is operational and less risky.
- *Debt* – The government may want to help provide or mobilize debt for infrastructure projects themselves or through an intermediary. Acting as lender is a difficult function for many governments that do not have the due diligence, oversight, implementation, and other key governance functions of financiers. Once the project is operational, and the risk profile is lower, less expensive, lower-risk debt can be used to refinance the project, often from the capital markets.

Box 6.7. Arguments for Government Equity Holdings in PPP

Some argue that government should be an equity holder in infrastructure transactions. The argument usually runs that government needs the following:

- A share in the upside of very profitable projects, to ensure that government gets a piece of the action. Counterargument: Equity distributions in infrastructure are hard to control and harder to forecast. If government wants to share in the upside, it should require a share of revenues or a fixed lease payment instead.
- Control of the sector, to maintain government influence over the project and the sector. Counterargument: Private partners are likely to limit real government control over the project as equity holders to mitigate conflict of interest and ensure that decisions are made on a commercial rather than political basis. Government would do better maintaining control through regulations and regulatory powers.
- Access to information. Government may see equity as a mechanism for accessing company information. Counterargument: Private partners will inevitably establish a governance structure that isolates sensitive information. The government may find that regulatory powers and data gathering of its own will provide a more practical solution to information access.

- Long-term liquidity for commercial banks. Commercial banks may have staff and capacity to finance projects, but may not have access to sufficient long-term local currency capital. Often, their deposit base will be short term in nature, creating a liability mismatch if they create long-term assets. Also, commercial banks may be nervous about using what long-term capital they have on infrastructure (where competing opportunities are more profitable). The government can help by providing financial institutions (in particular, commercial banks) access to long-term liquidity, which they can then on-lend to infrastructure projects, for example, helping commercial banks access local capital markets or supplying/lending long-term funds directly to commercial banks.

Box 6.8. Chilean Infrastructure Bonds

Chile successfully tapped the bond market for a project to finance debt through infrastructure bonds amounting to an average of U.S.$1 billion a year during 1996–2001. This situation was aided by government revenue guarantees and even foreign exchange guarantees in certain cases; political and regulatory risks were mostly insured by DFIs.

6.3 Using an Intermediary

Infrastructure projects (in particular PPPs) provide an ideal opportunity for holders of long-term local currency. In addition to treasuries and real estate, infrastructure offers one of the better long-term placement opportunities for developing economies. It also creates economic opportunities, jobs, and growth.

However, most developing country financial sectors are ill equipped to respond to the opportunities of infrastructure finance. They do not generally have lending products with the long tenors, fixed interest rates, and grace periods needed by infrastructure investments. Also, the risk profile for infrastructure differs from the normal diet of local financiers.

Intermediaries can help. These are specially equipped entities that can provide advice, structure projects, and offer specialized financial instruments to help address the challenges faced by local financiers. These intermediaries can borrow from the local markets and convert these liabilities into the kind of financial instruments sought by infrastructure projects, and/or they can co-finance with local financial institutions and financiers to achieve together the lending products sought.

Creating such intermediaries (whether from existing entities or by creating new ventures) can be costly and time consuming. There is no easy or standard approach to intermediation. Each country will need to consider carefully its requirements, its legal framework, the make-up of its financial sector, and the kind of infrastructure that is to be financed before creating such an intermediary. Key lessons have been discussed previously, learned from countries that have significant experience in creating intermediaries for infrastructure finance.

Box 6.9. Pebble Commute Scheme Credit Enhanced Bond Style

In the financing of a penitentiary in Zaanstaad, the Netherlands, with Euro 195 M of debt, ING and NIBC provided 15 percent of the debt as a seven-year, first-loss protection subordinated loan to guarantee the other senior tranche. The subordinated loan is paid back first if the asset is performing, while it is used to absorb losses if the asset underperforms or defaults. After the end of construction, cash flows are directed to pay back the subordinated loan. The long-term, fixed-rate debt accounts for the remaining 85 percent of the total debt and was provided by institutional investors, both insurers and pension funds with a tenor of more than twenty years. The credit-enhancement facility, in this case, is aimed at guaranteeing the riskier construction phase and the beginning of operation, while the long-term management phase is left uncovered. The subordinated loan was also drawn first compared with the institutional tranche rather than simultaneously.

Source: www.nibc.com/nc/news/news/nibc-wins-european-ppp-deal-of-the-year-award.html.

6.3.1 Role of Intermediary

The government may want to provide a vehicle (an "intermediary") to provide financing for PPP projects and an intermediary for institutional investors who could or would not invest directly in projects. Such an intermediary is often created through state-owned enterprises, which provide a convenient nexus among the public, government support, and commercial/private context. Such an intermediary can help with the following:

- Use government and donor funding to leverage private sector funding
- Reduce the transaction costs represented by government and donor funding for individual transactions by creating a wholesale mechanism

- Increase transparency and consistency of government support by establishing an entity with governance mechanisms and operational guidelines establishing rules of the game
- Allow private sector salary scale to attract suitably skilled and expert staff and create a center of expertise based on larger volumes of transactions, with commercial selection criteria
- Use the leverage available through a financial institution to increase the amount of support made available from a limited capital base

6.3.2 Functionality

Three key functions for the intermediary that can help mobilize local finance include origination, liquidity, and refinancing.

Box 6.10. Tamil Nadu Urban Development Fund (TNUDF)

TNUDF was created as a trust fund with private equity participation and without state guarantees, the first such structure in India. Its paid-in capital combined with debt raised from a World Bank loan allowed TNUDF to issue the first nonguaranteed, unsecured bond issue by a financial intermediary in India, in 2000. The issue received a LAA+ rating from the Indian Credit Rating Agency (ICRA) due to credit enhancement and structured payment mechanism, low gearing, and strong repayment record. The proceeds from bonds are deposited in the fund and subsequently lent back to the participating local bodies as subloans to finance their infrastructure projects.

Source: www.tnudf.com.

Origination: Intermediaries originating infrastructure finance will assess a project, influence its design and structure, and then build a book of debt either alone, with a club of other lenders, and/or through syndication.

Liquidity: Long tenor funds can be made available to those financiers or as co-financing (senior or subordinated) to the project. Other instruments, such as take-out guarantees, can be used to extend tenors of debt.

Refinancing: Liquidity constraints, liability mismatches, risk ratios, single borrower limits, and other prudential requirements can constrain the amount and terms of support that local financiers can provide to infrastructure markets. After construction, the risk profile of a PPP project changes significantly, allowing the project company to source debt at lower interest rates and better terms. Refinancing involves the prepayment of part or all of a project's debt by borrowing from a new lender (possibly at a lower interest rate or longer tenor or on easier terms).

6.3.3 A Few Challenges

PPP financial intermediaries (FIs) can be particularly difficult to implement effectively. Some of the key challenges when creating an intermediary are discussed in this section. Section 6.4 provides a quick snapshot of some of the global FIs.

Staying demand responsive – the FI must address identified market gaps, with access to products and instruments designed to address those gaps, but also with the flexibility to use other instruments or approaches that respond to the changing nature of such gaps and market needs. The Indonesian Infrastructure Finance Facility (IIFF) was created after much effort at market analysis and coordination with other market actors. The Brazilian Economic Development Bank (BNDES) was a public bank that was adapted to address a growing market need.

In the same way, the FI must focus on the gap rather than squeezing out private investment. It must squeeze in private lenders and investors to give them new opportunities.

Once FIs are created, it is often difficult to get rid of them after they have served their purpose. Provision needs to be made for the FI to be wound up, sold off, or absorbed into another entity, or for it to evolve into some other mechanism that will be responsive to other market demands relevant at that time.

Box 6.11. Development Bank of Southern Africa (DBSA)

The DBSA is a development finance institution wholly owned by the government of South Africa that focuses on investments and joint ventures/partnerships in public and private sector financing. The DBSA can raise money on local and international capital markets and is publicly listed on the New York Stock Exchange. Its bond ratings are the same as South African Sovereign Ratings.

DBSA offers a variety of financial products, including grants, equity, debt (senior and subordinated), underwriting guarantees, and other credit enhancement.

Source: www.dbsa.org.

Governance and management structures – investment project selection must be based on sound commercial criteria, and not driven by purely political priorities; the risk of capture of the intermediary by political interests is high. This is generally addressed by developing the FI as a privately owned company, for example, the IIFF. At the same time, purely commercial motivation may be too risk averse for the investments available. The Emerging Africa Infrastructure Fund (EAIF) faced this challenge. The EAIF is a partnership between development financiers wanting to take risk and commercial financiers with a more risk-averse approach to project selection, creating a particular challenge in the early days when searching for an appropriate incentive mechanism for the fund manager.

Amount and source of original capital – any effort to make a significant impact on an infrastructure market is likely to require a large investment of capital in the FI. For example, the Indian Infrastructure Finance Corporation Limited (IIFCL) and BNDES were allocated funding from government bond issuances, giving them access to significant amounts of capital at a low cost. The National Infrastructure Fund (FONADIN) of Mexico was allocated the revenues from a portfolio of publicly owned toll roads. The IIFF and EAIF started from a smaller capital base.

Skilled staff and resources – newly formed FIs are a risky bet for financiers, and so an FI needs a solid, experienced management team to give comfort to the financial market and politicians. They must be able to attract funding from institutional investors and display a keen understanding of the infrastructure market. The management team also needs to be committed for a

---

Box 6.12. Fondo Nacional de Infrastructura (Fonadin) of Mexico

Fonadin is housed within Banobras, Mexico's national development bank, and was created in response to the tight credit market of the financial crisis to address risks that the market was not able to handle. It began with a sum of over 40 billion pesos (U.S.$3.3 billion) in 2008 and has its own revenue source from existing toll road assets that were rescued in a government bailout in the late 1990s and therefore does not rely on government support for its financing base.

Fonadin's role is to finance infrastructure. It offers a variety of instruments, including grants, subsidies, guarantees (for stock, credit, damage, and political risk), subordinated lines of credit, and grants for technical assistance.

Source: www.fonadin.gob.mx.

reasonable period; this is not the job for a political appointee, a retiree look-ing for something to keep busy, or a short-term consultant. The role of CEO is key, a politically acceptable individual but with good banking experience and the right incentives to take calculated risks. The IIFF and the African Finance Corporation both had challenges with their management teams in their early days in finding the right set of skills and personality. These skilled staff can also be sourced through secondments from shareholders, as was done for the Infrastructure Development Finance Company (IDFC), or through a management contract, as was done for the EAIF.

Identifying a solid pipeline – it is often tempting to focus on the market gap to be resolved by the FI. But the FI's first investments, the demonstra-tion projects, will be critical and must be carefully prepared as the FI is being created. This creates a timing challenge as the market is unlikely to wait for the FI. The Investment Promotion and Financing Facility (IPFF) of Bangladesh addressed this challenge by focusing on a series of gas-fired power projects in its first phase, projects that were well developed, easy to market, and limited to one sector. Phase two expanded to other sectors and riskier projects. The IDFC and IIFF spent their first few years provid-ing advisory services to the infrastructure sector and thereby developing their own pipelines of investments, the former by necessity and the latter by design.

6.4 Sample Intermediaries

The following provides a snapshot of a few of the global financing intermediaries.

Investment Promotion and Financing Facility (IPFF) (www.mof.gov.bd/en/budget/09_10/ppp/IPFF) of Bangladesh is a publicly held vehicle in operation since 2006 that provides long-term funding through eligible financial institutions that on-lend to qualifying PPP projects on market terms. The equity contribution of the sponsor (minimum of 30 percent) and the debt share of the local financial institution (minimum of 20 per-cent) ensure market-based incentives in selecting only commercially viable PPP transactions and successfully implementing them.

Fonadin (National Infrastructure Fund–Mexico) (www.fonadin.gob.mx) was established in February 2008 under the management of the national infrastructure bank Banobras. Fonadin was created in response to the tight credit market of the financial crisis to address risks that the market was not able to handle. It began with a sum of over 40 billion pesos (U.S.$3.3 billion) in 2008, which will build up to approximately 270 billion pesos (U.S.$22.2

billion) in 2012 through toll road revenues. Fonadin can offer credit guarantees to project companies seeking funding from commercial banks or financial intermediaries or for bonds issued by a concessionaire. Fonadin can cover up to 50 percent of the loan or issuance with its guarantee.

Infrastructure Development Finance Company (IDFC) (www.idfc.com) of India was set up in 1997 by the government of India along with various Indian banks, financial institutions, and IFIs. IDFC's task is to connect projects and financial institutions to financial markets and by so doing develop and nurture the creation of a long-term debt market. It offers loans, equity/quasi-equity, advisory, asset management, and syndication services.

India Infrastructure Finance Company Limited (IIFCL) (www.iifcl.org) started operations in April 2006. IIFCL accesses capital from the government, IFIs, and the financial markets (in some cases benefiting from a government guarantee). These funds are on-lent to PPP projects. The IIFCL does not have a sophisticated risk assessment function. It follows commercial banks, providing only part of the debt requirements of the project and therefore ensuring that the incentive to assess projects and ensure successful implementation rests squarely on the commercial equity and debt providers.

Indonesian Infrastructure Finance Facility (IIFF) (www.iif.co.id) is a private, non-bank financial institution, commercially oriented fund with private sector governance, mandated and equipped to mobilize local currency private financing. The IIFF is capitalized through equity investments and subordinated loans from the government, the private sector, and multilaterals. It will invest in PPP projects, with debt, equity, and/or guarantees, and by providing advisory services.

Emerging Africa Infrastructure Fund (EAIF) (www.eaif.com) is a U.S.$600 million debt fund which aims to address the lack of available long-term foreign currency debt finance for infrastructure projects in sub-Saharan Africa. The EAIF was created through a joint venture of development institutions and commercial banks. By mixing equity from donors and subordinated debt from development partners with senior debt from commercial lenders, EAIF seeks to reduce its cost of lending and provide midmarket debt managed by commercial lenders.

Indonesian Infrastructure Guarantee Fund (IIGF) (www.iigf.co.id) is a company, wholly owned by the Indonesian government, that acts as the single window for guarantees for PPP projects. It assists the MoF in its role of monitoring and allocating government support by assessing projects and helping to source any guarantees needed for that project, for example, from the World Bank, MIGA, its own capital, or the government.

Brazilian Economic Development Bank (BNDES) (www.bndes.gov.br) is a publicly owned commercial bank. Formed in 1952, BNDES raises money through the issuance of government securities in favor of BNDES. It also has access to the capital markets and can raise money through trading securities and all manner of derivatives; it also earns income from its loan portfolio and can issue debentures. With its long-term financing, BNDES has been fundamental in the growth of PPP in Brazil. It is a dominant force in Brazil's infrastructure market and provides debt for most of its PPP projects. As a government-owned bank, it received funds from the government and uses the government's credit position to offer very low rates for long-term debt. BNDES is also subject to criticism, in particular for squeezing out private lenders due to its dominant position, imposing long wait times for approval of loans, being overly risk averse, and requiring security from sponsors more appropriate to corporate financing than PPP.

Development Bank of Southern Africa (DBSA) (www.dbsa.org) is a development finance institution wholly owned by the government of South Africa that focuses on investments and joint ventures/partnerships in public and private sector financing. DBSA can raise money on local and international capital markets and is publicly listed on the New York Stock Exchange. Its bond ratings are the same as South African Sovereign Ratings. DBSA offers a variety of financial products, including grants, equity, debt (senior and subordinated), underwriting guarantees, and other credit enhancement.

Tamil Nadu Urban Development Fund (TNUDF) (www.tnudf.como) was created as a trust fund with private equity participation and without state guarantees, the first such structure in India. Its paid-in capital combined with debt raised from a World Bank loan to the government allowed TNUDF to issue the first nonguaranteed, unsecured bond issue by a financial intermediary in India, in 2000, three to four years after being established. The issue received a LAA+ rating from ICRA due to credit enhancement and structured payment mechanism, low gearing, and strong repayment record. The proceeds from bonds are deposited in the fund and subsequently lent back to the participating local bodies as subloans to finance their infrastructure projects.

Allocation of Risk

A successful project must benefit from workable, commercially viable, and cost-effective risk sharing. Given the differing interests and objectives of the parties involved, effective risk allocation will be an essential part of the drafting of the project documents and an integral part of the project's success. As discussed in Chapter 5, project finance lenders in particular are extremely sensitive to risk allocation and will look to see a contractual documentation that creates a "bankable" risk allocation.

> ### Key Messages for Policy Makers
>
> - *Don't allocate excessive levels of risk on the private sector.* It usually is not efficient and makes the project overly vulnerable to cost increases, change, and crises.
> - *Prepare for change during the project.* It is not possible to anticipate or make every risk decision in advance; mechanisms will be needed to address change and other challenges.

Risk management based on efficiency[1] is, of course, an ideal, a goal. In practice, risk tends to be allocated on the basis of commercial and negotiating strength. The stronger party will allocate risk that it does not want to

---

[1] An oft-quoted approach to "efficient" risk allocation places each risk on the party best able to manage that risk. While a useful rule of thumb, this is a gross simplification. See chapters 1–3 of Delmon, *Project Finance, BOT Projects and Risk*. For example, risk also needs to be borne by the party that has an interest in managing it proactively, has or will obtain the resources needed to address risk issues as and when they arise (the sooner the better) in a manner intended to reduce their impact on the project, has access to the right technology and resources to manage the risk when it crystallizes, can manage the risk at the least cost, and delivers value for money.

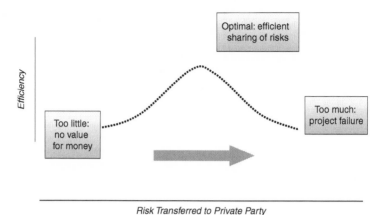

Figure 7.1. Efficient risk allocation.

bear to the weaker party. This scenario does not necessarily provide the most effective and efficient risk management.[2] Figure 7.1 shows this phenomenon from the government's perspective; allocating too much risk to the project company results in an expensive and unstable project, while allocating too little risk results in a loss of value for money and public resentment. Getting this balance right is notoriously difficult.

In most conventionally financed projects, it is accepted that certain risks (such as market risk, certain political risks, and completion risk) will be allocated by the contracting authority to the project company in relation to the role the project company plays in the project. For bearing such risks, the project company is compensated by higher returns on its investment. However, project financing is obtained primarily through the lenders, rather than the investment by or liability of the shareholders. The lenders will attempt to limit their assumption of project risk; they will require the project company to allocate as much of its risk as possible to the different project counterparties (e.g., the offtake purchaser, the construction contractor, and the operation and maintenance [O&M] contractor). The effort to transfer all project risk to these subcontractors is known as "back-to-back" risk allocation. Complete back-to-back risk allocation will result in the transfer of all project risk assumed by the project company to the other project participants. Rarely, if ever, will a PPP project achieve complete, absolute back-to-back allocation, although the most developed PPP markets such as the United Kingdom achieve something close to it.

---

[2] Business Roundtable, *"Contractual Arrangements" A Construction Industry Cost Effectiveness Project Report* (October 1982).

The following risks are of concern to parties, in particular in relation to the potential for increase in costs, reduction in revenues, or delay in payment.

7.1 Political Risk

The contracting authority may accept bearing a certain amount of political risk (such as events of war, rebellion, default or failure of public sector entities, change in law, and delays by authorities) as the sole party who may be able to influence its advent and mitigate its effects. However, host governments may not be willing to bear all political risk and may require the project company to bear certain aspects or the majority of this risk, as would other companies investing in that country.

Political risk includes the following:

- Changes in law or regulations, in particular the risk of discriminatory changes in law (those changes that are specific to the sector involved, private financing of public projects generally, or the project itself) and changes in technical parameters through permits, consents, or import licenses.
- Expropriation: it is a basic principle of international law that a sovereign government has the right to expropriate property within its territory for public purposes, but must compensate the owner.[3]
- Regulatory decisions that differ from the commercial arrangements underlying the PPP.
- Ability of the project company to access justice, in particular enforcing the government's obligations.
- Whether the contracting authority (or other key public parties) has the right or the power (vires) to enter into the obligations involved in the project and what administrative or legal requirements must be satisfied before those obligations can become binding.

The project company may look to methods of mitigating this risk, such as the following:

- The consideration of the host government's (and other political actors') interests and their implementation in the project
- The involvement of local lenders and local shareholders or subcontractors
- Political risk insurance, MLA involvement, or specialized risk mitigation products (see sections 7.10, 7.11, and 8.10).

---

[3] A sovereign state holds the power of disposition over its territory as a consequence of title. Brownlie, I., *Principles of Public International Law*, 4th ed. (1990), at 123.

7.2 Legal and Regulatory Risk

Certain critical legal issues need to be addressed as a prerequisite to implementing PPP. These issues include the following:[4]

- Authority of the contracting authority to undertake the project
- Procurement rules that permit PPP arrangements
- Security rights over assets and/or shares sufficient to provide the lenders with enough protection
- Access to justice (ideally international arbitration) and a reasonable mechanism for and history of enforcement of judgments/arbitral awards against the government

A host of other legal issues will be important to ensure the proper functioning of PPP, for example, land acquisition, labor relations, tax and accounting (e.g. transfer costs, depreciation, VAT offsetting), and regulatory mechanisms.[5]

7.3 Completion Risk

The construction phase involves potentially the most costly project risk. The nature of PPP is such that an incomplete project will be of limited value. PPP allows the contracting authority to package completion risks in a more efficient manner, often known as single-point risk allocation. This means that design construction, installation, commissioning, operation maintenance, and refurbishment risk are all allocated to and managed by one entity. Single-point responsibility reduces the interfaces between different project functions that can result in errors, delays, and a "claims culture" (where different contractors blame each other for any defects discovered – the number of interfaces facilitates such blame games). Under single-point responsibility, these interfaces are managed by the project company (which is likely more capable of performing this function than the contracting authority) and allocated to the construction contractor.

The implications of completion risk can be divided into three key categories:

---

[4] Legal and regulatory risk represents the application of political risks and decisions, discussed further in section 7.1. The close relationship between these sections results in some overlap in the discussions here.

[5] A full discussion of these issues can be found in chapter 8 of Delmon, *Private Sector Investment in Infrastructure*, 2nd ed.

- Cost of construction – a PPP project, in particular using project finance, is a delicate balance of financial covenants, ratios, and commitments that will be extremely sensitive to changes in cost. An increase in cost would require adjustment to these and the need for one of the parties to provide additional funding (unlikely to be provided by the lenders), possibly through standby facilities arranged before commencement.
- Time for completion – the project company will want to commence operation of the project as soon as possible in order to earn maximum revenue and improve return on investment. Similarly, the contracting authority and the offtake purchaser will have put the project out to tender owing to a pressing need for the service to be rendered and will therefore want the construction completed in the shortest amount of time possible. Therefore, timely completion of construction will be a key concern of the principal project parties and will be monitored and sanctioned accordingly.
- Quality of finished works – the finished works must satisfy certain tests and inspections in order to demonstrate compliance with the project specifications, successful connections with any external network (such as a power grid or a water system), and proper management of interfaces between different equipment and technologies used in the project. The finished product must be capable of delivering output in accordance with the project expectations; any shortfall would require financial restructuring to enable project revenues to meet project costs and service debt.

Completion risk includes the following:

- The adequacy of the design of the works
- The nature of the technology to be used and the availability of equipment and materials, including transportation, import restrictions, pricing, services necessary for construction, financing costs, and administrative costs
- Unforeseen events or conditions, such as weather or subsurface conditions
- The availability of labor and materials, whether skilled labor can be procured locally, the extent to which both labor and materials will need to be imported, visas and licenses required for such importation, and restrictions imposed by local labor laws (including working hours and holiday entitlement)

- The availability of associated infrastructure and services, such as access (road, rail, and air links), water, and electricity
- The program for completion, whether the construction methodologies are appropriate given seasonal climate, the approvals process, coordination among subcontractors, and testing and commissioning programs

Completion risk is generally allocated to the construction contractor by the project company.

7.4 Performance Risk

In order for the project to maintain sufficient revenues to satisfy debt servicing and to provide a return for the shareholders, the project must deliver infrastructure services to specified levels. Performance risk results in the inability of the facility to deliver the services in the manner and timing required and agreed. Possible issues include the following:

- Errors in the design of the facility
- Environmental issues that impede the operation of the facility
- The use of inappropriate technology
- Improper operation of the facility
- Insufficient quality of input used or inappropriate manner of offtake or use of project services

Therefore, performance requirements are imposed on the project company by the contracting authority and/or the offtake purchaser, whose requirements are then passed on to the project participants (in particular, the construction contractor and the operator). Whether these requirements are fulfilled by the completed works will be verified by performance tests as part of the construction regime. During operation, the facility will be tested periodically to ensure service delivery. The importance of these performance requirements leads lenders to insist on the use of proven technology. The project company may also wish to obtain further guarantees from suppliers and designers where relevant. These other entities may be best able to cure certain defects or to update technology as necessary.

7.5 Operation Risk

Clearly, the project must operate to given performance levels in order for the project company to earn the revenues needed to pay operating costs, repay debt, and achieve the levels of profit needed. The project company will be required to operate the project in a proper and careful manner, so as to comply with applicable law, permits, and consents and to avoid damage to the project, the site, local or related infrastructure facilities, and neighboring properties. Operation risk will include the following:

- The risk of defects in design equipment or materials beyond the construction contractor's defects liability period.
- The availability of labor and materials, the cost thereof, whether skilled labor can be procured locally, the extent to which both labor and materials will need to be imported, visas and licenses required for such importation, and restrictions imposed by local labor laws.
- Changes in operating requirements owing to changes in law, regulations, or other circumstances.
- Proper maintenance of the project and the cost of asset replacement and major maintenance.
- The availability of experienced management committed to the project for the duration of the concession period.
- The program for operation and maintenance and whether that program follows a logical regime, correlated with the offtake purchaser's needs, and a realistic approach given the nature of the site country, government regulations on labor, and operation and the technical requirements of the project.
- Where the project requires input for operation, and where the market for such inputs is not sufficiently flexible or there is some concern as to its future viability, the lenders may require that the project company enters separate input supply arrangements to ensure, for example, availability of fuel, electricity, chemicals, or other inputs or services, such as disposal of sludge or ash.

7.6 Financing Risk

Financing risk relates to the sources of financing to be accessed for the project, the nature of lenders and borrowers, and the constraints imposed by the financial markets at the time of financial close and during the life of the project. This risk can result in increases in the cost of financing and will have a fundamental influence on the financial viability of the project. For example, PPP projects are sensitive to the following:

- Sufficient tenor of debt (projects with large upfront investment in long lifecycle assets usually look for twelve-to-twenty-year debt) and the availability of takeover or refinancing for short tenor debt.

- The ability to roll up interest (i.e., pay it later) during a grace period sufficient to address any lack of revenue during the construction period.
- Interest rates: Project finance looks for fixed-rate debt given the fixed nature of the revenue stream. If fixed-rate debt is not available, increases in interest rates beyond debt manageable through the revenue stream will need to be hedged or otherwise managed.
- Foreign exchange rates (where the currency of revenues and debt are different – the risk of movements between their exchange rates).
- The cost of hedging (where interest rate, foreign exchange, or other risks are managed through hedging arrangements) and the cost and availability of such hedging instruments.
- The availability of working capital financing to cover short-term financing needs.
- The credit risk of key project participants, including any available third-party warranties, bonds, and guarantees.

Much of financing risk is managed by the project company with the lenders. The cost of financing is likely to be uncertain, to some extent, until financial close, since the project company is unlikely to implement any of these financing mechanisms before then. Therefore, the contracting authority will generally share the risk of changes in the cost of financing between bid date and financial close.[6]

To the extent that hedging is not a viable option to manage specific risks (in particular, interest rate and foreign exchange), the contracting authority may wish to provide protection against such financing risks. For example, contracting authorities or offtake purchasers often help manage foreign exchange risk to give the project company the flexibility to use foreign currency debt (which can reduce the cost of debt). They may provide takeout guarantees, promising to provide financing at a specific tenor and interest rate at a future date. This protects the project company from the risk that refinancing might not be available at a reasonable price in the future, where long tenor debt is not otherwise available on reasonable terms.

---

[6] During this period, there should be a degree of alignment between the interests of the contracting authority and the private partner to achieve financial close promptly. Any change in the base interest rate between bid date and financial close is generally borne by the contracting authority, though often limited by a cap or collar.

7.7 Currency Risk

Monetary regulation and market conditions can limit the extent to which local currency (capital, interest, principal, profits, royalties, or other monetary benefits) can be converted to foreign currency, how much foreign currency is available, and the extent to which local and foreign currency can be transferred out of the country. These restrictions cause significant problems for foreign investors and lenders, who will want to have access to distributions and debt service in foreign currencies and to service their debt abroad. As a principally regulatory risk, this risk is often managed by the contracting authority in developing countries, for example, by obtaining waivers or preapproval for the project company for transfer of foreign currency.

7.8 Offtake Risk

Offtake risk involves any reduction in or failure of the use of the services provided by the facility, for example, with respect to the levels forecast – fewer people using the toll road, less electricity taken from the generator, fewer passengers or aircraft using the airport, and so on. It can be caused by, for example, reduced demand for the offtake, inability of the offtaker to pay for the offtake, technical or practical difficulties with delivering the offtake, and public reaction resulting in a boycott against the offtake (affecting overall demand).

Future forecasts of demand, cost, and regulation of the sector in any site country will be important to private sector investors considering the revenue prospects of the project. For example, they may wish to do the following:

- Review the demand profile for project offtake in the context of the extent to which the project company will bear project risk and will be able to influence demand
- Examine demand projections and information on the historical willingness of consumers to pay tariffs and to pay such tariffs on time
- Analyze prospects for growth, demographic movements, current tariffs, and projections of consumer attitudes toward paying increased tariffs
- Where tariffs are based on indices, assess projections of the future movement of such indices and their relation to actual costs, including

operating costs, finance costs, capital expenditure requirements, and other such costs

- Review the extent to which consumer tariffs cover utility costs and depreciation

Where these assessments result in specific risk concerns, the project company may need to obtain third-party protection (for the lenders and possibly for equity), such as the following:

- Undertaking(s) to purchase offtake in a quantity and at a pricing structure designed to provide the revenue needed (see sections 5.2 and 7.8)
- Revenue guarantees to ensure a minimum level of revenue
- Demand guarantees to protect the project company from the impact of, for example, traffic lower than forecast/assumed at bid
- Partial risk guarantees to protect the project company from shortfalls in the revenue stream associated with specific project risks

The private sector is generally better at delivering retail infrastructure services to consumers, and therefore the contracting authority may want the project company to bear some portion of offtake risk to ensure the project company is incentivized to innovate and improve service delivery.[7]

7.9 Environmental and Social

Environmental and social laws and regulations will impose liabilities and constraints on a project. The cost of compliance can be significant, and will need to be allocated between the project company and the contracting authority. Equally, in order to attract international lenders, in particular IFIs, the project must meet minimum environmental and social requirements that may exceed those set out in applicable laws and regulations (see Box 7.1). This process is made easier where local law supports similar levels of compliance.

Infrastructure projects generally have a substantial impact on local communities and quality of life, particularly in the delivery of essential services such as water and electricity or land-intensive projects such as toll roads. Project impact on society, consumers, and civil society generally can result in resistance from local interest groups that can delay project implementation,

---

[7] For a discussion of private sector performance in water and electricity distribution projects, see Andres et al., *The Impact of Private Sector Participation in Infrastructure*; Gassner et al., *Empirical Assessment*.

increase the cost of implementation and undermine project viability.[8] This "social risk" should be high on a lender's due diligence agenda, though it often is not. The lenders and the project company often look to the contracting authority to manage this risk. The contracting authority in turn may underestimate its importance, since the social risk paradigm for public utilities is very different (it is usually easier for consumers to complain about, or sue, private companies than public utilities; therefore, public utilities may not be as sensitive to social risk). The contracting authority may not have experience of the implications of social risk for private investors, and all parties may be caught unprepared for its implications. Therefore, the parties need to pay particular attention to this risk, and access to expert advice is important.

Box 7.1. Equator Principles

The Equator Principles[9] constitute a voluntary code of conduct originally developed by the International Finance Corporation (IFC) and a core group of commercial banks, but now recognized by most of the international commercial banks active in project finance. These banks have agreed not to lend to projects that do not comply with the Equator Principles, which follow the IFC system of categorizing projects, identifying those that are more sensitive to environmental or social impact, and requiring specialist assessment where appropriate. During project implementation, the borrower must prepare and comply with an environmental management plan (EMP).

7.10 Risk Allocation and Mitigation

The management of risk in PPP is a complex and intensive task, but a number of mechanisms have been developed to address these risks to make a project bankable and to benefit the different project parties by managing risks more efficiently. Such mechanisms include the following in particular:

- The project company will enter into contracts with specialist counterparties or parties better placed to bear and manage certain risks. This is discussed in more detail in Chapter 8.

---

[8] Delmon, J., Implementing social policy into contracts for the provision of utility services, in Dani, A., T. Kessler, & E. Sclar, eds., *Making Connections: Putting Social Policy at the Heart of Infrastructure Development* (2007).

[9] www.equator-principles.com.

- Insurance will be obtained for key insurable risks, in particular in relation to construction, equipment, buildings, staff, and force majeure events (see section 8.9).
- The government may provide guarantees or subsidies for specific risks (see sections 3.4 and 5.3).
- MLAs, BLAs, and ECAs will provide debt, equity, insurance, and guarantees for specific risks (see Chapter 5).
- Other financial instruments may be used to manage risk, such as hedging, monoline insurance, catastrophe bonds, and so on (see sections 7.8 and 7.10).

Clearly, an important part of risk mitigation is organizing the project and its risk assessment efficiently. When performing due diligence on a project, the following actions may be taken:

- Risks can be plotted on a risk matrix to help identify the gravity of specific risks.
- Risk interfaces (e.g., where the whole of the risk profile is greater than the sum of its parts and where risks are intertwined such that when addressing a risk, one must address those related risks) can be identified and plotted to ensure each is addressed.
- Risk management priorities can be identified to help allocate funding and resources.
- The tasks to be performed to prepare and implement the project can be plotted on a critical path, showing dependencies between them (e.g., which tasks need to be completed before other tasks can commence).

The preceding will help to identify the order in which these tasks should be performed and resources should be allocated to maximize efficiency.

7.11 Risk, Efficient Risk Allocation, and Risk Noise

Risk is key to our perception of our world. The private sector is sensitive to risks in PPP projects, particularly those located in the developing world, and will increase the cost of a project where risk is allocated in a manner that the private sector perceives to be inappropriately burdensome. This increase in cost may relate to the price charged by the private sector to perform services or give specific undertakings, or it may relate to the cost of money, being a combination of the cost of debt and equity. Therefore, a number of different private sector entities (lenders, investors, and service providers) influence the cost implications of risk allocation, complicating the analysis. Despite its complexity, maximizing efficiency in risk allocation in infrastructure projects can reduce costs, reassure investors, and thereby release additional resources into the market to improve infrastructure services. To reduce poverty and increase quality of life across the globe, it is essential to increase risk allocation efficiency, releasing more funding for infrastructure.

The commonly accepted approach to efficient risk allocation is well established in risk literature and risk allocation practicum in the infrastructure sector; it argues that risk should be allocated to the party that is able to bear that risk at the lowest price and that has the most control, the necessary resources, and the necessary availability or opportunity to manage the risk. This literature argues that adoption of the commonly accepted approach would increase project efficiency and reduce project costs, which in turn should make financing more easily available at a lower cost and on better terms.[10]

But project-financed transactions fail to implement accepted approaches to efficient risk allocation due to inaccurate perceptions of risk driven by inadequacies in information management, subjective assessment of information and biased reaction to risk, that is, risk noise.[11]

"Risk noise" describes the various factors that impede an individual's ability to assess risk based purely on an objective interpretation of accurate and complete information. The word "noise" evokes the distraction and frustration involved in endeavoring to transmit a signal or information and having that signal altered or tainted by some internal or external influence. This imagery of "noise" provides a good metaphor for the influences that impact the ability of an individual to assess a risk accurately and therefore apply an efficient risk allocation methodology.

Risk noise can be divided into three categories: *lack of knowledge, anchoring,* and *familiarity.*

Lack of knowledge refers to any failure in information or its interpretation. The individual making the risk decision must apply her own assessment in order to fill the gaps in her knowledge and the information available.[12]

---

[10] Delmon, J., *Risk Noise: Increasing the Efficiency of Risk Allocation in Project Financed Public Private Partnership Transactions by Reducing the Impact of Risk Noise – Part I*, 135 ICLR (2015).

[11] Ibid.

[12] Starr, C., The precautionary principal versus risk analysis, *Risk Analysis* 23 (2003), at 1; Tversky, A. & D. Kahneman, Belief in the law of small numbers, *Psychological Bulletin* 76 (1971), at 105.

Familiarity causes us to grasp on to what is familiar, internally, even against information that may indicate that other risk decisions might be more efficient.[13] Risk assessment based on past experience with similar risks or similar issues results in extrapolated or "imagined" knowledge, which tends to be exaggerated, since the past is only a partial indication of the future.[14] Individuals seek certainty and to that end tend to ignore uncertainty or believe that chance events are influenced by skill and are somewhat within the individual's control.[15] Under ambiguity, individuals prefer probabilities about which they have an acceptable amount of information.[16] Risk perceived as more immediate is taken more seriously.[17] Similarly, the more recent the risk, the more recent the memory that the individual has of the occurrence of the risk and of its effect, and the more the individual can imagine its occurrence and appreciate the potential impact of its occurrence (leading to an overestimation of risk simply on the basis of temporal proximity of a similar risk).

Risk assessment is often based on the experiences of others or by association with some other experience;[18] this is known as *anchoring*.[19] Anchoring is similar to familiarity but created by external influences against which we measure risk. For example, where the immediacy of a risk, its external influence, is great, we have a tendency to *anchor* our risk assessment against that immediacy and assign to that risk a greater value. Anchoring may be an important part of the individual's sense of belonging (e.g., *anchoring* against *cultural, sociological, or political context*, or institutional rules/processes). It may be based on the sense of the power or powerlessness of the individual in his or her context.

Risk noise is one of the key drivers behind the failure to implement the commonly accepted approach of efficiently allocating risk; it influences the way individuals assess and allocate risk, making an objective analysis of

[13] Langer, E. J., The psychology of chance in Dowie, J. & P. Lefrere, eds., *Risk and Chance: Selected Readings* (1980).
[14] Fischoff, B., S. Lichtenstein, P. Slovic, S. L. Derby, & R. Keeney, *Acceptable Risk* (1981).
[15] Maslow, A., *Motivation and Personality* (1954).
[16] Kahneman, D. & A. Tversky, Prospect theory: an analysis of decision under risk, *Econometria* 47 (1979), 263–291; Slovic, P., M. L. Finucane, E. Peters & D. G. MacGregor, Risk as analysis and risk as feelings: some thoughts about affect, reason, risk and rationality, *Risk Analysis* 29 (2004), no. 2, at 311; Wildavsky, A. & K. Dake, Theories of risk perception: who fears what and why? in Lofstedt, R. & L. Frewer, eds., *The Earthscan Reader in Risk and Modern Society* (1998).
[17] Bjorkman, M., Time and risk in cognitive space, in Sjöberg, L., ed., *Risk and Society* (1987).
[18] Kahneman, D. & C. A. Varey, Propensities and counterfactuals: the loser that almost won, 59 *Journal of Personality & Social Psychology* 1101 (1990).
[19] Crouch, E. & R. Wilson, *Risk/Benefit Analysis* (1982).

efficient risk allocation more difficult. But risk noise can be reduced if it can be identified, isolated, and filtered. Once the cause of a component of risk noise is understood, a filter can be provided that improves the position of the project, thereby reducing the cost of capital and releasing additional capital, available to invest in more infrastructure. Since the commonly accepted approach represents a method for increasing efficiency and therefore reducing the cost of an infrastructure project, filtering risk noise can increase efficiency, reduce cost, increase profitability, increase availability of financing, and, most importantly, increase the amount of infrastructure that can be procured with currently available resources.[20]

Every project-financed transaction should – must – implement such a methodology and those involved in the task should be aware of their own risk biases, as a commercial and moral imperative, consistently and effectively, to increase investment opportunities and improve infrastructure, in the hopes of providing a better future for so many, to save the lives of the most vulnerable.

---

[20] Delmon, *Risk Noise.*

8

The Contractual Structure

As discussed in Chapter 1, PPP structures are ultimately flexible. Instead of endeavoring to dissect contractual structures and risk allocation for every possible PPP structure, this chapter will use the example of a project financed BOT project, as exemplified by a power generation PPP (also known as an independent power producer, or IPP) to show how risk can be managed in the context of PPP. Project-financed BOTs are highly structured, risk-sensitive projects and therefore a convenient opportunity for a discussion of the key issues that arise in any PPP project.

Key Messages for Policy Makers

- *Stability is the goal.* Prepare for every eventuality, but accept that it is impossible to anticipate every eventuality.
- *Ensure a practical fallback position that protects consumers.* Make sure that if all else fails, the public (or a third party) is in the position to take the infrastructure and services back quickly to ensure continuity.
- *Keep the revenue stream as certain, foreseeable, and ring-fenced as possible.* It is the lifeblood of the project.
- A failed project costs everyone time and money; *it is generally worth the extra money or effort to make the project a bit more robust*, obtaining information, improving planning, allocating and managing risk, and considering options.
- There will always be changes in circumstances and even full-blown crises, many of which will not be predictable, so *a proactive, collaborative framework must provide partners with the platform for resolution of conflict as and when it arises.*

The BOT project places the responsibility for financing, constructing, and operating the project on the private sector. The host country grants

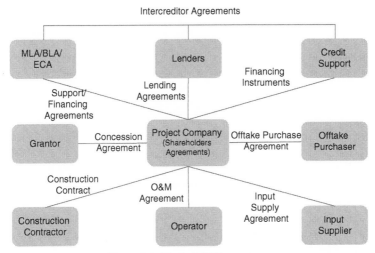

Figure 8.1. Typical BOT structure.

a concession to the private company to build and operate the facility over a period of time. The private company will then use the revenue from the operation of the facility to service debt and provide the investors with a return. Where the host country is also the offtake purchaser, the project is likely to be treated as payment for a service rather than financing of infrastructure. This can keep the project debt from being counted against the country's debt ratios or public sector borrowing requirements.

BOT projects are highly complex, commercially driven projects, requiring extensive documentation and negotiation. A BOT project represents a serious investment of money and time by everyone involved. The project company, and in turn the lenders, will undertake technical, financial, and legal due diligence exercises to analyze risk allocation for a project. A robust contractual structure with commercially appropriate risk allocation will be a deciding factor in the bankability of the project (see Figure 8.1) and whether the lenders will wish to go forward with the project financing.

8.1 Concession Agreement

Under the concession agreement (also known as the "implementation agreement"), the contracting authority grants a concession (a series of rights) to the project company to build and operate infrastructure (often what traditionally would otherwise be a public service) for a predetermined period, the concession period. The concession agreement may also set out the legal and tax regimes applicable to the project, including the environmental obligations of the project company. In practice, the concession agreement, the offtake purchase agreement, and/or the input supply agreement (to the extent each is needed) can be combined in one agreement.

The contracting authority needs to have the legal right to enter into the concession agreement, that is, the contracting authority's acts must be *intra vires*. Acts which are *ultra vires* (beyond the power of the party performing the act) may be unenforceable or subsequently rescinded or invalidated under applicable law; that is, if the contracting authority did not have the right to sign the contract, the project company may have trouble enforcing the contract. (It might even be deemed never to have existed.)

The primary issues addressed under the concession agreement will generally be as follows:

- *Completion date.* The contracting authority's need for the infrastructure in question is generally immediate/as soon as possible (often as much for political as practical reasons).
- *Condition of assets.* Where existing assets are transferred to the project company, the condition of those assets should be described, with a mechanism to address the possibility that the assets are not actually in the condition anticipated.
- *Performance of the project.* The contracting authority's requirements will cover issues such as input consumption, efficiency of operation, maintenance needs and costs, lifecycle, health, safety, environmental, quality/quantity of the output/service generated, and cost of operation.
- *Maintenance regime.* In order to mitigate the detrimental effect of operation on the project during the concession period, the contracting authority will want to ensure that the maintenance regime (including replacement of parts and materials) implemented is sufficient given the nature of the works involved. This is even more important late in the project; the incentive for the project company to invest funds in maintenance during the final phase of the concession period may be diminished, owing to the imminent transfer of the project to the contracting authority. The contract may offer a final bonus payment pending quality of the facility to incentivize appropriate maintenance for the entirety of the life of the contract.
- *Construction and operation.* The contracting authority will want to ensure that the project company's construction and operation activities meet certain minimum standards, both those imposed by law and those specified by the contracting authority to ensure the quality of the services provided and the protection of the public.

- *Government guarantees.* The government may provide guarantees for public sector bodies taking part in the project whose credit risk is otherwise insufficient, and these may be set separately or in the concession agreement where the government is a party.
- *Exclusivity.* The contracting authority may supply the project company with some form of exclusivity rights over the service to be provided to ensure a bankable revenue stream with careful consideration of future requirements, such as demographic changes and the needs of unserved communities.
- *Know-how transfer.* The contracting authority may want to maximize the interaction between the project company and local partners or the contracting authority's personnel in order to ensure the proper transfer of know-how.[1]
- *Government interference.* The contracting authority may undertake that the host government will not act against the interests of the lenders, the shareholders, the project company, the performance of the project company's obligations, or the project itself to protect the project company from a specific subset of political risk.
- *Concession fees.* The project company may be required to pay concession fees for the privilege of obtaining a concession and to offset contracting authority costs, payable before commencement and possibly periodically during the concession period, for example, as a share of revenues.
- *Restrictions on share transfers.* The contracting authority may want to place restrictions on the transfer or change of shareholding in the project company. The contracting authority may want to disallow any transfer (direct or indirect) until a certain point in time after completion of construction (a lockup period) or a right of approval over the identity of any transferee. The authority may also seek to maintain some guarantee from the original shareholders.
- *Contracting authority step-in/continuous operation.* The contracting authority may want the right to continue operation of the project where it terminates the concession agreement, sometimes referred to as the "right to continuous operation," to ensure continuous delivery of services.
- *Hand-back.* At the end of the concession period, the contracting authority will either put the project out for retender or it will require the project company to transfer the project assets to the contracting authority or to a replacement project company.

---

[1] For further discussion of the transfer of technology and know-how, see United Nations, *UNIDO Guidelines for Infrastructure Development through Build-Operate-Transfer* (1996), at 75–90.

8.2 Offtake Purchase Agreement

The offtake purchase agreement allocates the market risk of demand and the price for project output to an offtake purchaser. The offtake purchaser, although there may be more than one, is generally a local utility, public service provider, or operator that will purchase the output from the project company and then sell the output on the market, either directly to end-users or to other offtake purchasers. The terms "offtake" and "output" may be misnomers, as the project may provide access to facilities (e.g., a hospital or school), treatment of waste (e.g., waste water treatment or solid waste management), or access to networks (e.g., electricity transmission, gas pipelines, or telecommunications backbone). No matter the terminology, these project generally require similar offtake purchase arrangements.

The offtake purchase agreement defines and delimits the revenue stream to be received by the project company, and therefore the lenders and shareholders, over the life of the project (usually fifteen to thirty years). It will define not only the amount of the revenue stream but also when it can be interrupted, modified, or terminated. It is often the offtake purchaser itself that has identified the need for the output and initiated or influenced the putting of the project out to tender; the offtake purchaser may also be the contracting authority.

The provisions of the offtake purchase agreement must reflect the nature of the output and the specific market of the project. They are common to power projects (the "power purchase agreement"), water treatment projects (often called "water purchase agreements"), and other production projects, such as industrial plants (for example, aluminum smelters and oil refineries). This section assumes the output is an asset produced by the project and sold on to the offtake purchaser. Where the project involves an output that is a facility or service, such as a road or bridge, or possibly a hospital or prison whose facilities will be made available to the offtake purchaser, the provisions of the offtake purchase agreement described in this section will need to be modified accordingly.

Where the contracting authority benefits from the offtake of the project, a more common approach is to include the elements of the offtake purchase agreement (set out later in this section) in the concession agreement. In such cases, this section should be read together with section 8.1.

PPP projects can also be structured without an offtake purchase agreement, such as tunnels, roadways, and bridges, where no physical offtake is produced and the project company collects tariffs directly from consumers, for example, where the contracting authority needs more assistance improving retail service delivery (such as water or electricity concessions, where output is delivered directly to consumers) and therefore looks to the project company to provide better services to consumers and bear more demand risk. Such projects often require the support of a sector regulator. However, no matter the approach taken, demand risk will still need to be managed as between the contracting authority and the project company, particularly regarding the issues discussed later in this section.

The key terms addressed in an offtake purchase agreement will include the following:

- *Performance standards.* The offtake purchaser will want to define closely the technical parameters of operation in order to satisfy performance and other technical requirements, for example, levels of secure, clean, and safe operation within certain ranges of technical, climatic, and other operating parameters. The project company will then be penalized where the project does not satisfy these basic requirements.
- *Completion standards.* The transition from the construction period to the operation period, completion, and commencement of output production should be identified by the passing of defined tests or the issue of a certificate. Completion under the offtake purchase agreement should correspond to completion under the construction contract.
- *Offtake price.* The offtake purchase agreement obliges the offtake purchaser to procure a certain amount of project output or pay for an amount of project service (under certain formulations such as "take-or-pay," whether or not it is used) over a given time. A dual payment system is often used, including a capacity (or availability) charge and a usage (or offtake) charge. The capacity charge is that amount paid for making the project available and will compensate the project company for its fixed costs. The usage charge is paid for the amount of project output actually taken, or used, and compensates the project company for the variable costs of operation, such as the cost of input (see section 8.3), some or all of the equity return, and variable maintenance costs.
- *Payment risk.* The credit risk associated with the offtake purchaser will be of particular concern to the project company and the lenders. Where the offtake purchaser is not a good credit risk, it may be required to provide credit enhancement such as escrow accounts, revolving bank guarantees, or state/federal/MLA guarantees for its payment obligations (see section 8.10).
- *Foreign exchange.* Some or all of the foreign exchange or other financial risk (see sections 7.6 and 7.7) may be allocated to the offtake purchaser,

for example, where part of the payment obligation is indexed to foreign exchange rates.

- *Offtake infrastructure.* The offtake purchaser may be required to provide certain infrastructure and continual access, for example, to connect the project to its facilities (e.g., to the power grid or the water system). The offtake purchaser may bear any risk in connection with the operation of the project that is related to the transportation/transmission system or the offtake purchaser's acts or omissions.

- *Regulation.* PPP projects tend to involve heavily regulated sectors. In many cases, the sector regulator may be a new creation or otherwise unaccustomed to interfacing with the private sector. Project arrangements will need to be coordinated with the relevant regulation and regulator, realizing that generally regulators cannot be bound by contract to perform their mandate in a specific manner, and therefore the project company may look to the contracting authority or the offtake purchaser to protect it if a regulator imposes requirements (e.g., performance criteria or tariff levels) different from those originally envisaged in the project contracts.

8.3 Input Supply Agreement

The PPP project may need some form of input in order for it to operate, such as fuel for thermal power generation or electricity for water treatment. The project company may not want to bear the risk that required input will not be available when it is needed and at an appropriate price in view of the project's revenues. Therefore, the project company will often enter into a contract with an input supplier to provide the necessary input to the extent of the project's needs or to the minimum level necessary for the project's operation.

The input supply agreement involves an input supplier contracting to provide a certain amount of input of a given quality at a given price.[2] For example, coal suppliers for a coal-fired power plant will have long-term capacity, using the promised income from an input supply agreement to finance the development of new coal fields. Input may be a misnomer for certain projects where the required service is effectively an offtake arrangement. For example, in waste water treatment, the project company will need to subcontract for the removal and disposal of sludge, or in hospital projects

---

[2] The necessary input may be provided by the contracting authority and/or the offtake purchaser. In such cases, the input supply provisions discussed in this section may be incorporated in the concession agreement or the offtake purchase agreement. This section may therefore need to be read in conjunction with sections 8.1 and 8.2.

the removal of medical waste may need to be subcontracted. This type of agreement will require many of the same conditions and raise similar issues to other input supply agreements.

The key terms addressed in an input supply agreement will include the following:

- *Price.* The cost of input will include the cost of export from the source country, import into the host country, and transport to the site. The input supplier will generally be responsible for obtaining the proper permits and licences for importing the input into the host country. Any failure on the part of the input supplier to provide the amount required will result in liquidated damages[3] or a decrease in the price paid for the input delivered.
- *Quality, quantity, and timing.* The input supplier will also be allocated some of the performance risk for the project, in as much as it is required to provide a given quantity of input at a given quality and at a given time. The input supplier will be responsible where the input is provided late or is insufficient.
- *Duration.* The length of the input supply agreement will depend on the risks associated with the specific input and the ability to use other sources of input. There may be resetting or renegotiation of the agreement scheduled to adjust with the market over time.
- *Transport.* The project company may need to enter into a long-term contract for transportation of the input, even where the project company and the lenders are willing to take market risk on procurement of the input itself.
- *Testing and inspection.* To ensure proper operation and requisite performance levels, the input must be inspected and tested accordingly.

8.4 Construction Contract

The project company will allocate the task of designing and building the project to a construction contractor. The construction contract will define the responsibilities of the construction contractor and the project company and their relationship during the period of construction.[4]

The construction phase of the BOT project is generally governed by a turnkey construction contract, sometimes also known as a "design and

---

[3] A fixed monetary penalty, defined in the contract.
[4] For further discussion of construction contracts, see generally Scriven et al., eds., *A Contractual Guide to Major Construction Projects.*

build" or an EPC (engineering, procurement, and construction) contract. The term "turnkey" suggests that after completion one need only "turn the key" to commence operation of the constructed facility. Where a single turnkey construction contract is not available, the lenders will want the several contracts to work together as a turnkey contract or will want a completion guarantee from the sponsors to cover any gaps in risk allocation.

The turnkey construction contract places single-point responsibility for the design and the construction of the works on one party, the construction contractor. Single-point responsibility simply means that the construction contractor is bound to provide to the project company a completed project in accordance with the contract specifications and will be held accountable to ensure that the performance and the quality of the works comply with all of the contractual requirements, so that where there is a problem, the project company has a single point of reference. Where tax liabilities or other considerations necessitate construction under several different contracts (e.g., where combining tasks in one contract will attract a higher rate of taxation for the whole of the contract), single-point responsibility can be achieved, but with some additional challenges (see Box 8.1).

Single-point responsibility will require several important obligations to be placed on the construction contractor. The construction contractor will be required to design the whole of the works, coordinate design and construction interfaces, and complete the works to satisfy the completion and performance targets, all in accordance with a specified contractual standard of care. Thus, where the project company wishes to make a claim concerning a defect in the works, it need not specify whether the defect was caused by inadequate design or faulty workmanship since responsibility for both of these elements of the work falls on the construction contractor.

Other key terms addressed in a construction contract will include the following:

- *Time for completion.* In PPP projects, timely completion is essential, as penalties may apply under the input supply, offtake purchase, and concession agreements for late completion. Revenues will generally not be sufficient to meet debt servicing obligations until construction is complete, and the lenders will defer payment of debt service for only a specified grace period. Turnkey construction contracts are conducive to a fixed time for completion since they combine all design and

---

Box 8.1. Splitting Contracts

In some jurisdictions, turnkey contracts performed in that country have the unfortunate habit of increasing the tax liabilities and consequently increasing the overall cost of construction.[5] In such circumstances, the parties may wish to consider splitting the single turnkey construction contract into a number of separate construction contracts, with work performed by separate companies in the various jurisdictions.[6] This split would be implemented so as to manage the risks related to tax exposure and other costs while maintaining the "turnkey" nature of the construction arrangements.

---

construction tasks under the single-point responsibility of one construction contractor.

- *Construction price.* Turnkey construction contracts generally use a fixed-price, lump-sum structure, wherein the contractor is paid one lump sum for the design and construction of the works, with limited opportunity for price increases, thus providing greater price certainty for the project company and the lenders. The use of a lump-sum price combined with payments on the completion of stages of construction (for example, milestone payments) can result in an increased rate of progress, since the faster the contractor finishes the construction, the faster it gets paid.[7]
- *Performance risk.* The completed facility must perform to a certain standard to achieve the revenue stream required to satisfy the debt servicing, provide a return on investment, and cover any other costs. The construction contractor will be responsible for constructing works capable of attaining the performance levels required under standard operating conditions, taking into consideration the site conditions

---

[5] For more detailed discussion of splitting turnkey contracts, see Delmon, J., Splitting up is hard to do: how to manage fiscally challenged turnkey contracts, *International Construction Law Review* 30 (2003).

[6] The performance of works by branches located in different jurisdictions or subcontracted to companies in those jurisdictions will not achieve the desired effect. It is the use of a single contract for these different works that tends to attract the adverse tax treatment. See also Scriven et al., eds., *A Contractual Guide to Major Construction Projects* (1999), chapter 9.

[7] Wallace, N. D., *Construction Contracts: Principles and Policies in Tort and Contract* (1986), at 331.

and any other projects-pecific limitations. Performance tests will verify, for example, input requirements, heat rate, waste output, climate variations, lighting, accessibility, ventilation, consumption of input, temperature, and environmental impact

- *Site conditions.* The allocation of site risk will depend on the nature of the parties and their expertise. Site conditions, such as geographical, geological, and hydrological conditions, are difficult to define with great accuracy, even after extensive site investigations. Non-natural or manufactured obstructions or conditions may be dealt with separately when allocating this risk, because they are even more difficult to assess accurately by site investigations.

- *Defects liability.* For a period after completion, the construction contractor will remain responsible for the remedy of defects in the works. The period during which the construction contractor is liable for defects is generally called the "defects liability period," although it may also go under the name of "maintenance period" or "warranty period." Certain jurisdictions establish minimum defects liability periods at law.[8]

8.5 Operation and Maintenance (O&M) Agreement

After completion of construction of the works, the project company will need to operate and maintain the project during the concession period. This function is essential to protect the revenue stream of the project (see Figure 8.2). The O&M function will involve managing the operation of the project, providing maintenance for and replacing materials and equipment, receiving and managing inputs, and developing the relationship with the offtake purchaser. In order to allocate the risks involved in O&M, the project company may contract with an O&M contractor, also known as the operator. The operation of the project will require an understanding of the local market; the demands on operation in developing countries, such as availability of materials and labor for maintenance and repairs; as well as the importance of relationships with local authorities.

Risk allocation under an O&M agreement is generally not as clear-cut as under the construction contract or the input supply agreement, where a more substantial transfer of project company risk may be possible.

---

[8] For example, decennial liability under French law, Civil Code Article 1792, which makes contractors strictly liable for ten years for all damage, including that resulting from soil conditions, which renders them improper for their intended use.

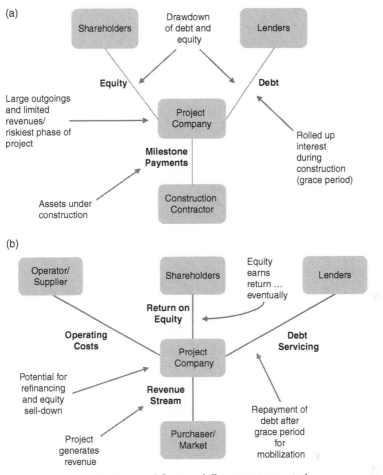

Figure 8.2. Financial flows in different project periods.

This is often explained by the fact that the construction contractor and the input supplier provide products, while the operator provides a service. Equally, the O&M agreement may not provide a pricing structure as fixed or certain as the construction contract, or the operator may not bear levels of liability (e.g., liquidated damages) sufficient to indemnify the project company completely. This is partly due to the long-term nature of the operator's obligations, but also the lower amounts of profit earned by the operator.

The operator's obligations should mirror those set out in the concession agreement, the offtake purchase agreement, and those required to ensure continued and efficient operation of the project. The key terms addressed in an O&M agreement will include the following:

- *Performance risk.* The operator will be required to work to a standard of performance generally based on the performance standard or operating requirements set out in the concession agreement, the offtake purchase agreement, the construction contractor's operation and maintenance manuals, and any other supplier instruction in order to maintain relevant warranties. The operator will deliver the proper operation and maintenance of the works to achieve the required levels of output or availability. Ideally, the level of penalties applied to the operator will match the liability of the project company for such performance failure; however, those levels of penalties are often too high relative to the fee paid to the operator.
- *Operating cost.* The agreement may use any of the following approaches:
    - (i)   Provide a fixed price for operation
    - (ii) Provide variable costs but be subject to controls to ensure mitigation of cost
    - (iii) Provide short periods (possibly three to seven years) during which the operator's fee is fixed, at which point market testing is carried out and the operator's fee is modified accordingly or a new operator is selected.
- *Public face of services.* The operator is in a very sensitive position as the operator of a public service in the host country. Therefore, the operator's methods of operation and his or her relationship with the employees and local communities will be critical to the project.

8.6 Lending Agreements

Financing arrangements for PPP projects follow a rough two-step progression. First, funding is provided by the lenders and the shareholders during the construction phase, which is generally considered the riskiest phase of the financing arrangements, since money is being utilized but no significant assets can be seized in the event of default. Funding during this first phase will include upfront fees, development costs, design, and construction. The lenders will advance funding progressively during the construction phase; payments are usually linked to milestones and verified by an independent expert acting for the lenders and possibly the contracting authority. During this first phase, the lenders will insist on a careful balance of equity and debt funding and may require recourse beyond project assets, to the shareholders or some other guarantor, to cover the risk of any delays or cost overruns that have not otherwise been transferred to the construction contractor.

The second step is final completion of construction followed by operation. Completion of construction includes performance tests to ensure that the project is capable of earning the necessary revenue stream. Approval of final completion will release the construction contractor from certain liabilities and will therefore be carefully controlled by the lenders. During operation, once the project has begun to produce output, the debt is serviced solely by the project revenue stream (see Figure 8.2).

The lending agreements will therefore set out protections for the lenders, such as the following:

- Drawdown schedule and the conditions precedent that must be satisfied before each drawdown, in particular those related to completion of construction milestones and aggregate paid-up equity
- Lender rights over warranties from contractors, delay liquidated damages, performance liquidated damages, contractor-supplied performance bonds, standby equity and debt undertakings, and other mechanisms to mitigate construction risk
- Funding and control of reserve accounts where the project company must set aside money for contingencies, in particular to cover a number of months of debt service in the event of revenue shortfall, periodic major maintenance expenses, and annual costs such as insurance and taxes
- Events of default, such as failure to satisfy ratios (debt service cover ratio, loan life cover ratio, debt:equity, etc.), late payment, defaults under project contracts, changes in management, or project contracts without consent
- The right of lenders to stop disbursements to the shareholders, control voting rights and other project company discretions ("reserved discretions"), and seize funds in the event that things are not going as well as the lenders would like (e.g., where events of default arise or might arise)

Security rights (over different project assets and in favor of creditors) are both "offensive" and "defensive": they are offensive to the extent the lenders can enforce the security to dispose of assets and repay debt where the project fails; and they are defensive to the extent that security can protect the lenders from actions of unsecured or junior creditors. If comprehensive security rights are not available, the lenders may seek to use ring-fencing covenants in an effort to restrict other liabilities, security over project company shares to allow the lenders to take over control of the company, or the creation of a special "golden share" that provides the lenders with control in the event of default. Security rights may also allow the lenders to take over the project rather than just sell the project assets, since the value of the project lies in its operation and not in the resale value of the assets.[9]

The lenders and the contracting authority may enter into direct agreements with the project participants setting out step-in rights,[10] notice requirements, cure periods,[11] and other issues intended to maintain the continuity of the project where the project company defaults and/or falls away. A project may not require direct agreements where appropriate provisions can be included in the relevant project document or where some other solution is available.

8.7 Hedging Arrangements

Some financial risks can be shared through financial instruments known as derivatives, swaps, futures contracts, or hedging. These complex arrangements, in effect, require one party to compensate the other party in the event of a specified risk, in exchange for a fee. In some cases, the parties may swap risks, each compensating the other in the event of specified risks. For example, exposure to foreign exchange risk can be mitigated by swapping currency requirements with another market participant or by agreeing to buy one currency at a fixed price in another currency at a future date. Other risks such as interest rate and commodity risk can be managed through the use of derivatives. These arrangements are usually managed under the common terms set out in the International Swaps and Derivatives Association (ISDA) master agreement.[12]

Hedging arrangements can have significant impacts on the project, including the following:

---

[9] Lender rights to run the project rather than just sell off the assets will require consideration of the applicable legal system and its treatment of security and insolvency. Rights over project company shares may achieve the desired security, but may also involve the lenders taking on project risk.

[10] Where one party to a contract is in default, the right (usually of the lenders or the government) to take over that party's position in the contract, in an effort to keep the contract from termination.

[11] Where one party to a contract is in default, the right (usually of the lenders or the government) to be notified of the default and to be given the opportunity to cure that default.

[12] See www.isda.org.

- Hedging arrangements will influence the cost of debt and the breakage costs to be included in termination compensation. Therefore, hedging counterparties (and the hedging bank) should be selected competitively to keep these costs down.
- Hedging arrangements may have significant breakage penalties, which may make prepayment of or modifying financing arrangements more expensive.
- Hedge counterparties, or possibly a hedging bank, will be a party to the intercreditor agreement to formalize the sharing of security and arrangements on default (see section 8.8).

To the extent hedge counterparties benefit from project security, in theory their hedges should also be limited recourse.

If hedge counterparties get paid out when they suffer a loss when they close out their hedge, then lenders will argue that they should share any windfall profits.

8.8 Intercreditor Arrangements

Financing for the project is likely to come from several sources, such as commercial banks, multilateral organizations, international financial organizations, and possibly the capital markets, including different levels and classes of debt and equity. An intercreditor agreement will often be entered into by the lenders in order to address key issues,[13] such as the following:

- Choosing the order of drawdown of funds
- Coordinating maturity of loans
- Selecting the order of allocation of debt service payments
- Subordination amongst the different lenders
- Holding and acting on security rights and exercise of discretions
- Voting on decisions, for example, variations of lending agreements, waiver of requirements, acceleration, enforcement of security, and termination of hedging arrangements

Security and other rights tend to be managed through trustee arrangements, with one of the lenders or a third party acting as agent for the lender group, holding and acting on security rights.

---

[13] For more detailed discussion of intercreditor agreements, see Wood, P. R., *Project Finance, Securitisations and Subordinated Debt*, 2nd ed. (2007).

8.9 Insurance Arrangements

Although the project participants may each provide insurance for the project, it is generally more efficient for the project company to provide or ensure provision of comprehensive insurance coverage for the entire project. In this way, the interfaces between different insurance packages, the coverage provided by different insurance providers, and the overlapping of the tasks performed by the various project participants will not result in overlapping insurance or gaps in insurance coverage.

Generally, the following insurances will be required:[14]

- Materials and equipment during transportation to the site, including equipment to be integrated into the works, temporary plant, and the construction contractor's equipment, from the location of manufacture or assembly (ex works) to delivery at the site.
- Construction all risk (CAR) or construction and erection all risk (CEAR) insurance will cover all operations and assets on the site during construction.
- Professional indemnity (PI) insurance for design faults or other such professional services provided by the construction contractor or its designers.
- All risk operational damage insurance, including, in particular, insurance of property damage during operations.
- Third-party liability insurance for any claim by third parties for the acts or omissions of the project company and any of the contractors, subcontractors, or other persons for whom it may be responsible.
- Consequential loss insurance, including delayed startup, advance loss of profit, and business interruption insurance.
- Mechanical or electrical failure not otherwise covered under the operational policy.
- Automobile liability insurance for all vehicles to be used on site, which will often be mandatory under local law.
- Workers' compensation/employer's liability insurance.
- Directors' and officers' liability insurance.

The contracting authority will indicate in the concession and/or offtake purchase agreement the insurances it expects the project company to maintain, and to ensure the following:

---

[14] Delmon, *Private Sector Investment in Infrastructure*, 2nd ed., section 15.5.

- That sufficient coverage is obtained and maintained.
- The contracting authority is co-insured (not joint insured) and that there is no risk of vitiation.[15]
- The insurer waives its subrogation rights.[16]
- Where insurance payments relate to damage to assets that are part of the project, those monies are used to fix the damage or replace the assets and are not otherwise captured by the lenders or other creditors.

Required insurance may become too costly or unavailable. The parties will need to agree how to manage risks that become "uninsurable" and how to define this term. For certain risks, and in certain markets, the contracting authority may agree to be the insurer of last resort, effectively stepping in to insure risk in exchange for the payment of the premium last paid when the insurance became "uninsurable" or some other agreed rate. However, the contracting authority will want to be sure that the increased costs are not due to project company failure or actions.

Applicable law may require insurance to be obtained locally, in which case the project company may seek to reinsure those risks internationally in order to obtain additional insurance protection. Local law may limit the extent to which reinsurance can be used. Lenders will likely seek cut-through arrangements with reinsurers, to allow direct payment from reinsurers to the project company and/or to the lenders to avoid the risk of insurers not paying or going insolvent after they received payment from the reinsurers.

8.10 Guarantees and Credit Enhancement

A third party (e.g., the government, a BLA, or an MLA) may provide some form of credit enhancement to reduce the cost of debt or make investments available. This enhancement may be provided to lenders and/or equity investors, compensating them in certain circumstances, or ensuring that a certain portion of their debt service or equity return will be protected. Rating agencies may be consulted when structuring the project to maximize the credit rating for the project (in particular, when bond financing is

---

[15] Where the project insurance involves several insured parties (with varying interests in the insured risk) under the same insurance policy, and the insurance policy becomes unenforceable (with all of the insured parties losing their coverage) due to a breach by one of the insureds of its obligations under the policy (in particular, the obligation to disclose relevant information to the insurer).

[16] The right of an insurer to take over the rights in action (i.e., right to sue) of its insured to recover the amount it paid out to the insured.

involved), and credit enhancement can result in much higher credit ratings and therefore lower cost of debt (in particular, where the credit enhancement brings debt above investment grade – i.e., Standard & Poor's BBB). Credit enhancement can include the following:

- Funding/supporting direct payments or grants
- Providing financing for the project in the form of loans or equity investment
- Providing guarantees, including guarantees of debt, exchange rates, convertibility of the local currency, offtake purchaser obligations, other supplier obligations, tariff collection, the level of tariffs permitted, the level of demand for services and/or termination compensation, and so on.
- Providing an indemnity, for example, against failure to pay by state entities
- Providing tariff subsidies for consumers from whom the project company would have difficulty in collecting debts due
- Waiving fees, costs, and other payments that would otherwise have to be paid by the project company to a public sector entity (e.g., authorizing tax holidays or a waiver of tax liability)
- Funding shadow tariffs and topping up tariffs to be paid by some or all consumers
- Providing capital assets or other direct, in-kind investment

Credit enhancement providers will usually perform their own due diligence on the project, with associated time and cost implications. Providers of credit enhancement may also look for government or other counterguarantees or security rights, in particular to mitigate the moral hazard of credit enhancement protecting a defaulting party with the perverse incentive for that party to default. Credit enhancement may therefore involve a counterguarantee from the party whose obligation is being supported.

8.11 Sponsor Support

The lenders may want access to nonproject assets to protect their interests, where the project does not provide sufficient protection to the lenders. So-called sponsor or shareholder support provides the lenders with a guarantee or undertaking from the shareholders (which may need to be supported by bank guarantee, parent company guarantee, or otherwise) giving the lenders further security or comfort that the shareholders are committed to the project. Sponsor support may include standby subordinated financing for construction cost overruns, guarantees of borrower warranties (in particular, those within the control of shareholders), indemnities against environmental hazards, guarantees of cost of materials, or demand for project offtake. The shareholders, however, have entered into project financing in order to benefit from limited liability and limited recourse. They will not want to provide further support or increase their liability for the project.

8.12 Shareholding Arrangements

The shareholders' agreement governs the relationship between the shareholders within the project company. The shareholders' agreement may involve several documents, for example, a development agreement for the prefinancial close phase, and for postfinancial close a joint venture agreement. It may include articles of association or incorporation or whatever constitutional documents exist for the project company, as well as shareholder loans, standby credit, standby equity, and other similar documentation. The shareholders' agreement will cover topics such as the allocation of development costs, the scope of business of the project company, conditions precedent to its creation, the issue of new shares, the transfer of shares, the allocation of project costs, and the management of the project company, including decision making and voting. Such an agreement will often also include a noncompetition clause, providing that the shareholders may not enter into activities directly or indirectly in competition with the project company.

8.13 Other Key Contractual Issues

8.13.1 Dispute Resolution and Renegotiation

PPP projects have characteristics propitious to recurrent and often debilitating disputes involving parties from a variety of legal, social, and cultural backgrounds;[17] they represent long-term, complex commercial and financial arrangements that may require renegotiation to resolve. Failure to address such disputes early can have devastating impact on a PPP project. Conflict management, dispute resolution, and renegotiation are discussed further in sections 9.9 and 9.11.

---

[17] Straub, J. L., J-J. Laffont, & S. Guasch, *Infrastructure Concessions in Latin America: Government-Led Renegotiations* (2005). PPP database (preliminary figures): for 2003, 34 percent of contracts (by investment amounts) in the water sector were classified as distressed and 12 percent were canceled, in transport 15 percent were distressed and 9 percent canceled, while in energy 12 percent were distressed and 3 percent canceled. See PPP. worldbank.org.

8.13.2 Force Majeure

Certain events, beyond the control of the parties, may inhibit the parties from fulfilling their duties and obligations under the project agreements, for example, extremely bad weather, earthquakes, or acts of war. Given the extreme and unforeseeable nature of these events, the parties will prefer to avoid immediate termination of the contract and instead provide some excuse of contractual obligations that have been so inhibited. Each legal system will define force majeure events in a different fashion. In order to avoid the potential vagaries and uncertainties as well as the delays involved under applicable law, contracts often provide for a specific regime for force majeure, along with a definition of which events shall qualify for special treatment. The parties will generally provide in the force majeure provision a list, which may or may not be exhaustive, of examples of force majeure events. Force majeure events generally can be divided into two basic groups, natural events and political events. The party prevented from performing by a force majeure event is generally excused from the resultant breach, for example, for a maximum of six months, but is not compensated (insurance may be available for these costs), and after those six months one or both parties may decide the contract needs to be terminated.

8.13.3 Choice of Law

The governing law of a contract will to some extent define the obligations of the parties and provide the basis for interpretation of the intent of the parties as expressed in the contract. The project documents may be subject to the influence of different legal systems. Each contract will normally include a choice of law clause, and parties will want to apply a legal system with which they are comfortable and whose laws and contractually implied terms support that party's intentions. Having the project documents subject to more than one legal system increases the likelihood that gaps will appear in back-to-back risk allocation. However, the commercial reality is that mismatches in choice of law will often occur and need to be managed accordingly.

Project Implementation

Managing the PPP agreement starts at the inception phase of the PPP project cycle, designing appropriate solutions and managing input from different advisers. It continues through the selection of the investors and then during implementation of the project. Despite common conceptions, after the exuberance of financial close, the real work begins. This is a critical point, and one often ignored by policy makers, to their detriment.

Key Messages for Policy Makers

- *Put in place the right contracting authority team.* The project will not manage itself; failure to assign a sufficiently expert team to manage project implementation (i.e., after financial close), with necessary funding, can turn the best project into a failure.
- *Prepare for the future.* Decide up front what happens later in the project; deferred decisions only become more expensive and contentious. Decisions to make changes need to be made in advance; such decisions later in the process, during implementation, can be expensive and time consuming.
- *Be flexible and prepare for conflict resolution.* No contract can contemplate every eventuality, so plan to resolve challenges collaboratively; that is, a PPP should be managed like a partnership.

After procurement, the government must manage the development phase, transitioning the project toward delivery of services. This involves the following:

- Establishing the government management team
- Approving construction arrangements, design, and detailed design

- Establishing performance monitoring systems
- Arranging asset, property, and staff transfers
- Monitoring and assisting with applications by the project company for approvals and permissions
- Monitoring and managing subsidy payments (including triggers for payments) and government liabilities
- Approving construction completion and commencement of operations
- Establishing the mechanism for periodic review of performance and end-user requirements

The development phase ends once key capital expenditure has been completed and approved. It is followed by the delivery phase (construction and operation), during which the government does the following:

- Establishes its internal protocols to manage the project, monitor project company compliance with its obligations, and ensure contracting authority compliance with its obligations
- Conducts regular project review meetings
- Audits and reports to relevant bodies on payments, performance, and achievements
- Monitors the financial viability of the project, including the financial management of payments made and to be made, liabilities incurred, potential future liabilities. and sufficiency of project funding
- Encourages early anticipation, identification, and resolution of conflict.

Figure 9.1 sets out a number of the key contract management functions.

Each of the issues discussed in this chapter needs to be considered by the government before starting procurement, to ensure solutions are in place, established by contract and/or by law, and properly resourced from the very beginning of project implementation.

9.1 Operation Manual

PPP implementation is a complex process and obviously essential for project success. An operation manual maps out the implementation and is invaluable for the public and private parties. The operation manual will provide guidance on every aspect of this process, including the following:

- A list of required licenses and permits and key steps in processes to obtain them.
- All required testing and commissioning regimes indicating which party is responsible and framework for supervision and approval.

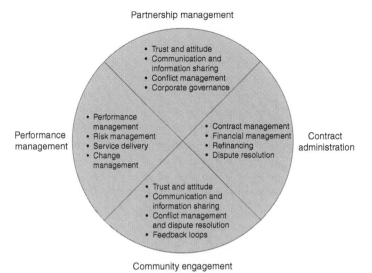

Figure 9.1. Management functions.
Source: www.ppp01.20.rsa.gov.

- Sample approval letters, change orders, and other key communications needed for smooth project implementation.
- Model process schedules and action plans for such items as performance assessment.
- A summary of rights and obligations under the project agreements, with time frame for when things must be done, and so on.
- A risk matrix and management plan, addressing each risk and how it is to be allocated, monitored, mitigated, and managed. Ownership of each risk should be clearly identified on a risk matrix, setting out a clear mitigation strategy.
- Other practical assistance for project implementation and contract administration.

The manual will help ensure that the rights and obligations under the contract are implemented in accordance with the terms of the contract, keeping track of risks and issues that arise related to the contract.

The operation manual should also include a communications strategy (see section 2.6) to ensure regular and ongoing communications on projects and the program and proactively identify and resolve issues as they arise. Good communication builds trust and enhances the partnership and success of the project and the program.

The government can use the transaction advisers to help it prepare for the role of managing the project, in particular the drafting of the operations manual.

Box 9.1. Squeezing the Stone

As part of its 2012 PF2 reform process, the United Kingdom identified and implemented potential savings during implementation, including the following:

- Renegotiating the scope of contracts, removing services no longer required
- Improving risk allocation by taking back energy consumption risk and improving energy efficiency through improved technology and using government purchasing power to lower utility and consumables costs
- Cutting waste by finding alternative uses for underutilized assets
- Avoiding additional costs through better contract management

Source: Infrastructure UK, *A New Approach to Public Private Partnerships*

9.2 Management Team

The government will need to form a project team, with appropriate skills, focused on the transaction (the key management tasks are unlikely to be part time jobs), and familiar with the project contracts. The team will need to include financial, legal, and technical specialists with access to external advisers. Most importantly, the team leader must inspire confidence in relevant government officials and the private markets, in particular potential investors. The government needs to allocate sufficient budgeting and funding for the team and its functions. The pursuit of funding should not be permitted to distract the team from its key functions or from its access to key resources, including expert advisers.

Management of a PPP project is not a classic public sector management function, and therefore those establishing the project team and managing relevant budgets and staffing functions need to appreciate the nature of a PPP project and the demands to be placed on the project team. To this extent, the team leader should be sufficiently senior to enable the team to implement its role and to access support and information from other government departments/agencies, with clear lines for decision making.

9.3 Financial Close

The signing of a PPP contract does not necessarily lead immediately to the beginning of construction. The project company will likely receive some (20–50 percent) of its total investment needs from its private owners as equity, and it will want to raise the majority of its finance (50–80 percent) as debt from lenders. However, the lenders will insist on performing their own detailed due diligence on the project before providing this level of debt. This process can take three to six months to complete (and up to one year for larger, complex projects). The financiers may start due diligence before project award. If they complete due diligence before bidding and the offer of finance is firm, then the bid is "underwritten." Further assessment by the lenders may be required after award but before the offer of financing becomes firm. This involves a second event called "financial close," at which point all conditions precedent have been satisfied or waived and first draw-down of debt can be made.

Reaching financial close can be a very demanding process. Financial close is part of the relationship between private investors and their lenders; however, governments or contracting authorities may need to be involved, for example, where the lenders

- Require additional information from the public sector
- Wish to propose changes to the project agreements
- Require direct agreements with or other support from the government/contracting authorities

In order to establish its role in ensuring timely financial close, the contracting authority may want to do the following:

- Give the project company a maximum period to achieve financial close, generally twelve months from contract award.
- Ask to be informed about progress of negotiations, with weekly updates and more detailed periodic reporting, for example, monthly. The contracting authority may also want access to the lenders to assess whether the project company is proceeding diligently toward financial close.
- Respond diligently to requests from lenders for additional information.
- Stand ready to enable/encourage timely financial close, including where the investors do not have prior experience in raising project financing for PPP projects, the project appears too risky for lenders to finance, changes in the consortium members are required, or other challenges arise.

While the contracting authority will not want to take over financing responsibility, failure to reach financial closure is a costly experience for all parties and will merit efforts by the contracting authority to support the process.

Box 9.2. Debt Competition

Mobilization of debt may be achieved through a competition. The bid process will contemplate that once the preferred bidder is selected, a competition will be run among potential financiers. The successful bidder, in coordination with the contracting authority, will run a competition to obtain debt at the best terms. The competition is usually based on a common due diligence report and term sheet produced by the contracting authority. The lending consortium able to commit to the term sheet at the lowest cost provides debt to the project company.

9.4 Construction, Commissioning, and Performance Monitoring

The private partner will develop a construction and commissioning plan, approved by the contracting authority. The plan will need to be implemented by the project company and overseen by the contracting authority. Issues to be monitored include those related to design, construction, commissioning, defects liability, and other issues that arise during construction.

During the construction stage, the contracting authority, through the PPP team, will need to monitor and verify that each of the following has been achieved:

- Financial closure has been reached.
- All of the land that the project requires for construction to begin has been provided.
- Permits and licenses needed for construction have been obtained in a timely manner (environmental permits, zoning permits, building permits, import approvals, etc.).
- All interconnection facilities, such as approach roads to the site or electricity, water, and sewerage interconnections, have been completed on schedule.
- Review and approval of project design have been completed.
- The performance bond has been received.

- All testing during construction, including testing of materials before delivery and installation of the works and associated facilities, have been reviewed.
- Each completion test for each milestone, commissioning of each phase of the works, commissioning of the whole of the works, and performance testing has been reviewed and approved.

During operation of the facility, the parties will need to comply with their obligations, including meeting performance obligations and delivering services to standards. Coordination during operation is essential to ensure efficiency and address issues, including conflicts, as they arise.

During the operational phase of a PPP, the contracting authority, through its PPP team, will need to monitor and verify the following:

- Compliance with the project company's obligation to maintain the assets and implement major maintenance programs
- Compliance with performance requirements, including capacity levels achieved, for example, heat rate (how much fuel is required to generate a given level of electricity) and volumes of water treated in a period of time
- New connections or conversion of illegal connections for water, electricity, or natural gas
- Output quantity and quality are satisfactory, for example, consumer satisfaction or demand levels achieved
- Performance levels, for example, the percentage of time that the service is available less regular, planned "shutdowns" for periodic maintenance

The contracting authority needs to prepare for the costs and physical requirements of gathering, analyzing, and verifying performance data. This will include a steep learning curve for contracting authorities that are not familiar with managing PPP project data.

9.5 Regulatory

The government may be assisted in its monitoring/management function by third parties. For example, an independent specialist may be appointed under the contract to act as the monitor of compliance with contract obligations by the parties, setting tariffs or assessing investment plans.[1] Equally,

---

[1] Tremolet et al., *Contracting Out Utility Regulatory Functions.*

the sector regulator (e.g., the water sector regulator) will be monitoring the project company's performance in any event, and may agree to monitor generally some or all of the parties' compliance with their obligations under law, which may well coincide with their obligations under the relevant contracts. The sector regulator may also be responsible for setting tariffs, ensuring affordability, and setting performance standards.

The difficulty is the need for the regulator to operate in accordance with its mandate, with the usual discretion given to regulators. Often, this discretion cannot be limited (or "fettered"), and therefore the regulator must comply with his legal mandate first and the contractual role as a secondary function. The parties will need to manage the risk that the duties enforced by the sector regulator are not inconsistent with the parties' obligations under the contracts. The regulator's requirements are likely to change over time, and the contracting authority is likely to bear the risk of any such changes.

9.6 Tariff Changes

There are two main options for setting and adjusting prices for long-term PPP projects to balance incentives to reduce operating costs and invest in new assets over time:

- *Rate of return*: To the extent the assets of the PPP project company are "used and useful" and where PPP operating expenses are "prudent and necessary," the service provider will earn a return on capital. This forms the basis for the charges to be permitted under the PPP for the next period. This approach provides an effective incentive for new investments in long-term assets but does not encourage operating efficiency.

- *Price-cap*: Fix the maximum price(s) that the private service provider may charge during a given period, such as five years pegged to a common price index, minus an efficiency factor, "X." This is an effective way to incentivize improved efficiency and reduce operating expenses but does not encourage new investments. Also, monitors need to be more vigilant to make sure that operating cost reductions are not overly aggressive at the expense of the technical quality and reliability of their services.

Changes may need to be made on an extraordinary basis to a PPP contract's prices or tariffs, in responses to specific changes in circumstances. Procedures should be agreed upon in advance in the PPP contract for

adjustments to PPP prices and tariffs. These procedures may be driven contractually and/or under the applicable regulatory mechanism.

9.7 Refinancing

After completion of construction, once construction risk in the project
has been significantly reduced, the project company will generally look
to refinance project debt at a lower cost and on better terms, given the
lower risk premium. In developed financial markets, the capital markets
are often used as a refinancing tool after completion of the project, since
bondholders prefer not to bear project completion risk but are often able to
provide fixed rate debt at a longer tenor and lower margin than commercial
banks. In countries with less developed capital markets, pension funds and
other institutional investors may provide refinancing, given their long tenor
liabilities.[2]

This refinancing process can significantly increase equity return, with
the excess debt margin released and the resultant leverage effect. While
wanting to incentivize the project company to pursue improved financial
engineering, in particular through refinancing, the contracting authority
will want to share in the project company's refinancing gains (for example,
in the form of a 50–50 split) and may or may not want the right to insist
on refinancing when desirable. The contracting authority's project management team will need to have the resources and skills available to manage
refinancing issues.

Detailed provisions in the PPP contract generally set out a method for
determining and sharing the gains from future refinancing rather than rely-
ing on broad principles and full-blown renegotiation of the contract when
refinancing takes place. The specific contract drafting needs to address several points, including the following:

- Deciding when the financing is to take place (the contracting authority may be entitled to call for refinancing in certain circumstances)
- Calculating the expected refinancing gain to the project company
  shareholders (e.g., using net present value of profits)
- Determining the portion of the gain that should be allocated to each
  party (e.g., a 50–50 split)
- Deciding how the gains should be shared (e.g., lump-sum payment to
  the authority, reduction in the availability fee payable to the project
  company)

---

[2] For further discussion, see section 6.1.

The contract will include other details, for example, the discount and interest rates to be used in the calculations and the possible impact of a refinancing operation on termination compensation.[3]

**Box 9.3. Refinancing without Credit Enhancing
Mechanisms – A66 Benavente Zamora Road Scheme**

The A66 Benavente Zamora road scheme, which was signed by a Meridiam, Cintra, and Acciona consortium in August 2013, saw its long-term debt refinanced. The original twenty-one-year €160.5 million senior debt facility was established in 2013 by commercial lenders BBVA, Santander, Instituto de Crédito Oficial, and the European Investment Bank. The three partners in the project successfully priced the €184.5 million, twenty-seven-year bond at a 3.169 percent coupon.

Refinancing may be essential, for example, when the project can access only short-to-medium term debt (such as five to seven years) and project revenues are insufficient to repay the debt during this period. In such an instance, the project company may arrange to repay much of the debt principal in a bullet payment at the end of the debt term (see discussion of hard and soft miniperms in Chapter 5). This bullet payment will need to be financed. The risk of the inability to finance the bullet payment will need to be managed, for example, with standby debt or equity from shareholders, the government, or a third party such as a bank, MLA, or BLA. In some markets, such as Australia, PPP debt is often or even mostly funded with short-term debt. Generally, sponsors take the refinancing risk, often alongside the contracting authority. The availability of hedging can mitigate some of this risk.[4]

**Box 9.4. Refinancing Using Credit Enhancement
Mechanisms – A11 Belgian Motor Link**

In March 2014, the A11 Motorway in Belgium, a greenfield project for the construction and operation of a 12 kilometer stretch of the trunk road link A11 between the regional roads N49 for a period of thirty years, issued Euro 578 million in bonds with a maturity of thirty-two

---

[3]   EPEC PPP Guide: Sharing the gains from a refinancing, European Investment Bank, 2015. www.eib.org/epec
[4]   *Partnerships Bulletin*, Taking the risk, at 20.

years. The project used credit enhancements in the form of contingent debt (to be used if the project is unable to pay the bondholders) from the European Investment Bank (EIB). This helped improve the credit rating of the bonds by three notches to A3 according to rating agency Moody's. The EIB project bond credit enhancement instrument used a letter of credit representing 20 percent of senior debt.

Source: europa.eu/rapid/press-release_BEI-14-66_en.html.

9.8 Selling Down Equity

Many of the key sponsors are not normally long-term equity infrastructure investors, for example, the construction companies who are often the key investors in road PPP, or the equity funds that look for investments with short-to-medium term (three to seven years) exit opportunities. Investors will therefore look for the right to sell down their equity positions as soon as possible. The contracting authority will want the shareholders to remain invested until key project risks have been addressed, in particular construction risks. Some time after completion of construction (usually one to three years), investors are generally permitted to sell down part of their equity.

Strategic shareholders are those who provide critical skills/inputs to the project company. The contracting authority will want to ensure that strategic investors retain sufficient financial interests in the success of the project, to align their interests, for a period long enough to ensure that design and construction meet requirements. Strategic investors may be required to sell shares only to companies with similar skills, capacity, and financial stability to ensure that the project continues to benefit accordingly.

9.9 Renegotiation

PPP projects have the characteristics propitious to recurrent renegotiation; they represent long-term, complex commercial and financial arrangements, in heavily regulated sectors, subject to significant political sensitivities, vulnerable to changes in circumstances, and often grounded in uncertainty (e.g., the condition of existing assets, lack of information on business data and ground conditions).[5] Data from Latin America suggest that some

---

[5] Guasch, J. L., D. Benitez, I. Portabales, & L. Flor, L., The renegotiation of PPP contracts: an overview of its recent evolution in Latin America. Discussion Paper No 2014–18. International Transport Forum at the OECD, Paris (2014); Gifford, J., L. Bolaños, & N. Daito, Renegotiation of Transportation Public–Private Partnerships: The US Experience. Discussion Paper No. 2014–16. International Transport Forum at the OECD,

75 percent of transport PPP contracts and 87 percent of water and sanitation PPP contracts are renegotiated at some point.[6]

Renegotiation is often perceived as failure, as a fundamental flaw in the project or in PPP generally. This perception arises in particular from poorly managed or implemented renegotiation processes, which

- Can result in reductions in revenue flows and service standards (those most likely to be affected by such reductions in services and increases in costs are the poorest households)
- Often lack transparency and are particularly vulnerable to corrupt practices
- Can create a public and governmental backlash against private sector involvement in other projects or other sectors, reducing the scope of possible tools that the government will have available to it for improving and reforming its infrastructure services.

But this perception of failure as a generalization is erroneous. There is no doubt that renegotiation is a difficult process, but it is typical for long-term arrangements (be they PPP contracts, commercial partnerships, or marriages) to face change or conflict and need adjustment to address new information and circumstances. Renegotiation is a natural part of most projects and can be an opportunity to adjust the terms of a project to address the needs of the project (and the public) and actual circumstances encountered by the parties. It allows the parties to respond to unanticipated events and changes. To the extent it would be more beneficial for the PPP contract to be terminated, the renegotiation process can help facilitate the transition process and help reduce the cost of termination and the stress involved. PPP projects must therefore be designed to address change and conflict quickly and effectively and to facilitate renegotiation in a balanced manner in accordance with the spirit of the project.[7]

Paris (2014); Bitran, E., S. Nieto-Parra, & J. Robledo, Opening the Black Box of Contract Renegotiations: An Analysis of Road Concessions in Chile, Colombia and Peru. Draft Renegotiations in Chile, Peru and Colombia. Mimeo (2012); Engel, E., R. Fischer, & A. Galetovic, Public–Private Partnerships to Revamp U.S. Infrastructure. Hamilton Policy Brief, Brookings Institution (2011); Engel, E., R. Fischer, & A. Galetovic, Soft Budgets and Renegotiations in Public Private Partnerships. Discussion Paper No 2014–17. International Transport Forum at the OECD, Paris (2014).

[6] Straub et al., *Infrastructure Concessions in Latin America*. PPP database (preliminary figures): as for 2003, 34 percent of contracts (by investment amounts) in the water sector are classified as distressed and 12 percent were canceled; in transport 15 percent were distressed and 9 percent canceled); while in energy 12 percent were distressed and 3 percent canceled. See PPP.worldbank.org.

[7] Delmon, J., & D. A. Phillips, *Renegotiation of Private Participation in Infrastructure and the World Bank* (2007).

To provide some perspective, it may be useful to note that renegotiations, as initially defined, are pervasive in traditional procurement as well. In the context of cost overruns in road projects, for example, changes in the scope of the project during construction, "scope creep," is often identified as the primary cause of cost overruns.[8]

9.9.1 Why Renegotiation?

Most renegotiations occur shortly after financial close, even before construction. This creates a clear danger of diversion of the procurement process, which could undermine the value for money achieved through competitive procurement.[9]

Box 9.5. Renegotiations in India

India has few – if any – renegotiations, due to a very strict contract, which allows changes only due to defined change in law and force majeure provisions. The contract also allows very limited compensation for events outside the control of the concessionaire. This creates a perception of strict risk allocation but may be creating disputes and resolution outside of structured processes. This is changing to allow contracts to adjust, to address concerns of banks, and to attract more foreign investment, but within very strict limits.

The reasons for renegotiation are many, but some of the aggravating factors can be summarized as follows:

- One party is doing better/worse than it hoped – especially when the private sector makes more profit than is politically comfortable, or the project is not sufficiently profitable to hold the investor's attention. In some cases, an opportunistic firm makes an overly aggressive offer and must renegotiate after award to make the deal financially viable. The question of intentionality is a difficult one. Some complications might include the following:
  - An oddly low or aggressive bid
  - A contract that leaves openings for change without sufficient limitations or oversight

---

[8] Blanc Brude and Makovsek, Construction risk in infrastructure project finance (2013) provides an overview.
[9] Guasch et al., Renegotiation of PPP Contracts; Engel et al., Soft Budgets and Renegotiations in Public Private Partnerships.

○ The government has in the past allowed such negotiation, or has given indications that it would be open to such calls for negotiation
- An opportunistic contracting authority wants to expand the scope of works without having to obtain approvals or go beyond agreed fiscal limits, where permitted or where oversight is insufficient
- Parties lack of sufficient information on the project, such as where a full feasibility was not performed or was performed by a biased party, or where there is lack of time and opportunity during bidding process to obtain and assess data
- Change in circumstances after financial close (e.g., market volatility, cost increases, change in demand patterns, political/legal changes) when the PPP agreement does not contemplate such changes
- Change in contracting authority requirements provisions not fore-shadowed in the PPP agreement

---

Box 9.6. Renegotiation of PPP in the EU

EU procurement law and in particular the 2014 Directive on the award of concession contracts explicitly permits renegotiation of a concession contract where

(i) The value of the project is not increased by more than 50 percent, and

(ii) The modification was provided for in the initial contract in a clear, precise, and unequivocal manner and does not alter the overall nature of the concession, or

(iii) The modification is urgent and necessary, and procurement of a new concessionaire would involve significant inconvenience or substantial duplication of costs, or

(iv) A diligent contracting entity could not foresee the circumstances, and the modification does not alter the overall nature of the concession, or

(v) The modification is not substantial.

Source: Department of Economic Affairs: Ministry of Finance, *Developing a Framework for Renegotiation of PPP Contracts* (2014).

9.9.2 Developing a Framework for Renegotiation

South Africa has an elaborate and robust PPP legislative and regulatory framework. Since 2000, only three PPPs on average per year are executed. The reason for this is the time it takes to conclude a PPP successfully, with a total of thirty PPPs and sixty-four IPPs, which is usually twenty-four to thirty-six months from prequalification to financial close. To date, there have been thirty PPPs and sixty-four IPPs, and no projects have been terminated. A breach notice has been issued on one project that was remedied by the concessionaire upon threat of step-in by the lenders. Any material amendment due to renegotiations must meet the scrutiny and obtain approval of Treasury in terms of value for money, affordability, and substantial technical, operational, and financial risk transfer to the private party.

Box 9.7. Change in the United Kingdom

Under the change mechanism for U.K. projects, the public rather than the private sector has initiated most of the changes to requirements during the operational phase of projects. Broadly, there is flexibility to initiate change from either party at any time and to any value within the prescripts of the 2014 EU Directive on the Award of Concession Contracts (see Box 9.6). All changes are approved by the authority itself and are subject to its ability to pay for the change. For high-value changes, an extensive due diligence process is used to ensure that the public sector achieves value for money. Authorities must carry out substantial preparatory work in scoping this type of change before issuing a formal variation notice.

Chile has one of the most successful PPP programs among developing countries, with some U.S.$11 billion investment in public infrastructure, including more than fifty PPPs: twenty-six roads, ten airports, three prisons, two water reservoirs, five public transportation projects, and four other. Its PPP Act allows the parties to agree to change the works and services contracted in order to raise the service levels and technical standards by up to 15 percent (a figure that is established in the bidding conditions) of the approved capital value. The Ministry of Public Works must be able to justify the changes for duly substantiated reasons of public interest in a public report. The circumstances giving rise to the amendment must occur after the awarding of the concession, and could have not been foreseen upon its awarding, and awarding the new works to the original concession holder is more efficient than granting a new concession. If the increase exceeds 5 percent of the approved capital works, then it must be put out to open tender by the private partner. There have been 148 renegotiations of PPP contracts; on average, each contract had been renegotiated three times.

Box 9.8. Renegotiation in Australia

In Australia, under the country's PPP Guidelines, renegotiation of any significant areas of a PPP contract after it has been approved and signed by government will require the contracting authority to obtain Cabinet approval prior to commencing negotiations.

9.9.3 Practical Guidance on Renegotiation

A number of good practices have been developed on renegotiation. These include the following:

- Feasibility studies can help identify key issues early.
- Project contracts need to address issues as completely as possible and to provide mechanisms to address conflict, changes, and circumstances. Balanced risk allocation is key. Some contractual clauses are more likely to create dispute; for example, financial equilibrium clauses have been shown to complicate renegotiation.[10]
- Proactive conflict identification, management, and resolution help keep communication open and address problems as they arise.
- Transparency, competition, an efficient approvals process, a robust institutional framework, and public disclosure of PPP contracts are desirable.
- Involvement of independent monitors, such as sector regulators to respond to changes, is advisable.
- Some countries, such as Peru and Colombia, impose a holding period for renegotiations for the first three years of a project, to avoid the use of renegotiation to compensate for a lowball bid.
- Evaluate bids based on best overall economic bid rather than lowest price.
- If significant changes are to be made in the scope of works, such work must be tendered competitively, to avoid abuse of the renegotiation process.

Box 9.9. Lessons Learned from Australian Renegotiation

The ability to manage the changing environment by adapting contracts has been key to de-stressing projects. On the whole, the renegotiation outcomes in Australia have been beneficial and demonstrated

---

[10] Guasch et al., Renegotiation of PPP Contracts.

government commitment to managing PPPs in a manner that is in the public interest. The following are words of wisdom from an ex-official from Australia on the process of renegotiation:

Australian PPP agreements cater for changes in a variety of ways:

- empowered committees to apply specifications in a manner that drives efficiency in public facilities such as hospitals
- dispute resolution procedures permit mediation and facilitated agreements
- amendments are permitted and subject to the same oversight as the original approvals and gateways.

So far, the market works. The state governments have sent a strong message to the market that they will not guarantee any private sector debt and will not bail out projects. The projects do not go under, the concessionaire is liquidated, and equity is sold into a secondary market in a process led by lenders.

Source: National Public Private Partnership Guidelines, Vol. 6 (December 2014).

Key Lessons for Policy Makers

- *Be proactive.* Establish mechanisms intended to catch disputes as early as possible. Early in the process, options are varied, relative cost is low, and the likelihood of immediate value-added resolution is higher.
- *Facilitation can help.* Softer processes are designed to use and develop relationships as the basis for finding mutually satisfactory solutions and can work better than more formal processes.
- *Renegotiation can be an opportunity,* and can improve the PPP arrangements and protect the poor, if it is contemplated in advance, transparent, and well managed when needed.
- *Get good advice.* Do not try to manage disputes or renegotiations with internal staff alone, no matter how good they are. Get the best external advice. It will cost money up front, but will save money in the long run.

9.10 Step-in

PPP contract terminations are expensive for all sides involved, and that is why they are relatively rare in large, capital-intensive PPPs. Almost all sides find it is more cost effective to try to restructure and renegotiate these deals and to share the costs of revising these contracts when compared to the cancelation of PPP contracts.

Where the project company breaches the PPP agreement in such a way as to permit the contracting authority to terminate, the lenders will want the right of step-in, such that they can continue the project and avoid the termination of the concession agreement. The contracting authority will therefore grant the lenders step-in rights.

In the same way, the project is only of use to the contracting authority when it is in operation. The contracting authority may therefore want the right to continue operation of the project where it terminates the PPP agreement. This is often called the right to continuous operation, as it allows the contracting authority to ensure continuous operation of the project even in the event of termination. The contracting authority itself will often not undertake such operation, but rather pass such responsibilities on to the operator, the offtake purchaser, or some other third party.

The contracting authority may also wish to have a right to step in to operate the project where, during operation, the project company is temporarily unable to continue operation. Given the urgent need of the host country for the project, the contracting authority may need the right to step in during the temporary disability and ensure continuous operation. The contracting authority will not want to act on such a right if it is not technically and physically capable of undertaking operation. Generally, the following are good guidelines:

- Temporary step-in should not involve any reversion of risk to the contracting agency or the offtake purchaser except in cases of negligence.
- Neither party should gain an additional benefit from temporary step-in; for example, the contracting agency should be compensated for its reasonable costs of operation.

The lenders and/or the contracting authority may also want step-in rights in relation to the other project documents to ensure the continuity of the project structure and continuity of operation of the project. Thus, each project document, either in the project document itself or in a direct agreement with the lenders and/or the contracting authority, is likely to provide for step-in rights. The project participants may want to receive guarantees from the party stepping in that are at least as good as those given by the project company.

9.11 Conflict Management and Dispute Resolution

The long-term nature of PPP, the variety of stakeholders and interested parties, public and private sensitivities, and different methodologies for resolving conflict can result in frequent conflict and the potential for disputes. A well-designed PPP will pay special attention to conflict management, identifying conflict early and elevating it to the right level for resolution. Where conflict management fails, and the parties find themselves in dispute, the resolution of the dispute needs to focus on the project. A failed project is a disaster for the parties; there are seldom true "winners" from a failed project, no matter what might be reported by interest groups or board meetings.

Dispute resolution should be kept in the hands of those who know the project best, that is, the parties. Nonbinding forms of dispute resolution can be used to facilitate a settlement among the parties, and in some cases to reinforce the relationship between the parties – resolving difficult issues can cement a relationship and prove commitment to the success of the project.

Where nonbinding mechanisms are not successful, access to binding dispute resolution is essential. PPP projects often involve parties from a variety of legal, social, and cultural backgrounds. Identifying a national court capable of meeting the needs of such a diverse collection of parties, and acceptable to each of these parties, may be difficult. It is for this reason that parties to a PPP project generally prefer to submit any disputes to arbitration rather than to state courts.

It is important that the dispute resolution regimes in the different project documents are similar, if not identical, in order to facilitate the resolution of complex issues involving multiparty resolution before a single forum.

This section will discuss some of the mechanisms for conflict management and nonbinding and binding dispute resolution.

9.11.1 Conflict Management

Given the complexity of PPP projects and the diversity of parties, conflict management is key to project success. A culture of conflict management should permeate the project documents and the parties' interactions. Communication is critical, keeping dialogue open and constant. Where conflicts arise, they need to be identified and addressed early and proactively.

Projects can benefit from partnering, whereby all participants meet together prior to commencement to establish communications expectations and responsibilities. The partnering process is usually professionally facilitated, and the goal is to establish among all stakeholders and participants a reliable and mutually shared system of accountability for communications.

A clear mechanism of escalation of concerns and conflicts can help notify decision makers of the issues and engage their support in resolution. Of course, no one will want to bother a senior management or chief executive officer for minor issues, but these same small issues can grow to serious problems if not resolved, and maybe the support (or threat) of senior management involvement is what is needed to encourage creative solutions.

9.11.2 Early Evaluation

Early evaluation involves review of the dispute by an independent expert to seek resolution early and in a short time frame, without the cost of arbitration. Characteristics of the independent dispute resolution mechanism include the following:

- The decision may bind the parties unless or until the decision is overturned by an arbitrator or the courts. The procedure used is not generally subject to concepts of natural justice or due process and therefore provides fewer protections for the parties than arbitration.
- Appointment may occur as and when a dispute arises, to ensure that the skill set of the expert meets the needs of the parties. In order to provide faster and more continuity in conflict management, the expert may be appointed from commencement; such an expert is also known as a "standing," neutral, or "initial" decision maker.
- Jurisdiction may be limited by the parties to specific areas of dispute, by issue, by technical specificity, or by value.

A few common, early dispute resolution mechanisms include the following:

- The engineer/employer's representative, in international construction contracts, is the engineer. The engineer is appointed and paid by the employer and acts as the employer's representative throughout the period of construction and provides the dispute resolution mechanism of first instance. Parties to a PPP jointly appoint an independent engineer to oversee construction and operation, monitor testing, and play a dispute resolution role.
- Some countries mandate early expert assessment for certain disputes; for example, adjudication for domestic construction contracts in the

United Kingdom[11] is mandated before reference can be made to final and binding arbitration or the courts.

- Many large, complex projects adopt dispute resolution boards (DRBs), created at the time of the inception of the project, whose purpose is to monitor the project status and be available for stakeholders in the event of disputes.[12] The DRB members follow the project from commencement to completion, keeping up with issues that arise in relation to the project, the parties involved, and the various project obligations. From the data gathered by the DRB Foundation, dating back to 1975, 60 percent of projects with a DRB had no disputes, and 98 percent of disputes referred to a DRB did not result in subsequent litigation or arbitration.[13]

- Courts may mandate the use of alternative dispute resolution – for example, *early neutral evaluation* – to provide disputants with a frank professional evaluation of their claims and defenses. For example, the disputants may use a referee, (classically) a retired judge. (This is sometimes called "private judging".)

- In a *minitrial*, the parties present their legal and factual contentions to a panel of senior representatives of each party, a neutral third party, or both. In a *summary jury trial*, representatives of the parties present evidence in summary form before an independent panel of neutrals, a synthetic jury. The "jury" renders an advisory verdict.

9.11.3 Mediation

Mediation is a powerful mechanism for conflict and dispute resolution that is underutilized in PPP. Mediation is simply a facilitated negotiation, with no decision or factual interpretation.[14] The mediator may be called upon to give a suggested resolution (often called "evaluative" mediation or "conciliation" as compared to the "facilitative" model of mediation) but will not bind the parties.

Mediation is very flexible, allowing the mediator to structure the process in the manner most appropriate to the situation.

---

[11] *Part II* of the Housing Grants, Construction and Regeneration Act 1996.
[12] The Dispute Resolution Board Foundation (see www.drb.org) provides further information about DRBs and has branches in many major jurisdictions.
[13] www.drb.org.
[14] Delmon, & Phillips, *Renegotiation of Private Participation in Infrastructure and the World Bank*; Mackie, K. J., D. Miles, & W. Marsh, *Commercial Dispute Resolution: an ADR Practice Guide* (1995); Delmon, J., *BOO/BOT Projects: A Commercial and Contractual Guide* (2000), at 59, 248.

There are several points at which mediation can be used in PPP projects:

a. *Consultation* – During project preparation, governments need help consulting stakeholders (community groups, labor unions, land owners, government staff, etc.). During these processes, there may be an opportunity for a mediator to help facilitate dialogue and open processes for sharing of issues while managing stress and frustrations.

b. *Negotiation* – During negotiation, there might theoretically be an opportunity for a mediator to help resolve deadlock on specific issues or more generally to help bridge cultural divides between the parties in order to finalize the deal.

c. *Initiation* – At the very beginning of a project, once the ink dries on the contracts and the difficult work of implementation begins, it can be useful to bring the parties together and have a mediator walk them through the practical process of implementation (similar to partnering), setting out or affirming implementation plans and teasing out details of how things will be done in practice, such as who is responsible for what and when. Ideally, this is done through the negotiation of the contract, but in practice these issues are often overlooked or swept under the carpet in order to get to financial close. The goal is to establish among all stakeholders and participants a reliable and mutually shared system of accountability and communications to enhance the team's ability to identify problems at a very early stage, when solutions are cheapest and most plentiful.

d. *Deal* – There are a number of changes, conflicts, and challenges that arise in a project that do not amount to a "dispute" under the relevant contractual clauses. For example, where the parties need to agree a variation order or there is an opportunity for refinancing, there may be disagreements about timing, currency, and tenor that a mediator could help resolve, but that no one will want to bring up through the formal dispute resolution mechanism.

e. *Dispute* – Where there is a full-blown dispute, whether or not the parties have included mediation in the contract, access to mediation can help avoid costs and delay. It is common for commercial parties to agree, in their initial contracts, to a stepped dispute management process under which they require mediation prior to asserting claims to binding dispute resolution.

9.11.4 Litigation

Litigation is a public dispute resolution process, and is the default dispute resolution system where no other system has been stipulated by the parties, although it can also be expressly chosen. Unlike arbitration, where the parties bear the full cost of the tribunal, litigants pay only nominal fees to the court. However, this cost saving may be outweighed by the costs incurred by the parties in complying with the lengthy procedural requirements of litigation.

In the context of international projects, it is important to bear in mind that litigation is a national dispute resolution process, tied to a particular national system of courts. Problems may arise when the defendant is located in a different country from that of the relevant court. For instance, there may be various specific procedural requirements for commencing an action against a foreign defendant. There may also be a perception of bias against foreign litigants. Even if no actual bias exists, foreign claimants will prefer to submit to a process with which they are comfortable.

A further issue that arises in an international context is the enforcement of judgments. For enforcement of a foreign judgment, each country will have its own rules and will be party to different international conventions. Different procedures must be followed in respect of each of these systems, and there are different substantive grounds for the court to refuse enforcement. The process of enforcement of a foreign judgment is therefore generally more complex and difficult than that of an arbitral award, unless the judgment is subject to arrangements for reciprocal recognition, as, for example, under the Convention on Jurisdiction and the Enforcement of Judgments of 1973 (the Brussels Convention) and the Lugano Convention of 1988 among certain European nations.

9.11.5 Arbitration

Arbitration is most often used as the final method of dispute resolution (instead of litigation) because of its flexibility and greater ease of award enforcement.[15] Arbitration is a private dispute resolution process that produces a binding result, immediately enforceable at law under most legal systems through arbitration acts and treaties. The mechanism by which the tribunal reaches its decision, known as an *award*, is generally subject to due process, and each party must have a reasonable opportunity to present its case. The parties determine the type of arbitration and seek to agree on the appointment of the members of the tribunal. Like other private systems, arbitration is also private in the wider sense in that it is confidential. The parties' agreement to arbitrate may be a clause that forms part of a contract, or it may be a separate agreement entered into by the parties before

---

[15] See generally Sutton, D., Kendall, & J. Gill, eds., *Russell on Arbitration* (1998).

or after a dispute has arisen. The following addresses a few issues specific to arbitration:

(i) Confidentiality: Arbitration is a private process, and the parties can undertake a general duty to each other of confidentiality. This duty is either set out in the arbitration clause or, to a limited extent, set out in the arbitration rules selected by the parties. There are two aspects to this duty: the confidentiality of arbitral proceedings and the confidentiality of documents created or disclosed as part of the arbitration process. This duty of confidentiality is not normally absolute but qualified by exceptions such as compulsion of law or where production of documents is necessary to protect the legitimate interests of one of the parties. Confidentiality may be particularly important where technical processes or commercially damaging information is disclosed as part of a dispute.

(ii) Choice of arbitrator: The fact that parties appoint, directly or indirectly, the arbitrator or arbitral tribunal is particularly important in a context since technical issues may arise that are best resolved by someone with the appropriate technical qualifications. Arbitration allows the parties to appoint someone with experience of the subject matter of the dispute rather than entrusting the resolution of a technically complex issue to a legally trained, but scientifically inexperienced, judge. This may reduce the need for expensive and time-consuming expert testimony.

(iii) Enforceability of arbitral awards: PPP projects often involve parties from different countries. It is therefore very important that an award be capable of recognition and enforcement in different countries. Many countries have signed treaties providing for reciprocal enforcement of arbitral awards. These treaties, such as the New York Convention,[16] do not usually allow the enforcing court to open up the award and make a qualitative assessment of its merits except in limited circumstances. The enforcement of an arbitral award may be easier than that of a judgment obtained through the courts because of the wider application of international conventions relating to arbitral awards.

States generally benefit from two forms of immunity: jurisdiction and execution. State entities are immune from the jurisdiction of the courts of

---

[16] United Nations Convention on the Recognition and Enforcement of Foreign Arbitral Awards (1958).

another state. Sovereign immunity results from both the nature of the actor and the nature of the act. The actor must be a sovereign entity, because a creature of sovereignty cannot be subject to the jurisdiction of another without specifically submitting to such jurisdiction.[17] However, the designation of an actor as sovereign or not sovereign can be difficult, because public bodies become involved in essentially private/commercial acts, and those same public bodies may be wholly or partially privatized. One must then look to the nature of the act. Is it a governmental act (*jure imperii*) or a private/commercial act (*jure gestionis*)? Each legal system will classify acts differently, and these differences may be very pronounced.[18]

This immunity results from the belief that it would be inappropriate for one state's courts to call another state under its jurisdiction, since this would erode the principle of independent national sovereignty. However, this immunity can generally be waived by the state entity, and the adoption of arbitration often includes such a waiver. The state will also have immunity from execution, since it would be improper for the courts of one state to seize the property of another state. Just as courts do not have jurisdiction over foreign sovereign states under international law, they are also prevented from seizing the property of such sovereign states. This immunity is intended to protect the independence of a sovereign state.[19] Immunity from execution generally may also be waived.[20]

    (iv) Arbitrator's jurisdiction: Arbitration is a creature of contract; therefore, the power of the arbitral tribunal and its ability to hear a particular dispute derive from the arbitration provisions in the relevant contract. The arbitrator will need to be given jurisdiction over the parties to the dispute and the dispute itself.

    (v) Arbitration rules: The parties may stipulate the procedure to be followed by an arbitral tribunal. They may appoint an arbitral institution such as the International Chamber of Commerce (ICC), the London Court of International Arbitration (LCIA), the Arbitration Institute of the Stockholm Chamber of Commerce, or the Singapore International Arbitration Centre to administer the arbitration and run it according to the relevant institutional rules.

---

[17] O'Connell, *International Law*, 2nd ed. (1970), at 842.

[18] Ibid., at 845.

[19] Ibid., 864.

[20] Maryan, N. E., Jr., Negotiating with the Monarch; Special Problems when the Sovereign is your Partner, *Project Financing in Emerging Markets* (1996).

The United Nations Commission on International Trade Law (UNCITRAL) also has a set of arbitration rules but has no specific administrative body, though most of the other administrative bodies will implement UNCITRAL arbitrations. The assistance of an administrative body is of considerable benefit once a dispute has arisen, since the parties may have difficulty agreeing on procedure once their relationship has become contentious.

Where the parties to the contract include a foreign government, or a government entity, the private contracting party must take into consideration the difficulty of executing arbitral decisions against government assets. A separate arbitral body has been developed for this purpose under the International Centre for Settlement of Investment Disputes (ICSID), part of the World Bank Group. This body has greater powers of enforcement over its member states and has been successful in the resolution of investment disputes between private parties and sovereign entities. A strict procedure must be followed in order to submit disputes arising under a contract to ICSID.[21] Bilateral Investment Treaties (BITs) can provide a method for accessing ICSID arbitration if the same is not contemplated in the contract.

9.12 Expiry, Termination, and Handover

After delivery, whether the project is terminated early or expires in accordance with expectations, the parties will need to manage the exit phase, for example, to accomplish the following:

- Identify relevant assets and other things that need to be transferred and assess their value. Some assets will transfer automatically, and some only where the contracting authority so chooses.
- Assess the condition of assets to be handed over and ensure those assets are handed over in the agreed condition. In the run-up to expiry, a regime is normally agreed in the contract to assess the condition of assets and resolve any defects.
- Monitor and ensure remedy of any defects or deficiencies in those assets and resolve issues associated with the allocation of any costs of any such remedy.
- Procure a replacement project company (or provide access to information to do so) when needed.
- Monitor the transfer of assets, staff, and the business generally to the contracting authority or an appointed entity.

---

[21] www.icsid.worldbank.org.

Box 9.10. Transfer and Refinancing of Tunnels

The Lane Cove Tunnel (LCT) is a 3.6 kilometer tunnel in eastern Australia. It links the Gore Hill Freeway with the M2 Motorway, providing a key link in the Sydney Toll Road Network. The capital cost of the Lane Cove Tunnel and E-ramps project was estimated at over $1.6 billion, which was financed with $0.54 billion equity and $1.14 billion in debt of various maturities. While the tunnel and ramps were successfully completed and opened to traffic in 2007, traffic was much lower than predicted. (In 2009 there was 50,000 annual average daily traffic [AADT] versus a forecast of 120,000.) Cash flow problems due to high operating costs occurred when revenue was low. The concessionaire was placed in receivership in 2010. The concession was sold to Transurban in May 2010 for $630.5 million: $372.5 million of equity and $258 million of debt. The sale of the concession was managed by the lenders in terms of their step-in rights. The government did not pay any compensation as a result of the failure. The loss to equity participants was absolute, while the lenders may have minimized their loss through restructuring their loans

Source: www.treasury.nsw.gov.au/ppp.

Sector and Specific Project Issues

This chapter sets out some of the specific requirements of a few different sectors: transportation, telecommunications, power, water and sanitation, health, education, and small-scale projects. It also discusses the possibility of leveraging commercial revenues for PPP projects and the need to balance incentives. It does not attempt to provide detail, nor will it discuss all issues in all subsectors, but is specifically focused on the characteristics of each sector that will influence PPP.

Key Messages for Policy Makers

- *PPP is not one size fits all.* Each sector needs specific consideration, and possibly a bespoke PPP solution; adapt the structure to the context.

10.1 Transportation

Transportation projects – including airports, ports, roads, railways, light rail, buses, tunnels, and bridges – are traditionally financed by a combination of private and public funding. Governments are increasingly looking to the private sector for input in the development of new transportation schemes and the privatization of those already in existence.

Transport projects raise a number of specific issues:

Land acquisition. The need for access to large amounts of land and space to build transportation facilities makes them expensive, long-term, and politically sensitive undertakings. Public reaction to new transport facilities can be challenging; no one wants a railway line or new road running through the backyard. Generally, land acquisition is at the risk of the contracting authority. It is best for all land to be acquired before the bid process. It may be tempting to try to accelerate the process and commence bidding assuming that the land will be acquired in a timely manner; but this has been the downfall of many a project and has created massive liabilities for governments across the globe.

Capital subsidies. Transportation projects often involve quite significant capital costs, which may exceed the appetite of the private sector finance market or the revenue potential of the project while keeping tariffs affordable, and therefore government support may be essential to the financial viability of the project, whether through capital grants, availability payments, or other such instruments.

Regulation risk. Given the various safety risks, transportation is a highly regulated industry. Any construction or improvements will need to comply with regulatory restrictions and may need regulatory approval. Tariff levels in transport are generally regulated to ensure a balance between affordability and cash generation for capital investment. These regulatory matters will influence the timetable for project implementation and should be anticipated at the beginning of the process, in particular where user charges are to be introduced or significantly increased through the PPP project.

**Box 10.1. Optimism Bias or Bad Incentives:
How Planning Goes Wrong**

Planning and forecasting need to reflect benefit to the government, through cost-benefit or value for money assessments. But such assessments tend to involve incentives for those performing them to emphasize benefits and deemphasize costs, whether consciously or not. For example, where there is competition for resources between government authorities, there may be an incentive to overstate the benefits of the project. The assessment function therefore needs to be performed at a level where a more objective assessment is possible.[1]

There tends to be a similar bias toward new build, rather than refurbishing what exists and maintaining it properly. Maintaining a road properly is more than three times less expensive than maintaining it poorly and rebuilding later. But the sociopolitical incentive is to build something big and new that can carry the name or be identified with a

---

[1] See Flyvbjerg, Survival of the unfittest; McKinsey Global institute, *Infrastructure Productivity.*

politician or political party. Khan and Levinson (2011) highlight the failure in the U.S. national highway system to maintain roads properly due in part to the tendency for federal monies to be allocated to new build projects rather than maintenance or refurbishment.[2]

Examples of institutional mechanisms designed to manage such biases include the Private Infrastructure Investment Management Center in South Korea, which routinely rejects 46 percent of proposed projects (compared to 3 percent before its creation) at a savings of 35 percent to the government on poorly planned or selected projects. Similarly, Chile's national Public Investment System rejects 25 to 35 percent of projects proposed.[3]

Source: McKinsey Global Institute, *Infrastructure Productivity*.

10.1.1 Roads, Tunnels, and Bridges

Roads and bridges are historically financed with public money, and their operation is subsidized by local or national taxation. Private sector investment in roads and bridges is increasing significantly and comes with significant challenges:

- *Operating costs* – A road and bridge will not require high operation and maintenance costs, nor any other input. Therefore, the revenue stream will be devoted primarily to debt servicing; up to 80 percent of revenue can be allocated to debt servicing (during the period of repayment of the financing) and return to the investors.[4]
- *Revenues* – Demand is difficult to manage in roads, tunnels, and bridges; users may not want to pay tolls or may prefer free alternative routes. Alternate modes of transport may bleed traffic. Traffic forecasts often suffer from optimism bias (see Box 10.1) or from political orientation, where they are undertaken with the intent to show the need of the local economy for state investment in infrastructure rather than to provide an objective analysis of demand.[5] The challenge of demand risk is particularly difficult where the project revenues are based on the collection of tolls from users.

[2] Kahn & Levinson, Fix It First; McKinsey Global Institute, *Infrastructure Productivity*.
[3] Ibid.
[4] Macquarie Corporate Finance Limited, *Project Finance: The Guide to Financing Transport Projects* 12 (1996).
[5] Ibid.

Box 10.2. Toll Road Traffic Forecasts

Where the project company takes traffic risk, the toll regime for a transportation project should be based on reliable economic, technical, and financial assumptions. Lenders will generally undertake their own traffic forecasting exercises to verify those provided by the contracting authority and the project company. The inherent vulnerability of traffic forecasts to optimism bias was demonstrated more than fifteen years ago in a Standard & Poors study[6] from 2002 of traffic forecasts in user fee-based toll road schemes. Of thirty-two different projects, actual traffic was on average only 70 percent of that forecast, with a large majority of projects not reaching even 90 percent of the forecast traffic. Governments therefore often provide revenue or traffic guarantees to protect the project company and/or the lenders from a certain portion of traffic risk.

The contracting authority may prefer to use an availability payment mechanism to compensate the project company for making the road available to users, with deductions for defects in the road or deficiency of services provided by the project company. The availability payment mechanism places traffic risk firmly on the contracting authority but also provides the contracting authority with the upside if traffic exceeds expectations.

Box 10.3. Lekki Expressway, Lagos, Nigeria

The Lekki Expressway is a greenfield 49.4 kilometer dual carriageway. The contracting authority is the Lagos state government rather than the federal government.

Financial close was achieved at the height of the global financial crisis in November 2008. The overall debt-to-equity ratio was 83:17, and 68 percent of funding was from private sector sources. Substantial currency and political risks were covered by South African banks. In addition, twelve-year loans were obtained from local banks that had little previous experience of such long tenors.

Despite these achievements, the Lagos government was unable to secure the rights of way fully, and this resulted in delays and additional

---

[6] Standard & Poor's (2002).

costs. More critically, the imposition of tolls on a previously untolled but now improved road generated strong protests. Political reluctance to support tolling finally led to the government buy-back of the concession.

Source: Brocklebank, P., Private Sector Involvement in Road Financing, SSATP Working Paper #102.

- *Subsurface risk* – Road projects, in particular tunnels, are vulnerable to subsurface risk, where subsurface conditions encountered differ from those anticipated, requiring changes in construction methodologies and subsequent increases in cost and delays. Often, the contracting authority will bear the risk of unforeseeable subsurface conditions. Another common approach is to establish a baseline for anticipated ground conditions, sharing costs and delays to the extent the baseline proves inaccurate.

Box 10.4. Dakar-Diamniadio Toll Road, Dakar, Senegal

One of the only highways to be procured and implemented successfully through a PPP in sub-Saharan Africa, this greenfield dual carriageway 32 kilometer PPP concession was let through a procurement process that generally followed good international practice.

It achieved a debt/equity ratio of 87:13, which is very high for a PPP concession in sub-Saharan Africa. Debt was provided by IFC, the African Development Bank (AfDB), the West African Development Bank (WADB), and Compagnie Bancaire de l'Afrique Occidentale (CBAO – the largest Senegalese bank, majority-owned by the largest Moroccan bank, and the only private debt finance in the project).

Early access to technical assistance from development partners helped to ensure proper time and resources for preparation, full feasibility studies, and focus on the full spectrum of key project issues. Government/development partner funding was used to address some difficult project issues, such as relocating a dump site and resettling the community that was living on the site.

10.1.2 Railways

In the United States, private railway investment and land development went hand in hand, with private profits focused more on land than on payment for railway construction and operation. In the United Kingdom, the railway network was developed during the nineteenth century by the private sector, in exchange for certain benefits, including land.[7] As the government's interests in such forms of infrastructure increased, it nationalized the railways, only for them to be reprivatized in 1995.

- *Revenues* – Rail services are often unprofitable, particularly passenger services. Recovering operating costs alone can be difficult. Support from government is therefore critical to make rail projects feasible for PPP. In particular, public financing may be required for a large part of the capital costs for new railway lines or high-cost systems with tunnels and bridges. It may help to separate rail from rolling stock. Operators pay track access charges to the owner of the track to run their rolling stock on the network.[8] However, significant challenges have arisen with this model, in particular with Railtrack in the United Kingdom.[9]
- *Other transport systems* – Railway projects need to be linked to other transport services, which may suffer from operation and maintenance failures, inefficient scheduling, or high cost for users. This is why many rail PPPs are for high-speed rail or airport links, with fewer interfaces with the rest of the system.[10]
- *Government support* – Such support may be structured as an availability payment. This was done in the United Kingdom for the Nottingham Express Transit. Or the government may provide demand guarantees. For example, in the Barcelona Metro light rail system, the government assumed 50 percent of the risk of usage where it fell below a certain agreed level.[11] Such guarantees will need to be budgeted by government accordingly
- *Regulation and access* – Given the various safety risks and heightened public perception, rail is a highly regulated industry. Where work is to be done on an existing rail system, access to that rail system will be limited to those times when the track can be cleared (i.e., when it is not in use or to the extent it can be closed down). Construction work will need to take into consideration the specific requirements of existing signaling systems, rolling stock, and other issues associated with the management of services for the railway. Where the existing railway is

---

[7] Elliott, C., *Transportation Infrastructure: Recent Experience and Lessons for the Future*, Project Lending 137 (1992).

[8] Pritchard, *Project Financing the UK Rail Industry* Project Finance International 246 (July 24, 2002), at 29.

[9] www.parliament.uk/briefing-papers/SN01224.pdf.

[10] Dehornoy, J., PPPs in the Rail Sector – a Review of 27 Projects, MPRA Paper (April 2012).

[11] Pritchard, *Project Financing the UK Rail Industry*, at 29.

to be modified, the signaling system design will need to be amended to take into consideration changes in the physical infrastructure.

10.1.3 Airports

Airport projects generally benefit from a diversity of revenue sources (airside and landside – see Box 10.5), a strong monopoly position, and access to foreign currency revenues from international traffic and duty-free shopping.

Box 10.5. Airport Revenues

Nonaeronautical revenues represent a large proportion of total airport revenues. In the United States in 2008, an average airport earned 66 percent of revenues from nonaeronautical activities. The airports in Europe were some of the first to exploit nonaeronautical revenues. Even after the EU removed duty-free advantages for passengers traveling within the EU, the commercial efficiencies found in airports kept the products available in airports competitive with those sold in shops. In 2007, average spending per enplaned passenger was U.S.$13.90 for the United States and Canada, U.S.$14.40 for western Europe, U.S.$27.40 for Asia, and U.S.$39.00 for the United Kingdom/Ireland.[12]

- *Commercial issues* – Obtaining private investment for an airport raises issues associated with whole business management more than in other transport projects (sea ports aside). Where the contracting authority for a road or bridge will look first for an experienced builder of major civil works, the key investor for an airport is often an experienced operator. Since such experienced operators will have interests in other, competing airports, consideration should be given to excluding from any competition investors with interests in airports close enough to the project to create a potential conflict of interest (where traffic might be diverted from one airport to another to improve the investor's returns).
- *Revenues* – Airport projects involve a multiplicity of commercial arrangements. Terminal facilities, fueling facilities, cargo warehouses and handling, catering, parking, hotels, commercial businesses, and a variety of other support services must be provided by the operator or a

---

[12] Airport Cooperative Research Program, *Resource Manual for Airports In-Terminal Concessions* 2016, www.trb.org.

series of different operators. The contracting authority and the share-holders will need to allow the project company sufficient flexibility in order to improve revenue flow and investment in infrastructure on the site and the airport experience of passengers. Airport charges are often based on taxes that can be imposed on the use of airport services or other such fees and charges on airside facilities. By some calculations, 46 percent of airport revenue comes from nonairside sources, specifically landside facility and services.

- *Regulation* – Careful examination and regulation of private sector involvement in an airport are necessary to avoid substandard design and development as well as to achieve appropriate safety levels. Some governments impose an architectural design, at least for key features. For example, for Pulkovo, the airport of the City of Saint Petersburg, Russia wanted a dramatic roof structure reminiscent of the famous bridges over the Neva River. Not wanting to leave this design to the concessionaire, the city commissioned its design in advance, by a famous architectural firm, and required bidders to include it in their proposals.

10.2 Telecommunications and Fiber-Optic Backbone

Another traditional public sector service increasingly offered by the private sector is telecommunications. Increased demand and rapidly changing technology have exceeded the funding and commercial acuity available from the public sector, the monopolistic public utilities that traditionally dominated the sector. Some technologies, in particular mobile telephony, have created completely new markets. Together with power and transportation, telecommunications is one of the primary growth areas in PPP projects in developing countries.

While growth and investment in mobile and fixed telephony have been impressive over the last ten years – in particular in private investment in mobile telephony – the public involvement has been limited primarily to issuing of licenses. One might say that telecoms have outstripped PPP and are now fully private. However, some key activities are still undertaken through PPP models. This section will focus on PPP projects for fiber-optic backbone.

One of the key requirements in the telecommunications sector is the capacity to transmit the maximum amount of data and/or voice traffic to market-quality standards as widely, quickly, and inexpensively as possible. Governments have sought to increase connectivity of their populations to access the associated commercial and educational opportunities and encourage economic growth. India is an excellent example of this, with major investments in fiber-optic connectivity to certain key cities, such as Chennai and Bangalore. The explosive growth in these cities of outsourcing and other commercial activities requiring access to large bandwidth seems to validate the investments arranged by the Indian government. One of the best ways of achieving significant increases in telecommunications connectivity is the installation of fiber-optic cables. Government can let the private sector develop such backbones directly, but by using PPP models government can achieve the following:

- Ensure open access to the backbone infrastructure and therefore reduce the number of competing infrastructure installations (e.g., limiting the number of times the same road is dug up)
- Provide access to public buildings and more remote communities that would not be commercially viable enough to merit connection by a fully private backbone
- Increase competition to help bring down costs, improve access, and increase innovation

A number of fiber-optic backbone systems have been developed using PPP structures. The project company links key demand centers with fiber-optic cables and sells access to various telecommunications operators and Internet service providers (ISPs). Fiber-optic backbone projects raise the following specific issues:

10.2.1 Vendor Finance

This is an additional source of financing provided by suppliers of equipment as an incentive for the project company to procure from them

10.2.2 Technology Upgrades

Telecommunications involves rapid change, with new technology being produced and a need to interconnect, in certain cases, with other providers or with public infrastructure. The contracting authority will need to consider how it will manage upgrades of technology and to what extent it will allow the project company discretion in how it implements such upgrades.

10.2.3 Operation

The project company will need to monitor the operation of the network and move information through the network in the manner most efficient for consumers. This is normally performed automatically by specialist software. The project company will need to be in a position to remedy any defect or replace any faulty equipment as quickly as possible.

10.2.4 Access to Land

For terrestrial fiber-optic cables, property rights must be obtained, trenches must be dug, and ducts installed in order to house the fiber-optic cable and associated equipment. Access to land for installation and maintenance of cable and equipment can involve specific challenges, in particular in countries where telecommunications licenses do not provide specific rights to do so. Submarine cables must be armored and laid properly in order to protect them from ship anchors and other hazards. Landing sites may also be strictly regulated, in particular in relation to shipping movements, environmental risks, and tourism.

Box 10.6. Fiber-Optic PPP

Singapore's Next Generation Nationwide Broadband Network (NBN) is a wired network offering open access, competitively priced broadband through more than twelve different service providers and over forty fiber-based broadband access plans for consumers and enterprise users. The NBN comprises three distinct layers of private parties:

(a) The network company (NetCo) is responsible for the design, build, and operation of the passive infrastructure (such as dark fiber and ducts). It makes use of existing ducts and other underlying infrastructure to minimize disruption to the public.

(b) The operating company (OpCo) offers wholesale network services over the active infrastructure comprising switches and transmission equipment.

(c) The retail service providers (RSP) sell services to end-users and industry, on a competitive basis, covering such markets as Internet access and voice-over-IP telephony.

NetCo must fulfill all reasonable requests to install fiber termination points in homes, offices, and buildings.

NBN has catalyzed a greater range of innovative services for end-users in homes, offices, schools, and other locations and has enabled Singapore to exploit new economic opportunities.

Source: Infocomm Development Authority of Singapore, Next Generation Nationwide Broadband Network (June 2012), www.ida.gov.sg

---

10.3 Power Generation

The power sector is characterized by unique constraints in the delivery of electricity to public, commercial, and residential consumers.[13] Electricity is relatively easy to transmit over long distances but very hard to store, so it must be generated constantly and responsively to instantaneously meet demand in its daily and seasonal variations. Base load generating capacity will address the more consistent demand over time, with peaking capacity available where short-term demand exceeds this level. Midrange generation capacity will provide a combination of these two. Power generation is often fuel intensive, requiring careful management of fuel supply and transport, with the associated environmental and commodity pricing risks.

The ease of transmission makes it possible to create competitive markets, at least around generation and the customer-facing retail market. Competition in transmission and distribution can be more difficult given the practical and price implications of duplicated transmission networks. However, common carriage arrangements are feasible and increasingly successfully implemented.

PPP for retail delivery of electricity to industrial and domestic consumers faces many of the same challenges as water and sanitation, with a similar need to improve efficiency and profitability in order to fund capital replacement and extension. Further, electricity tariffs are often used (officially or unofficially) to subsidize certain sectors of society, for example, agriculture. For consideration of issues associated with the PPP retail delivery of electricity, please refer to similar issues addressed in section 10.4 on water and sanitation distribution.

Power generation has been one of the greatest beneficiaries of private investment through PPP and project financing structures. Generation facilities usually involve the construction of completely new, independent assets over which security can be provided to the lenders and whose revenue stream is easily identifiable. For this reason, generation facilities have widely benefited from private financing.

The offtake purchaser in a power generation project, and often other PPP power projects such as transmission, is called a power purchaser and will enter into a power purchase agreement (PPA). The power purchaser is generally the local power utility. The project company is also known as an independent power producer (IPP). The following are issues specific to IPPs.

---

[13] For a good general review of the power sector, in particular its regulation, see Hunt, S., *Making Competition Work in Electricity* (2002).

10.3.1 Credit Risk

The project company will need to consider the commercial viability of the power purchaser, in particular whether revenues are sufficient and whether they will keep track of increases in cost, such as fuel. Electricity tariffs are often carefully controlled to protect consumers. Investors will need to understand who has the right to charge tariffs, who owns the tariffs collected, and the basis on which tariffs are set (will they cover costs?) and how tariffs collected can be used (can investors use the money to repay debt and pay dividends?). Investors will also want to know how hard it is to collect; for example, can customers be cut off if they do not pay?

10.3.2 Associated Infrastructure

The ability to test and operate power generation and transmission systems is generally dependent on the reliability of associated electricity infrastructure. For example, the power purchaser may be responsible for providing transmission facilities to connect the project to the electricity grid from the site substation. The project company will want to assess the condition of the grid, including load balance in the area (ensuring that generation in different parts of the electricity grid is appropriately balanced), likelihood of grid failure, and risk allocation to protect the revenue stream from any likely defect in the grid and in the power purchaser's ability to offtake electricity.

10.3.3 Merchant Plants

The project company may be able to manage offtake risk where it is able to sell the energy that it generates into a competitive electricity distribution market rather than against a long-term offtake purchase agreement that will guarantee a revenue stream; therefore, a merchant power plant will have no PPA.

10.3.4 Tolling Arrangements

Under a tolling arrangement, the power purchaser delivers fuel to the project company and pays the project company for turning that fuel into electricity. The tolling arrangement therefore treats the generation project as if it were a process plant: the sponsor of the generation project provides the fuel and buys the electricity generated – in effect, it pays for the processing of fuel into electricity, assuming a certain level of efficiency. The project company earns extra profits if it exceeds the assumed level of efficiency.

10.3.5 Other Offtake

Power projects may generate other offtake. The project company may therefore want to enter into additional offtake agreements in order to allocate the market risk for the sale of the secondary offtake. For example, a hydroelectric project may also provide a reservoir for raw water that can be used for irrigation or treated and used as potable water. Many water-poor coastal countries use desalination to make up for their water deficit. Some desalination technologies use large amounts of electricity, so combined power generation and desalination plants, also known as independent water and power producers (IWPP), are popular mixed offtake plants. A combined heat and power (CHP) plant provides for the sale of the heat generated while producing power, and co-generation plants allows the purchase of steam bled from the steam turbine during certain hours of operation.[14]

10.3.6 Fuel Supply

IPPs can involve a number of different fuel sources. Classic thermal fuels such as coal and gas require specific arrangements for fuel transport and storage and long-term access to fuel supplies. Power generators can use certain technology to reduce greenhouse gas emissions, for example, pressurized, fluidized bed combustion; integrated gasification combined cycle generation; and carbon capture and storage for coal-fired power plants.[15] Other fuels, such as nuclear energy, require specific management, while hydro, wind, geothermal, and solar require careful forecasts of resource availability and risk allocation. The government may also provide incentives to the project company or the contracting authority to encourage the use of renewable energy or lower emissions, such as the following:

- Tax or license fees set against clean energy targets
- Higher feed-in tariffs for clean energy generators
- Access to concessional financing
- Tradable certificates associated with the carbon neutrality of certain activities, such as carbon credits

The project company will need to be able to rely on any government incentives over the long term, as political appetite tends to change over time.

---

[14] Vinter, Legal issues involved in co-generation projects, in Hornbrook, ed., *Project Finance Yearbook 1995/96* (1996), at 15, 32.

[15] Enkrist, P-A., T. Naucler, & J. Rosander, A cost curve for greenhouse gas reduction, *McKinsey Quarterly* 1 (2007).

10.4 Retail Distribution of Water and Sanitation Services

Water distribution is characterized by the high cost of transporting water, relative ease of storage, and significant social and political sensitivity. The high cost of transportation makes the creation of a competitive market for water and sanitation services particularly challenging. This heavily regulated sector is also one of the oldest, with key water and sanitation assets often old and buried, making it difficult to know their condition and to forecast investment needed in such assets without time-consuming and costly investigations.

Water and sanitation are public services, with specific impact on the environment and quality of life, and pricing has political, health, and environmental implications. Service distribution is therefore generally heavily regulated. This, combined with government efforts to keep service prices down, can have disastrous consequences for the sector. PPP has a long and complex relationship with water and sanitation.[16] While the greatest benefits can be obtained from PPP in water distribution and sanitation collection,[17] these are also the most difficult areas to achieve a satisfactory commercial and financial structure.[18] Unlike treatment, distribution is often a more challenging fit with the PPP model given the need to identify and allocate a more complex and extensive series of risks.[19] While this section will address issues specific to the retail delivery of water and sanitation services, very similar issues will need to be addressed when considering the retail distribution of electricity. Similarly, for those interested in the issues specific to water and sanitation treatment through PPP, reference should be made to the discussion of power generation PPP in section 10.3.

Global consumption of water doubles every twenty years, at twice the rate of human population growth.[20] The opportunities for private sector investment in the water and sanitation sector are vast.[21] Some of the commercial fundamentals of water projects create particular challenges for PPP:

- The low marginal cost of service delivery (since the pricing of raw water rarely if ever includes its environmental externalities) means

---

[16] Marin, *Public–Private Partnerships for Urban Water Utilities*; World Bank, *Public Private Partnerships for Urban Water Utilities: A Review of Experiences in Developing Countries.*

[17] Andres et al., *The Impact of Private Sector Participation in Infrastructure*; Gassner et al., *Empirical Assessment.*

[18] Delmon, J., *Water Projects: A Commercial and Contractual Guide* (2000).

[19] Gassner et al., *Empirical Assessment.*

[20] Barlow, M., *The Global Water Crisis and the Commodification of the World's Water Supply* (1999).

[21] Crocker, K., & S. Masten, *Prospects for Private Water Provision in Developing Countries: Lessons from 19th Century America* (2000).

that metering and other mechanisms to improve efficiency may not make commercial sense for the project company without appropriate incentive schemes being set in the contract.

- The public health externalities of water services mean that the contracting authority is likely to put a premium on new connections, in particular to low-income consumers, even where the potential increased revenues from connecting such new consumers do not necessarily justify commercially the cost of connection. The relatively high cost of connection may not be affordable to most unconnected households. This will necessitate incentives, not needed in other sectors, for new connections. Pricing can often be structured to accommodation for some cross-subsidies between higher- and lower-income consumers (but these too are subject to political and regulatory factors).
- Social risk[22] takes on a particular prevalence for water services, where local communities are particularly sensitive to access to water services and tariffs charged.
- The project company can use its position as guardian of an essential public service to press for renegotiation of the concession agreement and better commercial terms. The contracting authority will be sensitive to its vulnerable position and the potential political backlash if the project company abuses its position, and is therefore more likely to act precipitously, or positionally, than would be true in other sectors.[23]
- Many public services, such as water utilities, tend to be natural monopolies. The transportation of water is generally too expensive and the infrastructure too difficult and costly to duplicate to permit much competition between suppliers. While electricity is more easily divided among generation, transmission and distribution, and retailing, these sophisticated competitive markets are difficult to achieve and manage in the water sector.

The water sector, as compared to other sectors, tends to look to private sector investors to provide services directly to consumers, to improve aspects of the water or sanitation system that may not have a fixed or definable scope of work and to take the risk of the condition of existing assets, which are often located underground, by doing the following:

- Implementing modern management approaches and latest technology

---

[22] For further discussion of social risk, see section 7.9.
[23] Crocker & Masten, *Prospects for Private Water Provision in Developing Countries.*

- Improving distribution capacity, reducing leakages, and providing long-term maintenance to ensure that the condition of the distribution system is consistently monitored and improved

10.4.1 Revenues

The payment obligation in retail distribution PPP will vary depending on the quality of service delivered. Poor service delivery may result in penalties charged against the project company or a reduction in the levels of tariffs it can charge. Where raw water is obtained by the project company from the aquifer under an abstraction license, the project company will be concerned about quality risk on the water extracted. The extent to which the project company is sensitive to this risk will depend in part on the level of treatment provided by the relevant facility. For example, where tertiary treatment, or even reverse osmosis, is involved, the project company will be able to bear more raw water quality risk.

10.4.2 Leakage

Loss reduction is commonly one of the key performance indicators for retail PPP. The project company can be rewarded for the amount of, for example, water or energy saved by reducing leakage, which affords the public utility higher revenues as it has more water to sell and defers the cost of new treatment capacity. Caution should be used in the creation of incentives to reduce leakage. In one contract, the project company was paid a fee per leak eliminated. Of course, it is easier to eliminate small leaks, especially at meters and household connections, but these leaks have a limited impact on the system capacity. The project company was well paid, but the utility received less than anticipated aggregate benefit. Design the system under the assumption that the private sector will do what they are paid to do, not more. Then you can be pleasantly surprised when they do more.

10.4.3 Low-Income Consumers

The provision of services to low-income neighborhoods often encounters a variety of particular challenges, including the following:[24]

- Low-income households are often located in informal settlements or may be forcibly relocated once utility services are provided to the

---

[24] See also International Institution for Environment and Development, briefing papers series on urban environmental improvement and poverty reduction: Briefing paper 10 Public/private partnerships and environmental services for the urban poor.

neighborhood and housing prices increase. Government support directly to such residents might be interpreted as formalizing tenancy rights.

- Such households are often difficult to access due to narrow roads, steep slopes, or other obstacles that make those areas less attractive to wealthier residents, but more expensive for installing and maintaining the system.

- Low-income households are often not connected, but the capital cost for connecting mains and new residences is extremely high, and low-income households generally do not have funds nor access to finance to pay for connection.

- Low-income households earn money a little at a time, so large periodic bills or advance payments may not be feasible.

- Such households rely on small, periodic delivery of services, while wealthier households will have water storage facilities. Low-income households will be more vulnerable to service interruptions, in particular where the water vendors have been replaced by the new utility-based service provision.

- Residents of low-income households may not have access to bank accounts or other formal methods of payment, though increasing access to mobile phone payment systems help.

- Low-income households are often unaccustomed to government or industry dealing fairly or generously with them, resulting in commercial offers of provision of services being met with some suspicion.

- Such households may prefer a less expensive lower standard of service (e.g., smaller pipe diameter). This may not be consistent with the large institutional investor who does not make sufficient margins on low-tech informal arrangements and does not want to be seen to compromise its professional standards by building such systems; also, such service may not be consistent with regulatory service standards.

- Low-income households often share services; for example, multiple households may share a single tap. This makes new connections very difficult for the project company, since there is no individual who will take the risk for services. Further, some subsidy or cross-subsidy arrangements are based on volumes and numbers of consumers served, which is inconsistent with the tendency of low-income households to purchase services communally. Under rising block tariffs, for example, communal yard taps might be charged a higher unitary charge than richer households.[25]

10.4.4 Billing and Collection

The private sector often has superior billing and collection systems and methodologies than most public entities and can thereby improve revenues significantly. The project company will need to have the right to collect tariffs directly from consumers and to impose sanctions on consumers for failure to pay tariffs. For example, in certain legal systems it may be unlawful or impossible to cut off the services supplied to certain public establishments, such as schools and hospitals, or to an individual household in which a registered dialysis patient resides.

10.4.5 Metering and Measurement

The contracting authority may require metering improvement to help monitor performance requirements, for example, standards for unaccounted-for water and efficiency of treatment of raw water. An alternative would be for a separate authority to provide measurement services as a method of regulating and monitoring the project company. However, where the condition of the system is poor, the installation of meters may only make things worse, since for each meter two new connections to the existing assets must be made, multiplying the potential for leaks and further damaging assets.

10.4.6 Scope of Works

A service utility is likely a going concern, with many of the investments that will need to be made over time difficult to ascertain for bidders and financiers until they have been in control of the services for some time. The transfer of an existing business generally requires extensive due diligence by the project company to ascertain the extent of the risks inherent in such an existing business. Project assets may not be identified and categorized before the project company takes over control. The condition of those assets and need for replacement or refurbishment may not be clear until well after the project company takes control. The condition of existing assets represents a serious risk for the project company. The project company will be bound to general obligations to improve the quality of water delivered,

---

[25] Rising block tariffs are designed to charge higher rates to large volume users, but where poor consumers collectively use high volumes, this mechanism may penalize them.

reduce the level of leakage, and improve the quality of service rendered to consumers. This may necessitate rolling programs for capital investment against an investment program or budget based on the amount of income available to the project company or as required to satisfy the performance criteria placed on the project company.

10.4.7 Tariff Levels

Water tariffs are a useful political tool for governments and special interest groups alike. The needs of the water utility and the sector are often lost in the pursuit of such political interests. Where tariffs are kept low, the water utilities' financial viability may be supported by government subsidies (rarely defined in a sensible or transparent manner and therefore difficult for the utility or any external lender or investor to rely on) or through cross-subsidies from higher tariffs imposed on certain consumers.[26] Historically, water tariffs may have been used to subsidize certain elements of society, specific industries, or public sector entities. More often, public water companies are subsidized, and tariffs are not charged, charged at very low rates, or not collected. Private sector involvement may necessitate formal arrangements with the project company for government subsidies or financing, particularly where the government is not willing to put tariffs up to profitable levels or where substantial investment in capital works is needed or desired. Though challenging, this can be a healthy transition for the utility, formalizing the subsidy for the water sector and rendering transparent the burden on the public purse represented by artificially low tariffs.

10.4.8 Regulation

In order to protect consumers and ensure that the project is operated to a standard consistent with modern industry practice, the contracting authority will want to establish a progressive and reasonable regulatory structure (including economic and technical regulation). This structure should give the regulator sufficient latitude to supervise the activities of the project company without unreasonably restricting competitiveness or the ability of the project company to operate and finance its activities within the context of the market. Creating a regulatory structure can involve a substantial investment of resources by the contracting authority or the government. It also creates risk for the project company, where the regulator can impose obligations and standards different from the PPP agreement.

---

[26] Such support mechanisms are discussed further in section 3.3.

10.5 Health and Education

PPP provides a useful platform for delivery of social services, such as education and health. However, given the nature of these sectors, they involve important differences in design, stakeholder engagement, and approach as compared with other sectors. PPP in health and education spans models focused on infrastructure similar to other sectors (construction, financing, and operation), but also include models focused more on service provision, program support, and sector reform. Investors and service providers in health and education can include a larger variety of entities than other sectors, for example, community groups, nongovernmental organizations (NGOs), faith-based organizations, charities, corporate social responsibility entities, trade unions, private companies, small-scale informal providers, and individual practitioners.

10.5.1 Education

A number of different approaches and creative commercial engagements have been developed to support the education sector through PPP. For example, these approaches might be organized into the following:

- Infrastructure delivery
- Management services
- Service delivery

Infrastructure Delivery
A private operator is granted a franchise (concession) to finance, build, and operate an educational facility such as a public school, university building, or hostel. While arrangements can differ widely, infrastructure PPPs have a number of characteristics in common:

- The private sector partners invest in school infrastructure and provide related non-core services (e.g., building maintenance).
- The government retains responsibility for the delivery of core services such as teaching.
- Payments under the contract are contingent upon the private operator delivering services to an agreed performance standard.[27]

From an education perspective, infrastructure PPPs help governments to provide appropriate school buildings and to relieve teaching staff and

[27] LaRocque, N., *PPPs in Basic Education* (2008).

school administrators of maintenance duties that are outside of the primary scope of their work, allowing them to concentrate on meeting the learning needs of students.[28]

However, interface risks between school administration and facilities administration can be difficult to manage. A blame culture can arise, where coordination between the teachers and the project company is not achieved.

Management Services

Under this subcategory, private organizations manage either a single public school or entire school districts. The responsibilities that the contractor assumes under these contracts usually fall into three categories: financial management, staff management, and long-term planning. Within these contracts, schools, although privately managed, remain publicly owned and all nonmanagerial personnel continue to be public sector employees.

According to the World Bank, PPPs in the area of management services can work, but these services are inherently more difficult to contract out than some other services. Specifying and monitoring the performance of managers, as distinct from the organization overall, is difficult, and because many factors contribute to school performance besides the quality of management, it would be inappropriate to attribute changes in school performance simply to performance under the management contract.[29]

Service Delivery

The private sector may be contracted to deliver services to public students from the private party's facilities. A government agency, such as the Ministry of Education, purchases education services, for example, places for students in private schools. Payments should be demand driven; for example, a private school might be compensated for each non-fee-paying student it enrolls. The government may have different objectives for these arrangements, for example, improving quality and/or increasing educational access either generally or for specific groups.

A school voucher is a certificate or entitlement that parents can use to pay for the education of their children at a public or private school of their choice, rather than the public school that is closest to them or to which they have been assigned. Vouchers are issued by a public entity to parents or to schools directly on parents' behalf. Some programs may allow schools to charge fees on top of the value of the voucher, while others may not.[30]

---

[28] World Bank, *Understanding PPPs in Education* (2011).
[29] World Bank, *Understanding PPPs in Education.*
[30] LaRocque, *PPPs in Basic Education.*

Box 10.7. Secondary School Voucher Program in Colombia

Programa de Ampliación de Cobertura en Educación Secundaria (PACES) was launched in 1991 in order to provide access to secondary education for the poorest third of the population of Colombia by using vouchers to pay for attendance in private schools. The program, which ran until 1997, covered 125,000 children in 216 municipalities.

Due to oversubscription in the program, there were more applicants than vouchers, which were then awarded by lottery. This created a natural, randomized experiment that led to an impact evaluation of the program. Voucher beneficiaries had higher educational attainment: they were 10 percentage points more likely to finish the eighth grade three years after they won the vouchers. They were also 5 to 6 percentage points less likely to repeat a grade, scored 0.2 standard deviations higher on achievement tests than nonvoucher students, and were 20 percent more likely to take the college entrance exam than students who had not won a voucher in the lottery. In a study of PACES's longer-term effects, it was found that the program improved scores for both average students and those over the 90th percentile.

Source: World Bank (2006).

According to the World Bank,[31] voucher systems can enhance accountability as follows:

- Schools may be subject to competitive pressures when parents and students are able to choose from among public and private schools.
- School operators may be selected through competitive processes that give schools an incentive to improve their services.
- There is an improvement of engagement with preexisting school governance and oversight arrangements, such as school boards, boards of trustees, and parent committees.

Schools must meet certain criteria to enter the program; for example, they must be registered or meet other minimum standards relating to teachers and infrastructure.[32] By paying for students to enroll in existing schools, governments can quickly expand access without incurring any upfront expenditure on constructing and equipping new schools.

---

[31] World Bank (2006).
[32] LaRocque, *PPPs in Basic Education*.

Governments may also contract out students' enrollment in specialized services that are not available in the public sector. This type of contract can be targeted to specific students and groups, such as low-income, disadvantaged, disabled, or "problem" students.[33]

Box 10.8. Residency Programs and Continuing Medical Education in Eritrea

In 2004, there were only 215 physicians in Eritrea, or 4.5 physicians per 100,000 people. Eritrea had five formally trained general surgeons, three otolaryngologists, and two orthopedists, all of whom had obtained their higher degrees from medical schools in Ethiopia or Europe. The PPP – which ran from 2008 until 2012 – in Asmara, Eritrea, was developed to train native Eritrean surgeons and postgraduate residencies in different fields of medicine, including surgery for Eritrea. The PPP thus also addressed the lack of access to advanced medical education, which also contributed to brain drain. This partnership was based on humanitarian contributions. The George Washington University Medical Center provided academic support and administration, Physicians for Peace (a private NGO) provided financial support, and the Eritrean Ministry of Health provided in-country coordination.

Patient length of stay has decreased by 15 percent by emphasizing evidence-based care, and resource usage such as antibiotic use has decreased by 42 percent. The establishment of regular ward rounds that included examination of supply orders led to decreased use. These practices led to improved recovery times and faster discharges. The residency program improved practice standards, which improved postoperative care, decreased complications, and expedited discharges. A concomitant pediatric residency program was initiated with in-house residents on call, resulting in improvements in the consultation process, especially between surgery and pediatrics departments. The partnership continues to expand an obstetrics-genecology residency program launched on July 1, 2009, with plans for residencies in anesthesia and internal medicine.

Source: Marzolf, S., B. Zekarias, K. Tedla, D. E. Woldeyesus, D. Sereke, A. Yohannes, K. Asrat, & M. R. Weaver, Continuing Professional Education in Eritrea Taught by Local Obstetrics and Gynaecology Residents: Effects on work Environment and patient outcomes (July 2016).

---

[33] World Bank, *Understanding PPPs in Education.*

Educational Philanthropy

Support for education from private philanthropy is significant in developed and developing countries and includes the provision of infrastructure facilities, teacher training, information and communications technology integration, curriculum support, health and social services, policy advocacy, financing of scholarships/vouchers, and healthy meals. PPP arrangements can be used to make such educational philanthropic support more sustainable and better coordinated with government activities. Examples abound globally:[34]

- In the United States, where there is a strong tradition of private philanthropy, examples include the Bill and Melinda Gates Foundation, which has invested more than $1.5 billion in the creation of high-quality, high-performing schools and systems and the Broad Education Foundation.
- Aga Khan Education Services (AKES), one of the most well-established private initiatives, serving the education sector, currently operates more than three hundred schools and advanced educational programs in Pakistan, India, Bangladesh, Kenya, the Kyrgyz Republic, Uganda, Tanzania, and Tajikistan.
- In India, the Bharti Foundation supports nonprofit, private schools in the nation's poor rural areas.
- In the Philippines, foundations support schools, through the country's Adopt-a-School program and various other initiatives, coordinated by an umbrella group – the League of Corporate Foundations – which has developed a roadmap of corporate giving to the education sector.
- In Singapore, Orient Global, a private investment institution, in 2007 launched a $100 million education fund that invests in private education opportunities in developing countries, including a low-cost chain of schools.
- The U.K.'s Academies program supports publicly funded independent schools that provide free education to students of all abilities. Academies are established by sponsors from business, faith, or voluntary groups through partnerships with central government and local education partners.

10.5.2 Health

PPPs in the health sector have achieved important advantages, including more timely completion, delivery to cost, technological innovation, and

---

[34] LaRocque, *PPPs in Basic Education.*

service improvement, but some important challenges have arisen, including the following:

- The slow pace of policy change in the health sector
- Labor resistance
- The need for better monitoring and contract management
- Rapid technological change and the need to introduce flexibility into the contract to accommodate change[35]

Box 10.9. Italy Healthcare PPP

Since 1999, Italy has developed PPPs worth approximately 6 billion euros and a ranking of third in worldwide PPP health care by capital investment in 2011, just behind Canada and the United Kingdom.

To date, projects for nearly fifty major hospitals or elderly care facilities have been successfully awarded or are currently at procurement stage, including thirty hospitals of six hundred beds or more totaling 3.5 billion euros of investment. PPP in health care provision achieved the following:

- *Greater involvement of private risk capital* – 60 percent of private capital expenditure on average
- *On time, on budget project delivery* – compared to traditional procurement
- *Reduction of claims and disputes* – during construction
- *Enhanced design and construction solutions* – workable, cost-effective, cutting-edge innovative solutions
- *Profit-sharing clauses* – some cases of compensation paid back to contracting authorities

Source: UNECE, *Case Study: PPP in Italian Health Sector* (2012).

Health PPPs can be divided in two broad categories:

- Facility-based PPPs
- PPP health programs.[36]

---

[35] A major issue in hospital PPPs is the need to constantly update medical equipment to reflect advances.

[36] UNECE, WHO, & ADB, Discussion Paper: A Preliminary Reflection on the Best Practice in PPP in Healthcare Sector: A Review of Different PPP Case Studies and Experiences, for the conference PPPs in health Manila (2012).

10.5.3 Facility-Based PPPs

These PPPs resemble the models used in other sectors, such as roads or power, with a focus on infrastructure developments and management, based generally but not exclusively on long-term contracts and project finance.

The United Kingdom had vastly underinvested in its National Health Service (NHS) hospitals, many of which were built in the Victorian era (during the late 1800s). Beginning in the 1990s, through the Private Finance Initiative (PFI), the United Kingdom built approximately one hundred new NHS hospital buildings in twelve years.

Box 10.10. Canadian Health PPP

Since 2003, more than fifty hospital PPPs valued at over CAD18 billion have been developed in Canada.[37] Generally, the impact has been positive, with the following benefits:

- *Value for money*: PPPs are estimated to have saved hundreds of millions of dollars in costs to the taxpayer, integrating construction and maintenance and transferring risks.
- *On time, on budget delivery.*
- *Innovation*: Better, more efficient solutions have led to more efficient use of space and better environment for patients, visitors, and staff

However, health PPPs also have encountered problems with the following:

- Communications with and misperceptions of the public
- Opposition by trade unions, including the Canadian Union of Public Employees
- Complexity of transactions

Source: www.p3canada.ca.

Facility-based PPP can be divided into three subcategories:

(i) *Infrastructure PPPs* see the private sector deliver infrastructure and non-core services, such as cleaning, catering, security, parking, and so on, but not clinical services. This model has been deployed in, for example, the United Kingdom, Australia, Italy, and Canada.

(ii) *Integrated PPPs*, where the private sector delivers all hospital services, including supply of infrastructure and clinical services. This

---

[37] Ibid.

model has been adopted in, for example, Australia, Spain, Portugal, and Lesotho.

(iii) *Service PPPs* provide for private delivery of services in a public facility, where performance risk is transferred to the private sector, for example, for private management of a public medical facility.

Box 10.11. Turkey Health PPP

The government has launched an ambitious PPP scheme for the health care sector, including tenders for fifteen integrated hospital projects throughout Turkey. These fifteen projects represent more than 25,000 beds and total capital investment costs of more than $5 billion. Under the Turkish scheme, supported by the Healthcare Regulations (2006), investors will finance, construct (or renovate, as the case may be), furnish, supply, operate, and maintain the hospitals. The Ministry of Health remains responsible for providing medical services, but the project company provides support services, including imaging, laboratory, sterilization, and rehabilitation, and other support services would include building maintenance, cleaning, utilities management, information management, grounds maintenance, reception, car park, waste management, laundry, and catering.

Source: www.worldfinance.com/infrastructure-investment/project-finance/
transforming-turkeys-health.

Box 10.12. Service PPP

The National Kidney and Transplant Institute (NKTI) in the Philippines is a tertiary medical specialty center that focuses on the treatment of renal diseases. In 2003, after a competitive procurement process, NKTI entered into a Hemodialysis Center PPP to furnish the hospital with state-of-the-art machines for patients suffering from end-stage renal diseases.[38]

The first five-year contract was renewed in 2009. The center is serving more than 120 outpatients a day, with 47 machines in operation. There has been no price increase to patients, with cost per treatment considered affordable and minimal. NKTI was able to acquire the latest available technology in dialysis treatment and expand its services to more patients at the same cost of treatment and at less risk to the government.

---

[38] Ibid.

10.5.4 PPP Health Programs

This second category of health PPP projects involves health programs. Examples include the following:

- New products against diseases
- Access to commodities, such as medicine, vaccines, and diagnostics through technology transfer, local production, and distribution
- Public advocacy and increasing awareness
- Regulation and quality assurance systems, for example, to fight against circulation of substandard and counterfeit products
- Training and education

Examples of health program PPPs include the following:

- *Dialysis centers.* Traditionally, governments have purchased equipment and supplies from major manufacturers, but there has been a shift to governments buying complete services. This transfers the risks and responsibility to the private sector (which is best able to manage the risks). The major dialysis companies have also shifted to become complete service providers.
- *Outsourcing of clinical support services in hospitals,* including laboratory and inpatient imaging services within hospitals. Often hospitals lack such equipment because it is too expensive. The private operator would assume responsibility for initial capital financing of equipment and maintenance/repairs, and would be paid only if the equipment was working properly, creating an incentive for keeping everything functioning properly.

Box 10.13. Dialysis Centers, Andhra Pradesh, India

The government of Andhra Pradesh provides basic medical treatment to patients living below the poverty line (BPL) through the Arogyasri health insurance scheme (at no cost to the patients). A significant number of BPL patients needed dialysis services, and many state-run hospitals had limited or no capacity to perform dialysis. To address this issue, a private partner was selected in 2010 to establish and operate dialysis centers in eleven tertiary care state-run hospitals for a period of seven years. In return, the government of Andhra Pradesh pays the private operator a set price (about U.S.$23) for each performed dialysis. The dialysis is provided free of cost to the patients, who are covered under the Arogyasri insurance Scheme. Under the project, the government

---

hospitals provide space, uninterrupted power supply, water supply, and clinical nephrologists. Eleven hemodialysis centers have been established, with 111 hemodialysis machines in medical colleges and hospitals across the state.[39]

10.6 Small-Scale PPP

One of the most exciting and innovative spaces for PPP is small-scale PPP.[40] Close to those who need services most, responding to local demand and need, these projects, due to their size, also offer opportunities for local investors and financiers that may not be available from larger projects.

The PPI database shows that in 2013, approximately 40 percent of projects globally were of a value less than U.S. $50 million, and approximately 25 percent of projects less than U.S. $25 million, even though the PPI database is specifically focused on sectors more accustomed to larger projects. About 40 percent of projects on the U.K. PFI database are below GBP 30 million and 20 percent below GBP 15 million. Thirty percent of all projects on the Australia PPP database[41] have a value of AUD 50 million or lower in total project cost.

Many of these small-scale PPP projects are developed by local government contracting authorities, such as municipalities. Local government PPP projects may be small or large in size. This section will focus on small PPP but will note many similar challenges faced by local government projects, in particular the following:

- Scale
- Lack of capacity
- Credit position

10.6.1 Scale

Sometimes size matters. Small projects are relatively:

- Expensive to prepare, despite their size, because small PPP projects require disproportionate levels of due diligence and specialist support for the contracting authority and for investors compared to larger projects.
- Less attractive to experienced investors. In particular, investors coming from other countries generally prefer larger projects to absorb risk and bid costs.

---

[39] Ibid.
[40] World Bank, *A Preliminary Review of Trends in Small Scale Public Private Partnership Projects* (2014).
[41] All PPPs are by subnational entities.

- More difficult to get approved, where approval processes are designed for larger projects and where approval power lies at levels of government that may not be familiar with or interested in small projects.

Box 10.14. Approval Process

HM Treasury carried out an assessment of small capital value projects under GBP20 million in 2003, using a sample of thirty-five projects. While the performance of the small projects was found to be as good and in many cases better than large projects, average procurement time was around 2 to 2.5 years, which was similar to that of large projects. Also, small projects had transaction and bid costs that were similar to those of large projects for bidders as well as the authority due to the use of the same complicated legal and technical documentation and due diligence as required for large projects.[42] This relative complexity of approval processes makes small PPP more difficult to deliver and more expensive.

10.6.2 Lack of Capacity

Staff allocated to develop small-scale PPP projects, in particular from local governments, may have fewer technical qualifications, less exposure to commercial activities, and generally less capacity than large projects at the central government level. This is a reasonable allocation of resources given the size of the projects and their likely priority for the government.

Small PPPs may be financed most efficiently in local currency. Local bankers and financiers are unlikely to be familiar with PPP and may need help to understand PPP projects, their dynamics, the opportunities they provide, and how to address the challenges they raise.

10.6.3 Credit Position

Small projects, and those implementing them, may suffer from a weaker credit position than would a national agency. Where the revenue stream or important guarantees are to be sourced from the contracting authority, such a weak credit position can undermine bankability and increase cost of money due to a higher risk premium.

A growing practice in small PPPs has led to the development of mechanisms to mitigate some of these challenges.

---

[42] HM Treasury, *PFI: Meeting the Investment Challenge* (2003).

Box 10.15. Sheberghan City Bus Terminal, Afghanistan

Prior to the project, passengers had to wait for buses on the main road, sometimes for hours, without access to public latrines or other facilities. They also suffered from lack of organized parking for drop-offs and pick-ups, causing traffic jams and frequent road accidents.

The municipality built the bus terminal and made land available. The private investor operates and manages the bus terminal and built sixteen municipally owned shops at no cost to the municipality. In return, the private investor leases the shops from the municipality at no charge for a period of five years, during which it will be able to recover its initial investment in the project, as well as a reasonable return. After the initial five-year period, the private investor will begin making lease payments to the municipality, further contributing to the sustainability of the facility.

Source: United States Agency for International Development (USAID): www.usaid.gov.

10.6.4 Small PPP Processes

Approval processes in a PPP program are generally designed for large, national PPP projects, which represent significant liabilities for the government. Small PPP projects may merit a simplified approval process, sufficient to ensure quality and compliance, without the complexity and high-level participation of large-scale processes. Simplification may include the following:

- Fewer approvals and/or approvals at a more familiar (and more accessible) level of bureaucracy
- Some or all approvals from lower levels of government, possibly the central government authority responsible for local government or the relevant municipal council
- Less documentation (e.g., less extensive studies, reports, and consultations, or fewer of them)
- Fewer publication requirements (e.g., only local press)
- Fewer procedural steps (e.g., no prequalification required).

Box 10.16. How Small Is Small

In South Africa, all approval processes are undertaken at the municipal level for projects with an estimated capital value of up to R10 million (less than U.S.$1 million), while the normal PPP processes apply to projects greater than R10 million. Since these guidelines were adopted in 2005, the cap has been found to be too low.

Consideration should be given to the fiscal liabilities created by a project. Even where a PPP is small in project value, it may create significant fiscal liabilities, in which case the more comprehensive approval process should be used. The Tanzania mainland, Zanzibar, and Kenya are exploring formulations to identify levels of fiscal liabilities sufficiently low to justify simplified approval processes. This is not an easy formulation. Any project creates some form of liability, and quantifying those liabilities (actual and contingent) in an objective, consistent manner is difficult. Another approach is to limit the types of government support that a small PPP might receive. For example, a small PPP might be one that does not receive one of the following:

- An indemnity or guarantee from the public sector for lost revenues, lost profit, loan repayment (other than as a basis for calculating termination compensation), or other indirect damages
- Any grant, loan, investment, or other direct financial support from the public sector (possibly above a specified cap)

10.6.5 Centralized Support

A team of PPP specialists can be formed centrally, with a mandate to provide advice and support to small PPP. This team may be part of the central PPP unit or may be a separate unit.

The government may wish to provide extrabudgetary funding for expert support, feasibility studies, and transaction advisers for small PPP (see the

---

Box 10.17. Bus Terminal and Commercial Complex in Dehradun, India

Located 236 kilometers from New Delhi, Dehradun is the capital city of the newly formed state of Uttarakhand and a popular tourist and educational hub in northern India. The private sector was asked to design, finance, build, operate, maintain, and transfer a bus terminal and commercial entertainment complex, with a concession period of twenty years. Revenue to the concessionaire is from usage fees charged to the scheduled 750 buses per day, lease rental from the commercial-entertainment complex, and fees from other value-added services. No expense was borne by the city for the development of the facility.

Source: United Nations Development Programme, *UNDP Training Module: Financing, Fare Fixation, & Cost Benefit Analyses.*

discussion of project development funds in sections 2.8 and 3.3). It may be worth developing a fund specific to small PPP, rather than simply using the national project development fund, to ensure sufficient focus and support for small projects.

10.6.6 Standard Documents and Processes

Small projects must be made simpler to understand, implement, and manage for contracting authorities and investors alike. Standard documents can make the project easier and cheaper to develop, easier for investors and lenders to understand, and in the end easier to fund.

The risk premium for such projects will reduce over time as investors get comfortable with the model, as the model is tested and becomes familiar in the market. This can also facilitate refinancing, since project risk allocation in different projects will be similar and therefore easier to compare and analyze.

Standard documentation can facilitate the approval process, since the approving authority will find it easier to approve documents based on the model and will have fewer open issues to assess.

10.6.7 Pooling of Advisory Mandate

Under a large PPP, a consortium of consultants provides transaction advice for a single project. The size of the project and complexity often demands one consortium to ensure focus and sufficiency of staffing.

Box 10.18. Bundling Bridges

The Pennsylvania Department of Transportation aggregated the construction and maintenance of a few hundred small bridges into a single PPP project under its old bridges rehabilitation program. The average cost of the individual bridges is as low as approximately U.S.$2 million, which would not make for a viable single PPPP project. Multiple jurisdictions were not involved. By bundling, the department achieved economies of scale on due diligence, project preparation, and tendering processes, saving money. The final project was large enough to attract serious investors and significant competition, which would probably not have been achieved with multiple small projects.

Small projects may be pooled, where one consortium of consultants develops feasibility studies and/or provides transaction advice for more than one project. Economies of scale reduce total cost and may speed development. Using one set of advisers, can achieve the following:

- Leverage the presence of advisers and experts in-country
- Cross-fertilize lessons learned more effectively
- Ensure continuity of commercial terms and therefore make it easier and cheaper for bidders
- Coordinate closely when the projects are brought to market, to ensure best sequencing to encourage competition
- Use competition among the contracting authorities to motivate faster implementation

---

Box 10.19. Bundling Roads

The Tamil Nadu Road Development Company in India is engaged in bundling of road maintenance projects to improve scale and attractiveness of relatively smaller roads to the private sector. These are projects where the government has already completed construction and is looking for a partner for operation and maintenance.

10.6.8 Pooling of Investment

Projects can be pooled (or bundled) into one single project, making the project larger and more attractive for larger, more experienced investors and lenders. The cost of advisory services is reduced by combining multiple processes into one. The cost of funding for one large project should be lower than the cost of several smaller projects, by making the process simpler and less burdensome for due diligence and documentation of the project.

Box 10.20. Bundling Schools

In the United Kingdom, Partnerships for Church of England Schools (PfCS) was created to bundle several small schools with a new-build capital cost of around GBP2 million each into "geographically coherent" groups in order to facilitate the procurement of the private partner. At around the same time, the United Kingdom created the concept of "batched acute hospitals" bundled together projects for the construction, management, and finance of a major acute hospital for the purpose of procurement (saving money on due diligence, project preparation, and procurement) but with separate contracts being signed, given different risk allocation needs and counterparties.[43]

---

[43] HM Treasury, *PFI*.

10.6.9 Credit Position

Contracting authorities for small projects, in particular local government, often have, or are perceived to have, poor credit positions. The perception of a poor credit position may be a question of lack of information, on the contracting authority and/or on the project. A credit rating can help improve the availability of such information, in particular for institutional investors who often rely on credit ratings to make investment decisions. Where credit ratings are not available, shadow or synthetic ratings can be used to provide similar information.

Box 10.21. Bundling Services

SPIE Sud-Ouest and the local authority of Juvignac, France, signed a contract for the renovation, management, and maintenance of the public lighting installations, traffic lights, video surveillance, and the civil engineering works for the town's high-speed communications network. The eighteen-year contract worth 8.8 million euros was to reduce energy consumption by 40 percent and improve operation and maintenance. The project also included upgrading traffic management at six intersections, creation of a video surveillance network, and installation of a high-speed communications network.

Source: spie.com press release, September 16, 2013: http://www.spie.com/en/spie-sud-ouest-and-town-juvignac-herault-sign-public-private-partnership.

Weak credit positions can be addressed through credit enhancement from entities with a better credit position. A local authority with a weak credit position may obtain guarantees or indemnities from central government, insurance agencies, multilateral entities, or others to help enhance its credit position and thereby reduce cost of money or attract additional investors to compete for a project. Credit enhancement is discussed further in sections 5.2, 7.10, 7.11, and 8.10.

10.6.10 Sources of Finance

Small PPPs may be too small or too risky to attract international finance, but they may provide an ideal opportunity for regional financiers or local currency finance. Local currency finance provides a commonality of currency between revenues and finance, reducing or even eliminating foreign exchange risk and associated hedging costs and risks. However, local currency finance often involves higher interest rates, shorter tenors, smaller volumes, lower debt-equity ratios, and less generous grace periods than global currencies (see Chapter 6).

Box 10.22. Rooftop Solar Project, India

The City of Gandhinagar awarded a twenty-five-year project to finance and install solar photovoltaic panels on the rooftops of public buildings and private residences. The public authority provides access to rooftops of public buildings, facilitates the PPA with the power procurer, and monitors performance standards.

This project involved multiple agreements, including rental agreements with the private residential owners and the public entities owning rooftop space.

10.7 Leveraging Additional Benefits

PPP can provide a useful mechanism to mobilize commercial revenues to fund public services. Often, the revenues to be obtained from such services are insufficient to make the project financially viable. In order to replace some or all of the public funding that would otherwise be needed to make the project viable, the project can mobilize commercial revenues. As an example, the Oyster School in Washington, DC, USA, needed to refurbish its facilities, but the price was so high that the school could not afford the refurbishment. Instead, the school contracted with a private party to refurbish the school and develop commercially part of the school land. The revenues from the commercial development (an apartment building) offset the cost of the refurbishment (see Box 10.23).

Such commercial revenues can be mobilized for many PPP projects, alongside the public services. A public market may not be able to attract sufficient revenues to cover operating costs, much less depreciation or initial capital investment. Other commercial activities linked to the public market – for example, residential or office space – can provide the revenues needed and offer additional services in that location. Bus or truck terminals provide an opportunity for retail activities, selling goods and services to passengers and passersby. Government offices can be developed with commercial office space and mixed-use facilities to reduce costs to government. Convention centers are often developed with hotels, since revenues from convention centers are generally insufficient to cover costs.

**Box 10.23. James F. Oyster Bilingual Elementary School,
Washington, D.C., United States**

In 1993, the James F. Oyster Bilingual Elementary School was in danger
of closure due to a crumbling, inadequate building and lack of public
capital. Led by concerned parents and the Twenty-First Century School
Fund, a nonprofit PPP was formed between DC Public Schools, the
District of Columbia, and a national real estate development firm. They
divided the school property in half to make room for a new school and
a new residential development. The District of Columbia issued a thirty-
five-year, U.S.$11 million tax-exempt bond for the construction costs, to
be repaid entirely with the revenue generated by the private apartment
building. The private partner redeveloped the school on half the site,
built a new 211-unit apartment building on the other half, and agreed
to pay U.S.$804,000 a year for thirty-five years to repay the bond. The
design and construction of the school included the proper level of oversight by the school board and community involvement to ensure it was
built to standards. The school facilities included a computer lab, library,
gym, and classrooms designed to accommodate the school's bilingual
program and office space.

Source: National Council for Public Private Partnerships, James F. Oyster Bilingual
Elementary School, Washington, D.C., United States, http://www.ncppp.org/
resources/case-studies/real-estate-and-economic-development/james-f-oyster-
bilingual-elementary-school/.

The purists may cringe at this suggestion, as it may look like government meddling in a purely private space. However, these investments are
by nature public and private, and leveraging commercial revenues to fund
public services may provide a practical solution.

In some countries, the weakness or absence of regulatory functions and
sector oversight make PPP a viable option for commercial activities that
bridge public and private. PPP can provide an opportunity for those different counterparts to come together through a project structure that satisfies
requirements and can be used to support local communities, protect heritage assets, and manage natural resources (see Box 10.25).

The contracting authority can also capture commercial value created by
the PPP project through taxes, fees, and tariffs. For example, transport projects, such as bus rapid transit systems, result in increased land values and
commercial revenues for those located near access points, such as bus stations. A share of this increased value can be captured by the government,
for example, through property taxes. The Tax Increment Finance (TIF)

Box 10.24. How Level Is Your Playing Field?

Akaretler Row Houses, in Istanbul, Turkey, was originally built as housing for palace workers in the nineteenth century. It represents one of the best examples of 1870s civil architecture. Strict regulations for the preservation of historical buildings and extensive procedures for obtaining permits hindered its restoration for many years.

To overcome these regulatory and bureaucratic constraints, the General Directorate of Preservation of Cultural and Historical Heritage and the General Directorate of the Turkish Foundation approved a PPP arrangement. In addition to redeveloping the site, the private partner helped to market the area and assumed the management of surrounding public spaces (including a local park).

The restoration of 60,000 square meters was completed in 2008, including a luxury hotel with 134 rooms, shops, offices, cafés, restaurants, the Atatürk Museum, and a car park. It has contributed to the creation of new jobs in the area and a rising number of tourists.

Source: World Bank, *The Economics of Uniqueness, investing in Historic City Cores and Cultural Heritage Assets for Sustainable Development* (2012).

---

captures, for a predetermined number of years, the tax revenues generated by the enhanced valuation of properties within a "district" resulting from a project (see Figure 10.1). The tax revenues yielded, which exceed the taxes that would have been collected without the redevelopment, constitute the "tax increment," and the TIF captures that gain to support the redeveloped area.

Other benefits – such as environmental, social, and cultural ones – can be leveraged through PPP structures by creating commonalities and confluences of interests. Serious investors are keenly interested in the welfare of the local community, the sustainability of natural resources, local transport infrastructure, solid waste management, and so on. These are critical to the long-term viability of a PPP investment. PPP provides the opportunity to identify government needs in advance, and for investors and the government to agree upon the most important issues, how to allocate responsibilities, and how to work together to meet those needs. Box 10.26 provides an example of a partnership focused on natural resource management supported by the commercial energy of a tourism investment.

Historic and cultural sites are a key asset for government and investors alike. PPP can bring private investments to refurbish and maintain historic and cultural assets and in the process create an investment opportunity. An example would be PPP projects for the development of historic palaces

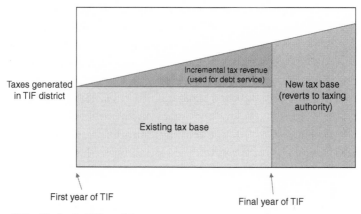

Figure 10.1. The basic TIF model.
Source: PriceWaterhouse Coopers, *Tax Increment Financing to Fund Infrastructure in Australia* (2008).

in Rajasthan, India. Faced with various historic properties falling to ruins due to lack of investment and maintenance, the government turned to PPP to commercialize the properties. These historic properties were leased to private investors through a competitive process that allowed them to redevelop the properties for commercial purposes, in many cases resorts and hotels. The investors have clear obligations to develop the properties in a timely manner, maintain their historic properties, and provide access to the public. (See Box 10.25 for discussion of a similar concept in Jaipur, India.)

Box 10.25. Jal Mahal Palace, Jaipur, India

Jal Mahal is an eighteenth-century pleasure palace located in the middle of a 300-acre lake surrounded by the Nahargarh hills, in the Jaipur-Amer tourist corridor. About 800,000 tourists visit Jaipur every year, including 175,000 foreign nationals.

The lake was an ecological disaster, with the dumping of untreated sewage from the city and general poor upkeep. After several failed attempts at restoration through other means, the government of Rajasthan awarded a ninety-nine-year lease for the 100 acres of land encompassing the site. Part of the site was allocated for private commercial development according to agreed parameters to generate revenues to fund the restoration and maintenance of the public space. Most of the lake restoration program has been completed with all requisite environmental approvals.

Source: www.ilfsindia.com.

Another example would be the redevelopment of historic ports. As cities grow and shipping transport increases and modernizes, ports are being moved out of city centers to areas more appropriate for industrial development. The historic port can be redeveloped to provide passenger terminal facilities (for both private craft and ferry/cruise liner traffic) surrounded by commercial space, for example, hotels, restaurants, pedestrian space, and residential. This has been successful in a number of cities, including Rotterdam, the Netherlands; Sydney, Australia; Buenos Aires, Argentina; Baltimore Maryland, USA; and Cape Town, South Africa; to name but a few.[44]

Box 10.26. Protecting Public Assets

Chumbe Island, a 55-acre island, is a successful self-sustaining marine park and forest reserve, covered by a coral rag forest and bordered by a fringing coral reef, which is home to over 420 fish species and 200 stone coral species. The marine and forest sanctuary is a partnership between a private company, Chumbe Island Coral Park Ltd (CICP), and the Revolutionary Government of Zanzibar (RGoZ). The revenues generated from ecotourism cover operational expenses, park management, and environmental education. CICP has a thirty-three-year lease and a ten-year management contract. CICP had to work with seven government departments and gain the support of area fishermen and local communities before the project was approved.

Source: UN Office for South-South Cooperation, *Chumbe Island, Tanzania, Coral Park Case Study* (November 2012). www.esc-pau.fr/ppp/documents/featured_projects/tanzania.pdf.

Box 10.27. Croydon Council (U.K.) Urban Regeneration Vehicle

The Croydon Council Urban Regeneration Vehicle (CCURV) is a twenty-eight-year joint venture with the aim of regenerating a portfolio of key sites across the London Borough of Croydon. The project involves the investment of land by the Croydon Council, with John Laing investing equity and providing development expertise. The partnership includes 2.2 hectares, 1,250 homes, and two forty-story towers to house 650 residential units (private and affordable).

Source: Croydon Observatory, *Capital Strategy 2010–2030*.

---

[44] en.wikipedia.org/wiki/Category:Redeveloped_ports_and_waterfronts; capeinfo.com/useful-links/history/115-waterfront-development.html.

One sector where commercial and public services converge is tourism. In some countries, the land, licensing, and regulatory system does not protect tourism investments sufficiently. In order to attract investment, and to ensure that tourism investment benefits local communities and fits with government strategy, PPP can help create a clear agreement and partnership between the public and private sector, with incentives built-in to protect investors, enable local staff and skill development, benefit local communities, and protect natural resources. Where the enterprise culture and business climate are weak, PPP can create a contractual arrangement more conducive and enforceable than would be the legal/regulatory system of the country. For example, in some developing countries, the tourism sector is the target of rent-seeking at different levels of national and local government. Investors find themselves faced with serial requests for payment and delays linked to permits, licenses, and other bureaucratic processes, whether or not fictional, without transparency or clarity. If well designed, a PPP regime can reduce or eliminate such rent-seeking and reduce the risk premium investors would normally apply. The Akaretler Row Houses project described in Box 10.24 was delayed for years due to the shortcomings and requirements of the legal and regulatory regime applicable to redevelopment of historic properties. The PPP arrangement helped to mitigate these risks and mobilize investment.

Box 10.28. Ecotourism Concession in Kruger National Park

In 2001, SANParks signed a concession with a consortium to outsource management of eleven restaurants, two shops, and three picnic sites in the Kruger National Park game reserve against a monthly concession fee of approximately 13 percent of its turnover. The concession has resulted in a significant increase in SANParks' profit, an upgrading of restaurants and shops, improvement in service and quality, skills development, and an incentives program for staff.

The concession has not been without its challenges, including staff resistance, due to new conditions of service (improved performance and strict control of stock).

Source: Peter Farlam Working Together, Assessing Public–Private Partnerships in Africa, The South African Institute of International Affairs, Nepad Policy Focus Series.

Box 10.29. Jozini Tiger Lodge, South Africa, 2010

Located in the Jozini Municipality, in northern KwaZulu Natal, the Jozini Tiger Lodge is a partnership between the community and a private sector investor (the Three Cities Hotel), which is responsible for the day-to-day management of the lodge. The National Empowerment Fund (NEF) funded the community interest and provided initial working capital of R28 million on the condition that a large number of employees of the lodge must be locals. The community made land available. Before the project, the community suffered from poor access to basic infrastructure, unemployment, and lack of social development. The lodge currently employs a total of seventy-nine staff, of which 80 percent are from the Jozini community.

A number of lessons can be learned from this project, in particular, mobilization of community partnerships is key to rural tourism success, and land ownership and security of tenure (licences and permits) can improve investor appetite.

Source: SA National Department of Tourism (NDT), Local Government Tourism Conference, *Tourism Development: Why Local Government Matters Report* (2013).

Aggregate Key Messages for Policy Makers

For reference, the following summarizes the key messages for policy makers provided in this book. Because these messages are often context specific, they have been roughly organized under the different phases of a project: selection, preparation, bidding, and implementation.

Conducive Investment Climate

Find the right champions. A good investment climate means working together with different ministries and agencies. The team of champions needs to be up to this task. A figurehead is not enough: political leadership and buy-in is key.

Seek balance: "the perfect is the enemy of the good" (Voltaire):

- There is no such thing as the perfect investment climate; stability, consistency, and certainty are more important to investors than the pursuit of perfection.
- Don't wait for a completed reform process before preparing projects, but a good investment climate will save a lot of headaches.

PPP is not one size fits all. Each sector needs specific consideration, and possibly a bespoke PPP solution; adapt the structure used to the needs of the sector.

Selection

Select projects purposefully. Work out exactly what you want from the project (more access, investment, lower prices?), and select accordingly.

Invest in development. Effort spent selecting the right project will earn benefits later. Get the project design right; changes made later cost more.

Select good projects. Garbage-in-garbage-out; just say "no" to bad projects:

- Select robust, viable projects for PPP. These are more likely to be financed on a competitive basis and are therefore more likely to provide value for money.
- Projects suffering from bad design, dubious demand, or weak fundamentals are more likely to fail and may weaken the entire PPP program in the process.
- A good, transparent selection process can reassure investors and increase competition. Projects selected for political reasons or priorities will create a perception of increased political risk among investors.

Confirm project viability periodically to avoid losing focus. First decide you want PPP on a rational, fundamentally sound basis, then keep reminding yourself why you chose PPP, as its implementation can be challenging, and periodically verify that the project is meeting those objectives.

Preparation

Be patient. PPP is not a quick fix; it takes time to develop and implement properly. Generally, more time spent in advance of procurement to prepare the project properly will save much more time and frustration later. Think through contingencies in advance and make sure you are happy with the project structure and specification before going to the market.

Prepare well. PPP requires upfront investment of staff and money to develop projects well, in particular to pay for expensive external advisers. Project development costs the government on average 3 percent or more of project construction cost. The benefit of this upfront investment is obtained over time, since PPP provides for management and funding for the whole life of the assets and therefore addresses project risks early.

Be ready for challenges. In any long-term relationship, change happens. PPP is above all a partnership; it needs to be designed with challenges, changes, and resolution in mind. Problems need to be elevated to appropriate levels of management before they become disputes or worse. As much as possible, potential challenges should be preempted and addressed in the contract.

PPP is by nature flexible. Look first at what you need, then design your approach based on those needs. Do not look first at what others have done, as your context may be very different. That said, learn from the experiences of others.

Consider all stakeholders. PPP will have a direct influence on some (in particular, employees and management) and may raise political or philosophical concerns among many more. While absolute consensus will never be reached, the government needs to understand fundamental concerns and address them.

Be flexible when considering sources of financing. Be ready to mix public and private money to improve value for money, especially in the early days of PPP or when private markets are weak. Public money also helps worthwhile projects that are not necessarily financially viable become more robust projects, increasing the opportunities for PPP.

Efficiency of financing is key. There is no free ride; someone will have to pay (consumers and/or taxpayers), so make sure you get the best value for money.

Beware creating significant risks when using highly structured financing. Overly complex, highly leveraged financing, while ostensibly cheaper, may create an overly vulnerable project – a robust project is often worth the higher cost in times of trouble – and trouble happens.

Project finance is complex. Get the right advice and be ready to pay for it. If properly managed, it can save you time and money.

Government money can be used effectively to improve PPP projects. Government is a key partner in PPP and government support a key element in successful PPP.

- Government support can improve financial viability and make a project more attractive for investors, but it will not turn a bad project into a good one.
- Use government support efficiently, in a targeted manner, to ensure government goals are achieved.
- Ensure that funding mechanisms are properly resourced and incentivized to avoid political capture or inertia.

Don't cram risk on the private sector. It usually is not efficient, is expensive, and makes the project overly vulnerable to change and crises.

Bidding

Do not cut corners on procurement. It may seem easier to enter into direct negotiations instead of using competitive procurement, but it isn't. In general, it takes longer and cost more money. Maximizing competition through good, transparent, public procurement is one of the most important benefits of a PPP.

Be clear to bidders about what you want. Indicate clearly what results, milestones, and indicators you want the investor to achieve. Help bidders to give you what you want; don't make them guess.

Be open to discuss your expectations; bidders might have some useful suggestions. Take the time to discuss with bidders, and use the competitive dialogue to improve the project.

Be cautious when selecting the winning bid. If a bid seems too good to be true (financially, technically, or otherwise), then it probably is. Look carefully at the detail, whether it is a fixed and complete bid; if anything looks unconvincing, it may be wise to reject it.

While protecting the contracting authority's interests, listen to lender concerns. Focus on the lenders' key needs and perceived risks, but don't let them drive the agenda. Take the time and effort to make life a little easier for the lenders. It is likely to make your life easier in the long run.

Implementation

Government must regulate and monitor PPPs. This must be an integral part of project design. PPP or not, the public sector is always the final authority and will be ultimately responsible for the provision of public services.

Prepare for change during the project. It is not possible to anticipate or make every risk decision in advance; mechanisms will be needed to address change and other challenges.

Stability is the goal. Prepare for every eventuality, but realize it is impossible to anticipate every eventuality.

Ensure a practical fallback position that protects consumers. Make sure that if all else fails, the public is in the position to take the infrastructure and services back quickly to ensure continuity.

Keep the revenue stream as certain, foreseeable, and ring-fenced as possible. It is the lifeblood of the project.

A failed project costs everyone time and money; *it is generally worth the extra money or effort to make the project a bit more robust*, obtaining information, improving planning, managing risk, and considering options. A proactive, collaborative framework must provide partners with the platform for resolution.

Put in place the right contracting authority team. The project will not manage itself; failure to assign a sufficiently expert team to manage project implementation (i.e., after financial close), with necessary funding, can turn the best project into a failure.

Prepare for the future. Decide up front what happens later in the project; deferred decisions only become more expensive and contentious. Decisions to make changes need to be made in advance. Such decisions later in the process, during implementation, can be expensive and time consuming.

Be flexible and prepare for conflict resolution. No contract can contemplate every eventuality, so expect to need to resolve challenges collaboratively – that is, it should be managed like a partnership.

Renegotiation can be an opportunity, and can provide the parties and all stakeholders with the opportunity to improve the PPP arrangements and protect the most vulnerable.

Be proactive. Establish mechanisms intended to catch disputes as early as possible. Early in the process, options are varied, relative cost is low, and the likelihood of immediate value-added resolution is higher.

Facilitation can help. Softer processes are designed to use and develop relationships as the basis for finding mutually satisfactory solutions and can work better than more formal processes.

Responding to the Economic Crisis

Crisis does not change the fundamentals of PPP, and PPP is sufficiently flexible to be adjusted to market conditions. Be willing to reconsider each aspect of the PPP to find the best solution. For example, phase or scale down investment to fit accessible finance and reduced demand, and consider replacing some of the desired private financing with public funding (to the extent public funding is available) until such time as market conditions make private financing a better value.

Make sure to continue developing the PPP pipeline during the period when private financing may not be available, to avoid a significant lag in the pipeline later. Similarly, sector reform to encourage PPP should continue, to the extent possible. Don't lose momentum.

Glossary

This glossary of terms, abbreviations, and acronyms is included exclusively for use as a reference aid and therefore should not be considered an exhaustive or complete discussion of any of the terms defined or indeed of all the terms relevant to PPP or project finance. Definitions are generally given under their spelt-out form, and the abbreviation refers to the spelt-out form.

affermage   A PPP structure originally created under French law, under which the private operator is responsible for operating and maintaining the utility/ business but not for financing investment. The project company does not receive a fixed fee for his services but retains part of the receipts collected from consumers, with a portion of the receipts going to the contracting authority as owner of the assets. The payment to the contracting authority will be a percentage of the receipts or a percentage of the total units of service provided.

arranger   The senior tier of a syndication. Implies the entity that agreed and negotiated the project finance structure. Also refers to the bank/underwriter responsible for originating and entitled to syndicate the loan/bond issue. The arranger may not necessarily also be the agent and may not even participate in the transaction.

availability charge   See *capacity charge.*

basis point (BP)   One hundred basis points equal one percentage point.

BBO   Buy-Build-Operate (similar to *BOO*).

BLA   Bilateral agency; see section 1.6.

BOO   Build-Own-Operate. The private entity will build, own, and operate the project just as in a BOT project, but there is no transfer back to the government. This method is often used where there will be no residual value in the project after the concession period or accounting standards do not permit the assets to revert to the contracting authority if the contracting authority wishes to benefit from off-balance sheet treatment.

BOOS   Build-Own-Operate-Sell. Same as a *BOT* except that the contracting authority pays the project company for the residual value of the project at transfer.

BOOST   Build-Own-Operate-Subsidize-Transfer (similar to *BOT*).

BOOT   Build-Own-Operate-Transfer (similar to *BOT*).

BOR   Build-Operate-Renewal of concession (similar to *BOO*).

BOT   Build-Operate-Transfer.

bridge financing   Interim financing, before a long-term financing is put in place.

BRT   Build-Rent-Transfer (similar to *BOT*).

BT   Build-Transfer. The project company builds the facilities and transfers them to the contracting authority.

BTO   Build-Transfer-Operate (similar to *BOT*). This often involves the contracting authority paying for construction of the facility, separate from operations, at or before transfer.

capacity charge   Payment by the purchaser to the project company for the available capacity of the project. This charge will cover fixed costs, including debt service, operating costs, and service fees. Also known as *availability charge*.

capitalized interest   Accrued interest (and margin) that is not paid but added ("rolled up") to the principal amount lent at the end of an interest period. See, for example, *interest during construction*.

concession agreement   The agreement with a government body that entitles a private entity to undertake an otherwise public service.

conditions precedent (CPs)   Conditions that must be satisfied before a right or obligation accrues. The matters that have to be dealt with before a borrower will be allowed to borrow under a facility agreement. These will be listed in the agreement.

construction contract   The contract between the project company and the construction contractor for the design, construction, and commissioning of the works.

contracting authority   The party that grants a concession, a license, or some other right.

credit risk   The risk that a counterparty to a financial transaction will fail to perform according to the terms and conditions of the contract (default), either because of bankruptcy or any other reason, thus causing the asset holder to suffer a financial loss. Sometimes known as default risk.

cushion   The extra amount, for example, of net cash flow remaining after expected debt service.

DBFO   Design-Build-Finance-Operate. The contracting authority retains title to the site and leases the project back to the project company for the period of the concession. Similar to *BOO*.

DCMF   Design-Construct-Manage-Finance. Similar to *BOO*.

debt–equity (D:E) ratio   The proportion of debt to equity, often expressed as a percentage. The higher this ratio, the greater the financial leverage of the firm. Also known as gearing.

debt service   Payments of principal and interest on a loan.

debt service cover ratio (DSCR)   The ratio of income to debt service requirements for a period. Also known as the cover ratio.

debt service reserve   An amount set aside either before completion or during the early operation period for debt servicing where insufficient revenue is achieved.

defects liability period   The period during which the construction contractor is liable for defects after completion.

direct agreement   An agreement made in parallel with one of the main project documents, often with the lenders or the contracting authority. Step-in rights and other lender rights are often reinforced or established through direct agreements between the lenders and the project participants.

discount rate   The rate used to discount future cash flows to their present values, often based on a firm's weighted average cost of capital (after tax) or the rate that the capital needed for the project could return if invested in an alternative venture. A higher discount rate may be used to adjust for risk or other factors.

ECA   Export credit agency; see section 1.6.

economic rate of return, also **economic internal rate of return (EIRR)**   The project's internal rate of return after taking into account externalities (such as economic, social, and environmental costs and benefits) not included in financial IRR calculations.

environmental impact assessment (EIA)   An assessment of the potential impact of a project on the environment that results in an environmental impact statement.

environmental impact statement (EIS)   A statement of the potential impact of a project on the environment. The result of an environmental impact assessment, which may have been subject to public comment.

EPC contract   Engineering, procurement, and construction contract (i.e., turnkey construction contract).

equity   The cash or assets contributed by the sponsors in a project financing. A company's paid-up share capital and other shareholders' funds. For accounting purposes, it is the net worth or total assets minus liabilities.

financial close   In a financing, the point at which the documentation has been executed and conditions precedent have been satisfied or waived. Drawdowns become permissible after this point.

financial internal rate of return (FIRR)   See *internal rate of return*.

fiscal space   Capacity in a government's budget (including borrowing capacity) that allows it to provide or access resources for a desired purpose without jeopardizing the sustainability of its financial position or the stability of the economy or otherwise breaching restrictions created by its own national laws, supranational bodies, or lenders (in particular, large lenders such as the IMF or World Bank).

fixed rate loan   A loan for which the rate paid by the borrower is fixed for the life of the loan.

floating interest rate   An interest rate that fluctuates during the term of a loan in accordance with some external index or a set formula, usually as a margin or spread over a specified rate. See also *variable rate loan*.

force majeure   Events outside the control of the parties that prevent one or both of the parties from performing their contractual obligations.

greenfield   Often used to refer to a planned facility that must be built from scratch, without existing infrastructure.

IFI International Financial Institution; see section 1.6.

input supply agreement The agreement entered into by the project company and the input supplier that defines the rights and obligations in relation to the supply of input for the project. It will be used to allocate the market risk of input cost and provision. This agreement will often be on either a take-or-pay or a take-and-pay basis.

intercreditor agreement An agreement between lenders as to the rights of different creditors in the event of default, covering such topics as collateral, waiver, security, and setoffs.

interest during construction (IDC) Interest accumulated during construction, before the project has a revenue stream to pay debt service, usually rolled up and treated as capitalized interest.

internal rate of return (IRR) The discount rate that equates the present value of a future stream of payments to the initial investment. See also *economic rate of return*.

limited recourse debt See *nonrecourse debt*.

liquidated damages (LDs) A fixed periodic amount payable as a sanction for delays or substandard performance under a contract. Also known as a penalty clause.

margin The amount expressed as a percentage per annum above the interest rate basis or cost of funds. For hedging and futures contracts, the cash collateral that is deposited with a trader or exchange as insurance against default.

mezzanine financing A mixture of financing instruments, with characteristics of both debt and equity, providing further debt contributions through higher-risk, higher-return instruments, sometimes treated as equity.

MLA Multilateral agency; see section 1.6.

monoline Specialist insurers whose business is the provision of financial guarantee insurance.

net present value (NPV) The discounted value of an investment's cash inflows minus the discounted value of its cash outflows. To be adequately profitable, an investment should have a net present value greater than zero.

nonrecourse (limited recourse) debt The lenders rely on the project's cash flows and collateral security over the project as the only means to repay debt service, and therefore the lenders do not have recourse to other sources, such as shareholder assets. More often, nonrecourse debt is actually limited recourse debt.

off-balance sheet liabilities Corporate obligations that do not need to appear as liabilities on a balance sheet, such as lease obligations, project finance, and take-or-pay contracts.

offtake purchase agreement The agreement whereby the offtake purchaser undertakes to purchase an amount of some or all of the project output, such as the power purchase agreement in the context of a power project and a water purchase agreement in the context of a water treatment project.

operation and maintenance agreement The agreement allocating to the operator the obligation to operate and maintain the project in accordance with its requirements.

option   A contract under which the writer of the option grants the buyer of the option the right, but not the obligation, to purchase from or sell to the writer something at a specified price within a specified period (or at a specified date). Also called purchase option, put option, hedge, futures contract, swap.

pari passu   Of instruments, ranking equally in right of payment with each other and with other instruments of the same issuer. From Latin: with equal step.

performance bond   A bond payable if a service is not performed as specified. Some performance bonds require satisfactory completion of the contract, while other performance bonds provide for payment of a sum of money for failure of the contractor to perform under a contract.

power purchase agreement (PPA)   An offtake purchase agreement in relation to a power project, for the purchase of electricity generated.

prequalification   The process whereby the number of qualified bidders is limited by reviewing each bidder's qualifications against a set of criteria, generally involving experience in the relevant field, capitalization, site country experience, identity of local partners, and international reputation.

project   The asset constructed with, or owned via, a project financing that is expected to produce cash flow at a debt service cover ratio sufficient to repay the project financing.

project documents or project agreements   The commercial agreements that are the subject of this book, including the concession agreement, the construction contract, the input supply agreement, the offtake purchase agreement, and the operation and maintenance agreement.

project financing   A loan structure that relies for its repayment primarily on the project's cash flow, with the project's assets, rights, and interests held as secondary security or collateral. See also *limited recourse debt* and *nonrecourse debt*.

rating agency or credit rating agency   A private agency that assesses credit risk of sovereign entities, companies, or investments, such as Standard & Poor's, Moody's, and Fitch. The agency applies a letter grade to indicate credit risk. Lenders and investors use the rating as an indication of the relative riskiness of a loan or investment.

recourse   In the event that the project (and its associated escrows, sinking funds, or cash reserves/standby facilities) cannot service the financing or the project completion cannot be achieved, then the lenders have recourse either to cash from other sponsors and/or corporate sources or other nonproject security. See also *limited recourse debt* and *nonrecourse debt*.

refinancing   Repaying existing debt by obtaining a new loan, typically to meet some corporate objective such as the lengthening of maturity or lowering the interest rate.

reinsurance   The procedure used by insurance companies to reduce the risks associated with underwritten policies by spreading risks across alternative institutions, portioning out pieces of a larger potential obligation in exchange for some of the money the original insurer received to accept the obligation. The party that diversifies its insurance portfolio is known as the ceding party. The party that accepts a portion of the potential obligation in exchange for a share of the insurance premium is known as the reinsurer. Also known as "insurance for insurers" or "stop-loss insurance."

reserve account   A separate amount of cash or a letter of credit to service a payment requirement such as debt service or maintenance.

return on assets (ROA)   Net profits after taxes divided by assets. This ratio helps a firm determine how effectively it generates profits from available assets.

return on equity (ROE)   Net profits after taxes divided by equity investment.

return on investment (ROI)   Net profits after taxes divided by investment.

RLT   Refurbish-Lease-Transfer (similar to *BOT*).

ROO   Rehabilitate-Own-Operate (similar to *BOO*).

ROT   Rehabilitate-Operate-Transfer (similar to *BOT*).

security   A legal right of access to value through mortgages, contracts, cash accounts, guarantees, insurances, pledges, or cash flow, including licenses, concessions, and other assets. A negotiable certificate evidencing a debt or equity obligation/shareholding.

shareholders' agreement   The agreement entered into by the shareholders of the project company that governs their relationship and their collective approach to the project.

special-purpose vehicle   An entity created to undertake a project in order to protect the shareholders with limited liability and limited or nonrecourse financing.

sponsor   A party wishing to develop/undertake a project. A developer. A party providing financial support.

step-in rights   The right of a third party to "step in" to the place of one contractual party where that party fails in its obligations under the contract and the other party to the contract has the right to terminate the contract.

subordinated debt   Debt that, by agreement or legal structure, is subordinated to other (senior) debt, allowing those (senior) lenders to have priority in access to amounts paid to the lenders by the borrower from time to time, and to borrower assets or revenues in the event of default. This priority may be binding on liquidators or administrators of the borrower. It does not include reserve accounts or deferred credits.

subrogation rights   The right of an insurer to take over the rights in action (i.e., the right to sue) of its insured, to recover the amount it paid out to the insured.

super-turnkey contract   Based on a turnkey construction contract, a contract that requires the contractor to contribute to the financing of the construction, often by agreeing to the deferral of the payment due to it until after completion or during operation.

swap   The exchanging of one security, debt, currency, or interest rate for another. Also known as a switch, hedge, futures contract, or option.

syndicated credit facility   A credit facility in which a number of banks undertake to provide a loan or other support facility to a customer on a pro rata basis under identical terms and conditions evidenced by a single credit agreement.

take-or-pay   In the event the project's output is not taken, payment must be made whether or not the output is deliverable. Also known as a throughput contract or use-or-pay contract.

tender process   See discussion of the bid process in section 4.5.

tranche   A separate portion of a credit facility, perhaps with different lenders, margins, currencies, and/or term.

turnkey construction   The design and construction of works to completion, so that they are ready to produce cash flow.

ultra vires   An act outside the scope of one's authority.

variable rate loan   A loan made at an interest rate that fluctuates with the prime rate, the London Interbank Offered Rate (LIBOR), or some other index.

variant bid   The contracting authority may wish to allow variant bids (in addition to compliant bids), which the bidder believes satisfy the contracting authority's needs but do not comply specifically with the requirements set out in the tender documentation. A variant bid may involve a technical innovation or some other change in approach, such as a different technology or tariff structure, that will reduce costs or improve efficiency.

variation or change   A technical term in construction contracts referring to a variation of the client's requirements ordered by the client, generally entitling the contractor to a change in the contract price, the time for completion, and any other obligation affected by the variation ordered.

vitiation   Invalidation of an insurance policy where the project insurance involves several insured parties (with varying interests in the insured risk) under the same insurance policy, and the insurance policy becomes unenforceable (with all of the insured parties losing their coverage) due to a breach by one of the insureds of its obligations under the policy (in particular, the obligation to disclose relevant information to the insurer).

weighted average cost of capital (WACC)   The total return required by both debt and equity investors expressed as a real post-tax percentage on fund usage.

works   A technical term in construction identifying the entirety of the facilities and services to be provided by the construction contractor.

Select Readings

While not an exhaustive bibliography, the following are key texts that will be of interest to those wanting an in-depth understanding of PPP.

Asian Development Bank, *Public–Private Partnership (PPP) Handbook* (2008).

Delmon, J., *Private Sector Investment in Infrastructure: Project Finance, PPP Projects and PPP Programs* (2016).

Public Private Partnership Programs: Creating a Framework for Private Sector Investment in Infrastructure (2014).

Private Sector Investment in Infrastructure: Project Finance, PPP Projects and Risk (2009).

Water Projects: A Commercial and Contractual Guide (2000).

Delmon, J. & R. Delmon, *Law Applicable to PPP and Project Finance Transactions in Key Frontier Jurisdictions* (2010; 2nd ed., 2012; 3rd ed. 2013).

Department of Treasury & Finance, Melbourne, *Partnerships Victoria* (2002).

Perth, *Partnerships for Growth: Policies and Guidelines for Public Private Partnerships in Western Australia* (2002).

Dutz, M., C. Harris, I. Dhingra, & C. Shugart, Public–Private Partnership Units: What Are They, and What Do They Do? Public Policy for the Private Sector Note No. 311, World Bank (2006).

Esty, B. C., *Modern Project Finance: A Casebook* (2003).

European Commission, *Guidelines for Successful Public–Private Partnerships* (2003).

Farlam, P., Working Together: Assessing Public–Private Partnerships in Africa, *Nepad Policy Focus Report* No. 2 (2005).

Finnerty, J., *Project Financing: Asset-Based Financial Engineering* (2007).

Green Paper on Public–Private Partnerships and Community Law on Public Contracts and Concessions, COM/2004/327, Brussels (2004).

HM Treasury, *Public Private Partnerships: The Government's Approach* (2000).

Industry Canada, *Public–Private Partnerships: A Canadian Guide* (2001).

Infrastructure Consortium for Africa, *Attracting Investors to African Public–Private Partnerships – a Project Preparation Guide* (2008).

International Monetary Fund (Fiscal Affairs Department), *Public–Private Partnerships* (2004).

International Monetary Fund, *Government Guarantees and Fiscal Risk* (International Monetary Fund, 2005).

Irwin, T. C., *Government Guarantees: Allocation and Valuing Risk in Privately Financed Infrastructure Projects* (2007).

Kerf, M., Concessions for Infrastructure: A Guide to Their Design and Award, Technical Paper 399, World Bank (1998).

National Treasury, South Africa. *South Africa PPP Manual* (2004).

Nevitt, P. K. & F. Fabozzi, *Project Financing*, 7th ed. (2000).

New South Wales Government, *Working with Government: Guidelines for Privately Financed Projects* (2006).

Organization for Economic Co-operation and Development (OECD). *Public–Private Partnerships: In Pursuit of Risk Sharing and Value for Money* (2008).

Posner, P., K. R. Shin, & A. Tkachenko, *Public–Private Partnerships: The Relevance of Budgeting* (2008).

PriceWaterhouse Coopers/Public–Private Infrastructure Advisory Facility (PPIAF). *Hybrid PPPs: Leveraging EU Funds and Private Capital* (2006).

Razavi, H., *Financing Energy Projects in Developing Countries* (2007).

Scriven, J., N. Pritchard, & J. Delmon, eds., *A Contractual Guide to Major Construction Projects* (1999).

The Public Sector Comparator: A Canadian Best Practices Guide (2003).

Tinsley, C. R. & R. Tinsley, *Advanced Project Financing* (2000).

United Nations, *UNIDO Guidelines for Infrastructure Development through Build–Operate–Transfer* (1996).

United Nations Commission on International Trade Law (UNCITRAL), *Legislative Guide on Privately Financed Infrastructure Projects* (2001).

UNCITRAL, *Model Legislative Provisions on Privately Financed Infrastructure Projects* (2004).

Vinter, G. & G. Price, *Project Finance: A Legal Guide*, 3rd ed. (2006).

Wood, P., *Project Finance, Securitisations and Subordinated Debt*, 2nd ed. (2007).

Yescombe, E. R., *Public–Private Partnerships: Principles of Policy and Finance* (2007).

Representative Websites

Australia – Victoria: www.partnerships.vic.gov.au

Canada – British Columbia: www.pss.gov.bc.ca/psb/

Partnerships U.K.: www.partnershipsuk.org.uk

South African Ministry of Finance PPP: www.ppp.gov.za

U.K. National Audit Office: www.nao.org.uk has a number of excellent reviews of specific projects and the PFI/PPP program.

U.K. Treasury: www.hm-treasury.gov.uk/documents/public_private_partnerships

U.S.A. National Council for PPP: www.ncppp.org

World Bank: www.worldbank.org

- PPP in Infrastructure Resource Centre – www.worldbank.org/pppirc – legal, contractual, and regulatory guidance, documents, and agreements for PPP
- Global Program for Output Based Aid: www.gpoba.org
- PPP database: www.ppi.worldbank.org

- Public–Private Infrastructure Advisory Facility (PPPAF): www.ppiaf.org – in particular the toolkits for different sectors and functions.
- World Bank PPP Lab: www.pppknowledgelab.org
- World Bank PPP Reference Guide: www.worlbank.org/Public-private-partnerships-reference-guide-version-2-0

Index